Dying of
Politeness

Dying of Politeness

Geena Davis

HARPERONE

An Imprint of HarperCollins*Publishers*

HarperCollins books may be purchased for educational, business, or
sales promotional use. For information, please email the Special Markets
Department at SPsales@harpercollins.com.

FIRST HARPERCOLLINS PAPERBACK PUBLISHED IN 2024

Designed by Bonni Leon-Berman
Illustrations by Geena Davis

Library of Congress Cataloging-in-Publication Data is available upon
request.

ISBN 978-0-06-311914-7

24 25 26 27 28 LBC 5 4 3 2 1

To Dan

"So to feel brave, act as if we were brave, use all our will to that end, and a courage-fit will very likely replace the fit of fear."

—William James, "The Gospel of Relaxation," *On Vital Reserves (1922)*

Contents

Chapter One
My Journey to Badassery

I toyed with the idea of writing a book a number of years ago and started jotting down things I could include. I just went back to look at my notes and saw that the very first thing I wrote down was "Mrs. Morgan's lawn."

I've never known a Mrs. Morgan, nor do I have any memories of her lawn. *Our* lawn, yes. I remember one day when I was a kid, our neighbor Mrs. Perkins called my mother to tell her there was something seriously wrong with me. My dad had set me up in the side yard with the power mower, and I was pretending the blades of grass were enemy soldiers that I was mowing down in a ferocious battle. Naturally I had to speak up above the roar of the motor as I gave orders to my troops. But to Mrs. Perkins, at least, it looked very odd to see a young girl shoving a big lawn mower around while angrily bellowing at the grass.

Actually, there were a lot of calls to my mother to say that something must have been wrong with me.

...

I kicked ass onscreen way before I did so in real life. The roles I've played have taken me down paths I never could have imagined when I dreamed of becoming an actor. They have helped transform me, slowly, in fits and starts, into someone of power. As my career progressed, I went all the way from playing a soap star in her underwear in *Tootsie*, to a housewife-turned-road warrior in *Thelma & Louise*, to a baseball phenomenon in *A League of Their Own*, to the first female president of the United States in *Commander in Chief*, and more. For everything I put into each of those roles, I've taken away far more. Acting has changed me every single time I've had the great good fortune to do it.

Some movies I've been in have even inspired the people watching them to feel more empowered—like, you know, *Earth Girls Are Easy*.

I've been blessed to practice living a different life onscreen—a bolder, freer, and more authentic one than my own. And though my characters were bold before I was, that boldness rubbed off on me, and transformed me into a fledgling—then full-fledged—badass. (I figure I'm permitted to call myself that because the magazine *The Mary Sue* ran an article in 2013 with the headline "Geena Davis Is the Most Badass Badass to Ever Badass.")

For people observing my life from afar, I imagine they picture my journey to badassery climbing upward in a nice even line:

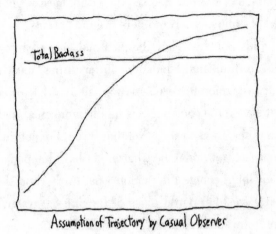

Assumption of Trajectory by Casual Observer

However, this is the actual graph of my journey:

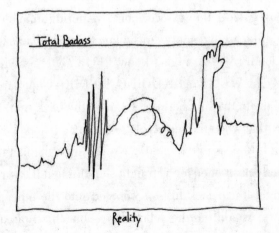

Reality

Setbacks are part of the process on any journey, of course, but the reason my road toward claiming my power is so meandering may, in part, be a result of growing up a cripplingly polite New Englander who was much too tall to hide.

I may be one of the few people who can honestly say they very nearly died of politeness. Two others are my parents, as you'll see. This dangerous politeness was bequeathed to me early on. I was conditioned to think that I mustn't ask for things, must never put anyone out; so trained to be insanely polite that I learned to have no needs at all: even if someone was handing me an already poured glass of ice water, I was to say, "No, thank you. I'm not thirsty." Because otherwise, well, imagine what might have happened! I could have conceivably become the person who, every time she showed up, needed a freshly poured glass of fucking ice water, and who would want to be such a person?

My polite near-death came when I was about eight years old. My *ninety-nine-year-old* great-uncle Jack was driving his wife, great-aunt Marion, my parents, and me back to their house after a dinner out. The lovely old fella was occasionally veering in and out of the oncoming, if blessedly empty, traffic lane. Rather than saying anything out loud, like . . . I don't know, "FOR GOD'S SAKE PULL OVER, JACK, WE'RE ALL GOING TO DIE"—my parents simply moved me to the spot between them on the back seat, thinking, I presume, that when the inevitable head-on collision occurred, I'd be killed a little less in the middle. (Never mind the fact that I was now perfectly positioned for a straight shot through the windshield.) Finally, great-uncle Jack full-on wobbled into the other lane and stayed there, straddling the yellow line—but this time a car was approaching.

Still, not a peep from my parents.

At the very last instant, with mere seconds before impact, Marion gently said, "A little to the right, Jack." I still remember the distorted faces of the occupants of the other car streaking past us, inches away, as he swerved just in time. The lesson being: Even if there is death in the offing (or of the offspring), don't say something that could possibly be perceived as impolite.

• • •

I think the big task of my life is to close the gap between when something happens to me and when I react authentically to it. And miraculously, the characters I've played have helped transform me, slowly, in fits and starts, into someone who can stand up for herself—and who on occasion knows how she feels about something right in the moment.

It wasn't until I played Thelma that I realized I may have wanted to become an actor so fervently because I could use acting to fill out the persona of someone confident in their abilities—someone I desperately wanted to be like in real life. You've heard the term "Fake it till you make it"—I would inelegantly paraphrase that as "Act like it enough and it might just rub off on you." At the very least, people will think you're like that in real life.

Before *Thelma & Louise*, I felt plagued by the strong currents of self-effacement coursing through me, so I decided to try taking a self-defense class (with Impact, a great company offering these kinds of classes). In this class, you face up against a man in a huge padded suit, like the Michelin Man—so you can fight him as hard as you can without any fear of hurting him. The first thing the instructor did was to have us stand in a line, and one by one the padded man would walk toward us. When it felt like he was about to invade our boundaries, we were to say "Stop!" One by one he approached my fellow class-mates, and the differences in when they felt he was getting too close showed how strong or weak their boundaries were.

And when it was my turn? He ended up walking right into me, because, somehow, I couldn't manage to say "Stop!" in time. Evidently, I thought I had no license to tell anybody to stop doing anything.

But by the time I reached my forties I'd become a middle-aged data geek and had my own institute on gender in media—and I became a mom. I had my kids late in life—at forty-six and forty-eight!—and I thought it was wonderful that this happened after I'd become more of who I was supposed to be. I could show them what it was like to be a strong woman and raise them to see women and men as equals.

For example, have you ever heard this riddle?

A father and son are in a terrible accident, and they are taken to different hospitals. When the boy is wheeled into the operating room, the surgeon exclaims, "I can't operate on him, he's my son!" Who is the surgeon?

An interviewer once commented to me that if anyone would know the answer it would be *my kids*, and I said, "You got that right!" So later, just for fun, I told the riddle to one of my five-year-old sons, knowing he would nail it.

He named every type of male relative that exists, then moved on to "the neighbor" before I stopped him to say it was the patient's mother.

"No way—women can't be doctors!"

Yikes.

Another time I was with my little twin boys in the park when they saw a squirrel. Wanting to reinforce the equality between males and females, I said, "Oh, isn't she cute?"

They both turned to me instantly and said in near unison, "How do you know it's a SHE??!"

. . . but I kept at it, to the point where if we were watching a cartoon and I started to lean over to say something to one of the kids, they'd stop me by saying, "I already noticed, Mom—not enough girls in that scene."

I'm optimistic that our culture will finally be able to recognize the unconscious bias in all of us if we keep pointing it out. I *must* be an optimist. I mean, how many times do I buy kombucha thinking, "Oh yeah, kombucha! Maybe this time I'll like it!"

. . .

Pretty much as soon as I learned that people had jobs, I knew what I wanted to do with my life. Lord knows where the idea of an acting career came from, and at such a young age, especially since my family was as far from showbiz as you could possibly get. I hail from Wareham, Massachusetts, which optimistically called itself "The Gateway to Cape Cod" because it was not a destination town itself—you had to drive through it to get to the Cape. It most certainly wasn't Hollywood.

My parents said I announced at three years old that I was going to be in movies—though I have no memory of this. I'm sure I did say it, though. Throughout my childhood, I maintained this sort of idiotic, unshakeable faith that I was going to be an actor. (By the way, I don't use the term "actress." I feel sure it will soon come to sound as quaint and old-fashioned as "doctoress" or "poetess." I consider myself a former waiter who became an actor.)

I began training for my future career early. Once when I was home with the flu, I lay on the couch for a whole week watching soap operas. I noticed that at the ends of scenes, very often one of the characters would raise one eyebrow to signal intrigue. I figured that must be a skill actors had to have—raising one eyebrow—so for three days I held one eyebrow down and raised the other as I watched TV. Then I thought, *What if the camera is on the other side?* So I switched, and taught myself to raise the other eyebrow, too.

Despite their homespun ways, when I told my parents that I planned to major in acting in college, they simply said, "Oh, okay." They reacted as if I'd told them I was going to study ophthalmology or business administration—something you could actually expect to get a job doing. But of course, my laser-like focus on acting was not news. They knew that was what I wanted to be from the beginning.

Bill and Lucille met in Wareham, at the White Rabbit Tea Room—where my mother waitressed and my father lunched—and in chatting they realized that when he was a boy, little Bill had had his teeth fixed by a dentist up in a little town in Vermont; that dentist had been none other than my mother's father. Turns out Bill and Lucille both came from very tiny and very adjacent towns in rural Vermont, but fate had brought them together, 250 miles south.

My dad was a humble New Englander, an engineering genius, a machinist, a carpenter, and he held patents in surveying inventions. Whatever was broken at a neighbor's house, be it their furnace, car, plumbing, or lawn mower, Dad was the one to fix it. Mom, likewise, worked hard and was driven: aside from raising my brother and me, she took a job at the nursing home across the street helping patients do crafts, and at the local elementary school as a teacher's aide. She also waited tables at Ben Howe's Chicken House.

And she danced with a broom, singing music-hall songs.

My brother Dan was two and a half years older than I was, and like so many siblings, we toggled between loving each other and building a wall of cereal boxes on the dining room table between us so we didn't have to look at each other.

• • •

My birth certificate reads, "Virginia Elizabeth," but on the way home from the hospital after I was born, my mom asked little Dan what he thought my nickname should be. I was named after my mom's sister, Virginia, who went by "Ginny," so it had to be something else. Dan said, "Geena" (or did he say "Gina"?) and my mom liked it so much that she said she wished she'd thought of it before naming me Virginia. I always thought it was funny that she didn't know how to spell it correctly.

We—Mom, Dad, Dan, and I—basically lived like my grandparents had back in the day, heating the house with a wood stove, kerosene lanterns always at the ready, and taking baths on Saturday nights. (We didn't have a shower.) Dan and I had to take turns with who would get the bathwater first; there was only one bath drawn to save water, and being second always gave us the heebie-jeebies.

Dad had a collection of about five hundred antique axes that were spread all over the house, including beneath the dining room table and under my bed. Mom grew all our food—all of it, from asparagus to zucchini—in a one-acre garden. She would often start the water boiling and then say, "Go pick the corn." It really was *Little House on the Prairie*, without the pinafores and gingham dresses. Or prairie.

My folks were raised to be deeply resourceful. They came from a time when people could do anything and everything themselves— build their own house, make their own clothes. Our collection of used foil was something to marvel at. In fact, I'm not sure they ever bought a *second* roll.

They were also the most deeply, profoundly polite people who ever lived. My parents would probably have been Amish, had they heard of being Amish. Their lives would have changed not a bit.

...

As I said, I chose my career very early: The Christmas when I was three, I asked Santa for sunglasses, because somehow, I already knew that movie stars wore them. (My mom said she had a hell of a time finding children's sunglasses in December in Massachusetts.) I would wear the sunglasses whenever I watched TV.

My skill at being no trouble to anyone also kicked in early. I was sitting on my mom's lap during a church service, and as one-year-olds are wont, I was fussing and jerking and generally moving around a bunch. Somehow, I managed to clock my head on the pew in front of us; the bonk of my skull hitting wood was so loud everything stopped. The congregation held its collective breath to see just how much bloody murder I was prepared to scream. And then, nothing. Mom said she grabbed me and held me tightly, quietly saying, "Shhh . . . shhh . . ." This became one of her favorite stories about me, which I heard many times: "And she didn't make a peep!" she'd say, proudly, as if I'd passed some kind of cosmic test in which I had maintained decorum and invisibility.

I tell the pew story because it is the signature moment of my earliest formative years, and its lessons have become one of the key push-pulls of my life: being invisible while being as visible as possible; assertive yet modest; loud yet shy. Something very New England, very self-effacing, was banged into my skull that Sunday.

. . .

My mother experienced tragedy at a young age. Her beloved father, the dentist, had died when she was just eleven. He had been the passenger in a car during a terrible snowstorm; at one point he put his head out the window to try to see where he and his fellow dentist friend were going and was killed by a passing road sign. My mother's family became desperately poor. My grandmother made a little money from selling homemade dinner rolls, and it was my mother's job to run as fast as she could with them to the customer's house while they were still warm. They'd be rejected without payment if they arrived cold.

My mother had only two dresses throughout high school, wearing one and washing the other every day. She worked as a nanny for a dollar a day, and she ended up putting her older sister through nursing school and her younger brother through college. Once they had jobs, though, they didn't pay for her to go to nursing school, as promised, and for the rest of her life she felt somewhat martyred, and quite rightly.

After Dan and me, Bill and Lucille had another son, Joel, who was stillborn. Dan and I were somehow kept completely in the dark about this, and didn't find out about him until our mom died; Dad wanted to rebury Joel with her. In hindsight, it was utterly heartbreaking to realize that all the times when we were kids that she'd said, "If I had another son, I'd name him Joel," she'd already *had* a son named Joel.

But Mom also had a tremendous zest for life. She was a performer at home (with broom and without), and had a broad comedic style, singing music hall songs at the top of her voice:

> *I'm the LONESOMEST gal in town . . .*
> *But I'm learning to roll my eyes,*
> *And someday you may be surprised,*
> *When,*
> *I steal someone's lover man and kiss him with a smack.*
> *I'll hug him and I'll tease him,*
> *But I'll never give him back . . .*

My father was the most handy, understated, modest New Englander who ever lived, but certainly no Spencer Tracy. This fact was about the only thing that disappointed my mother about Bill Davis, as she claimed Mr. Tracy was her "boyfriend."

My mother would frequently bemoan her looks in a self-dramatizing way. Dad may not have been a matinee idol, but his wit was drier than a pinot grigio:

"I'm so old and ugly!" she'd say.

Dad took a moment to consider.

"You're not so terrible, *awful* old."

. . .

I was incredibly shy and quiet as a kid, but even so, my rare bursts of enthusiasm always seemed to cause people to go out of their way to get me to tone it the fuck down. What I too often learned was that the moment when, for a change, I did something unselfconsciously, there'd be a big price to pay.

For example, sitting and watching my friend Lucyann's ballet class when we were maybe six years old: The teacher noticed how enthralled I was and kindly said, "Would you like to try?" *Yes, so much!* I waited in the line until it was my turn to leap across the room, which I did with great verve. When I came back, the teacher looked down her nose at me coldly and said, "You may sit down." Evidently my enthusiasm combined with lack of skill represented some sort of unforgivable ballet crime. I had stepped out of the shadows because I thought the coast was clear.

It was not.

I couldn't catch a break. A couple of years after the ballet fiasco, I was at summer camp, and on the first day there was a swimming test. The idea was to see how far we could get without putting our heads up for air. I didn't know how to swim, and I was terrified the other kids would find this out, so I was damn well going to try my hardest to get somewhere.

When it was my turn to swim, I put my face under the water and kicked and swung my arms like crazy until I was all out of puff. As I popped up, I thought, 'Oh man, I must've gotten really far by now . . .' only to find myself pretty much exactly where I'd started. The counselor was looking at me; the other kids were looking at me, each of their faces slack, like they'd seen the Loch Ness monster and it made no sense. I wanted to die.

• • •

I've always been tall. Hell, I was a tall *baby*.

Being tall can be a curse when you're young and/or female, as some of you may know. Standing out as a kid is the one thing you want to avoid at all costs, but when you're a significant bunch of inches taller than your peers, you're pretty much cooked on the not-standing-out thing. My fondest wish was to take up less space in the world, and as a result, my height surely contributed to my extreme shyness.

I spent an inordinate amount of time staring into the bathroom mirror, unable to recognize myself. I'd stand there and think, "Who is that? Who am I?" I was also fixated on trying to figure out if there was anything attractive about my face. I remember being heartened to discover that there was one angle from which I thought I might look pretty: with my head tipped all the way back. But as soon as I realized this, a second thought shooed the first away: This was not a position one could casually find oneself in, so how would people ever get to see me like that?

• • •

My dad had me do things with him from a very young age. If he was shingling the roof or grabbing the kerosene lanterns from the bulkhead during a hurricane, so was I. As a result, I grew up believing I could do anything, and apparently, he thought I could, too. One day, Dad managed to get himself a huge splinter under his thumbnail. Mom was going to pass out just from looking at it—she was a fainter at the sight of blood—but Dad already realized I was made of sterner stuff. He got tweezers and asked me if I'd help him out. "Yes!" toddler me said, as I dug right in.

Just as my mother loved to tell the pew story, Dad loved to tell this story. His belief that I could—and should—do everything and anything instilled in me the sense that if a person could do it, I could do it.

. . .

When I was little, my brother had a toy gun. All the neighborhood boys had guns, too, and were playing army all the time. I wanted to play army, too. So, the Christmas I was four, I asked Santa for a gun. He'd come through the previous year on the sunglasses, so I figured this was a done deal. By this point, I could read and write fairly well, so I composed a letter to Santa. My parents had no idea what I meant by writing "I want a gun," and I presume that when your beloved daughter writes to Santa, you can't break the spell by asking what the hell kind of gun she wants. So, on Christmas morning, I got a five-dollar bill from Santa tucked in a card that read, "Dear Geena, here is some money so you can pick out your own gun. Love, Santa."

I burst into tears. "This is Daddy's handwriting! It's not from Santa! There is no Santa!" That's what I got for being precocious enough to recognize my dad's handwriting at four. Just as well—I had already been torturing my mother for a while about the facts surrounding the existence of Santa, like:

"The chimney's too small for him to come through."

"Santa shrinks down to fit."

"Oh, yeah? Well, we have a Franklin stove, so tell me how that works out?"

I needed facts; I demanded answers. I'm sure that was loads of fun for my mom.

I bought myself that toy gun, though.

. . .

In third and fourth grade I had my first boyfriend. I was confident in David Karhman's affection and felt completely comfortable around him. He used his ice cream money (with his dad's permission) to buy me an ice cream at recess every day. I never worried about what he thought of me or how I should behave around him. I was myself, and I had a boyfriend—simple.

One day, our fourth-grade teacher, Mrs. Moore, was giving away random items from her closet and told us all to take something we might want. "Or might like to give to someone . . ." she said, shooting David and me a very warm, knowing look, and a secret smile. Our relationship was a given.

I sometimes think it was the most natural and uncontrived relationship I've ever had. Turns out it's quite a thing, not changing for somebody else.

Chapter Two
Fingertips on Glory

I think it's probably safe to assume that most people had a monster or two as a kid, and not to be Olympic standard about it, but I think I could medal in Weirdest Monsters and Most Monsters. I had a battalion of them, plus a couple of spare companies and a platoon or two standing by, all ready to go to war with me nightly, right up until I left home at seventeen.

It meant for a fairly exhausting childhood.

To list just a handful of them . . . I had the standard monster under the bed, of course, whom I could manage if I catapulted onto the bed from as far away as possible; that way, it couldn't grab my legs as I sailed over. Of course, once in bed, I couldn't let any part of myself hang over the edge because of all the grabbing. This monster under the bed was different from the one at the *end* of the bed—End of Bed would knock on the bottoms of your feet if you straightened your legs, so I always slept in a tight ball on the top half of the mattress. (I never slept flat out until I was long gone from Wareham.) There was a monster in the closet (obviously—what else are closets for?), and one behind the door (ditto doors). At least with this particular set of monsters it would be safe to go to sleep if I stayed within a very prescribed area of the bed.

Not so with the most challenging monster of my childhood, the one who could read my mind to find out where I was. If you think about it, this is a kinda fascinating, kinda horrifying thing to have to live with. Your standard monsters at least have the advantage of staying put—the one in the closet doesn't leave it and *wander about*, for heaven's sake! But here I had an invisible monster that could look inside my mind, who could find me at any time. And as the whole point of child-hood monsters is to avoid them and outwit them, when it can stalk you through your very thoughts, well . . . this control of my young mind meant that I had to maintain constant and exhausting levels of *vigilance* at bedtime. I had to train my brain to outsmart what was essentially a creation of that very same brain. Hell.

How it went was, if I was in bed and wanted to throw Read-Your-Mind off the scent, I'd think very fervently, "Well, look at me, here in the *kitchen*, having some Ritz Crackers!" The monster would be totally bamboozled by the level of detail and my general badassery. The bit about the snack was crucial as it gave an appearance of veracity to the thought that I was telegraphing. The trap laid, the monster would no doubt waft into the kitchen to get me, even though I was safely in my bedroom, successfully avoiding all the ones in there. But eventually, the strain of keeping this performance up—after all, I hadn't yet been trained as an actor—would become too much, and I'd think, "Ugh, I hope it doesn't realize I'm really in my room . . ." and then I'd have to rocket out of bed and into the hallway just in time as it slithered up the steps toward my bedroom. (I guess Read-Your-Mind couldn't see, since I never worried about it passing by me in the hall.)

"YES!" I'd think, out in the cold hallway, my heart pounding, a pale unfeeling moon at the window. "Yes, yes, I *am* in bed . . ."

None of this made for good sleep patterns.

I also managed to have a monster who existed *outdoors*—in the *daytime*—a feat of which I'm rather proud. This was a colossal giant who stood juuust beyond the curvature of the earth, and who would take a step toward me each time I did something wrong. Accordingly, I spent a lot of time staring at the horizon, trying to see if the top of his massive head had started to appear. With all these monsters, I had set up an elaborate way to torture myself. I could not bear to get anything wrong, and had to please all comers, whatever the cost.

There was a *real* monster, too, up the street. I'll get to that in a bit.

. . .

In the intervening years, I've tried to bring to mind just what kind of horrific crimes I was committing as a kid to merit this kind of surveillance. I was profoundly not a bad child. Nobody wanted to do everything right more than I did.

My monster-y childhood also contained an absolute terror of being poisoned: the second that Mom finished unpacking the grocery bags, I would be sneaking into the pantry to check if any of the cans were dented (to avoid botulism), scrutinizing the eggs to make sure none were cracked (salmonella), and then microscopically inspecting the chicken at dinner for the slightest hint of pink (campylobacter, or *Clostridium perfringens* bacteria). Mom caught me more than once staring at a slightly graying package of ground beef in utter horror. The one that bothered her the most was that I'd never eat a sandwich she made without opening it first to examine the contents.

"What do you think, I'm going to *poison* you?!"

Well, yes, evidently, I did.

One time my parents were out Christmas shopping, and I was home sitting in my dad's olive-green Naugahyde recliner in the living room, paging through their *Reader's Digest*. There was a mention in there about poinsettia plants being poisonous. I slowly tipped down the magazine to look at that very plant, which was right in front of me, on the coffee table. Holy crap. I wondered if it could be giving off fumes that would poison me from just being in the same room with it. I was irresistibly drawn to touch the tiny yellow flowers in the center, and something moist got on my finger.

I decided I was dying.

There was no use even washing my finger now, the damage had been done. I tipped back the recliner and started to feel the poison do its work. When my parents returned and came into the living room where I was, they found me wasting away.

"Mom, I'm sorry," I said, "but I'm dying. I touched the poinsettia."

"Oh, for heaven's sake—you'd have to EAT it," she said.

I was saved!

It was a mystery to me—and everyone else—how I could have become so phobic about being poisoned. Then one day I was hanging around in the church kitchen with my mom and some other ladies while they prepared dinner for a Mr. and Mrs. Club get-together. At some point, their conversation turned to breastfeeding, and I guess my mom thought I was out of earshot when she said,

"Oh, Geena did *not* want to stop nursing. I finally had to put some hot sauce on my nipples, so she'd stop."

BINGO! THERE we go!

• • •

With these torments of the mind, did I *also* need to have a bad case of hypochondria? I don't know—maybe it's an achievement to be so fancy, what with all the ghosts and poisonings and diseases and such. (Thankfully I got free of all this many years ago.) As a kid, every time I heard about a new disease, I was sure I either already had it or would soon get it. My mom had to give in and take me to the doctor to check for breast cancer at twelve, for example.

My longest-lasting affliction struck when I was watching an episode of *Quincy*, the TV show starring Jack Klugman as a brilliant coroner. In this particular episode, Quincy discovered that a high school football star had died from an aneurism.

"He had a ticking time bomb in his head," Quincy said, "just waiting to go off."

Deciding that it was quite likely that I, too, had a ticking time bomb in my head, I spent *the next two years* trying not to move my head—I kid you not. If someone next to me spoke, I'd turn my whole body to look at them.

• • •

I suppose my first major role was that of "daughter," and it was a sometimes challenging one. I absolutely worshipped my mother; she was loving and funny and kind. But my mom's dramatic way of viewing the world probably was a major factor in how *I* viewed the world.

We used to watch *Wide World of Sports* together every Saturday night, and once in a while bullfighting would come on. My mother was a huge animal lover, and she'd seethe, "I'll tell you what—I want to take one of those sticks and stab *him* with it! See how he likes it! I'd *stab* him!"

Of course, she was right about the animal abuse. It was more the "stabbing-the-matador" bit that was hair-raising. I looked over at my dad to check his reaction and he wryly observed, "Your mother doesn't have a lot of Christian charity."

This was especially true when it came to my dad's dad, who lived in the house right behind us. For whatever reason, "Pappy" was very unkind—cruel, even—to my sweet brother, Dan, and it made her blood boil (understandably). Many times, she'd tell me how much she hated Pappy, going so far as to frequently say, "That damn old man! When he dies, I'm gonna dance on his grave—dance, I tell you!"

When he did finally die, years later, I was terrified that she might do just that. She didn't, of course. Not the tiniest amount of dancing transpired.

When I was finally old enough to stay home alone while my folks went somewhere, my mother would try to convince me to come along by saying, "Well, I hope you won't regret not coming if we get killed in an accident." AND I WENT. Which means that what convinced me to go was the opportunity to die along with them, rather than suffer from survivor's guilt.

For all my childhood I didn't have any privacy at home. The

bathroom door had no lock and I had to leave my bedroom door open so that my parents could hear me if I needed something or had a nightmare. (That was the rationale, at least.) There was even a shared closet between our bedrooms, the doors of which also had to be left open. This had all started when I was little, as a way to keep tabs on me, but it didn't change, even when I was a teenager. Come to think of it, I never even thought to *ask* for more privacy . . . or to just go ahead and shut my own damn door.

. . .

When it comes to not talking about things—especially things that might be either embarrassing or bring out emotions—we New Englanders are world champion gold medalists. We will not talk about *anything.*

As an example, we had a cat when Dan and I were very young—Sunny—who one day just vanished. Mom told us that Sunny had run away, but "I'm sure he's with a very nice family now."

WHAT?!?

"We have to go *look* for him!" I cried. "How do you know he's with a nice family? He might be hurt or lost—we have to find him! Why should another family get to have *our cat?*" And on and on, relentlessly. It was beyond comprehension that our gentle, animal-loving parents would immediately give up all hope when our kitty had disappeared. From then on, anytime we were in the car, Dan and I would have our faces plastered to the windows, looking for any sign of Sunny. And if we ever caught a glimpse of a yellow cat, we'd howl for Dad to stop the car to see if it was him. But they were always positive it was not Sunny. Even if we were on vacation in another *state*, we'd be looking for yellow cats. This went on . . . *for years*.

The truth was that Sunny had been run over by a car all those years before, but these dear people wanted to save us the trauma of knowing our cat was dead . . . thereby replacing *that* trauma with literally years of worrying about him. I should have asked them later if they regretted making that choice; it had to be absolute torture for them as well, realizing they had spared us nothing. We were a family mute in cars that were about to crash; we stayed mum to prevent unwelcome emotions. We kept our peace.

In my family there was also an unspoken rule to never talk about bodily functions . . . especially anything to do with sex or reproductive organs. I was so naïve that I was always tripping over land mines without realizing they were there.

When I was about eight years old, I was hanging around in the living room with my parents and looking at a ladies' magazine. After seeing yet another ad cloaked in mystery about "feeling fresh," I asked with exasperation, "What the heck is a TAMPON, anyway?"

Here is a multiple-choice question about what happened next. Did my mom:

a. Sit next to me to look at the ad together?
b. Take me into the other room to explain what tampons are for?
   Or,
c. Pretend she didn't hear me?

The answer is: Fiercely whisper "I will tell you *later*" as my father quickly raised his newspaper up over his face. I therefore assumed tampons had something to do with *Dad*. (And oh, she *didn't* tell me later.)

One of the most mortifying things ever to happen to me resulted from reading an article in yet another issue of *Reader's Digest*. This one was about how it was actually possible to get pregnant from sperm *outside* the vagina, if they swam inside. (This was obviously very unlikely, but I took everything I read in that magazine as absolute gospel.)

My dad would go away from time to time for his work, and whenever he did, I got to sleep with Mom in their room. (No monsters in there.) The next time I went to sleep on Dad's side of the bed after reading that article, I thought, What if Dad left sperm on the sheet *and it climbs up my leg*? I had to make sure I was safe from that happening. Forget that I was far from puberty—what did I know? So I got out a clean sheet, sneaked into their room (so Mom wouldn't know), and spread it out on just Dad's side of the bed.

A few days later Mom said, "Oh, Geena, your dad is hurt that you would put a sheet down on his side of the bed to lie on." The sheet! I had forgotten to take it away! But of course I could never, ever speak of *my father's sperm*—I would much rather have died . . . so I was forced to let stand that I thought his side of the bed might not be clean. What agony.

As it was, I didn't get my period until I was well into my sixteenth year, yet I remember seeing blood in my underwear and thinking, *Well, it's curtains for me.* I even told my mother—for the second time—"I'm sorry to tell you this, Mom, but I'm dying." She quickly disabused me of that notion.

. . .

My battalion of monsters, various poisonings, phantom diseases, and undead pets kept me quite busy, but someone in my real life was a monster. I just had no clue that he was.

When I was ten, my parents asked my brother to give me half of his paper route, and he kindly gave me the half closest to our house. He had a bike, but I didn't yet, so I delivered the papers on foot. My special touch was to knock on the door and hand the paper directly to each customer, rather than leave it on the lawn.

Delivering papers gave me lots of time by myself, and I invented myriad ways to escape into my own world. Up the street from our house was a short stretch of my route where there were no houses, only a creek on both sides and pretty woods. For some reason, I imagined I was utterly unobservable during this part of my walk, so most days I would stop and look for twigs that looked either like a Y or a V. A stick in the shape of a Y meant "Yes, it is safe to go on." A V twig, much harder to find, meant Very—as in, "*Very* safe to go on." Then I'd stand on the little bridge for a while, throwing the twigs into the water and singing at the top of my lungs. The thing was, my elderly customers up the street were often so impatient to get their newspapers, they'd come out and look down the hill to find out what was taking me so long, only to see me down there yowling hymns at the stream. Sometimes, just as Mrs. Perkins had done about my lawn mowing, they'd call my mother to say there must be something wrong with me.

But this was not the worst thing to happen on my paper route.

Mr. Teller rented an apartment in the upstairs of a house on my route. I'd give Mrs. Keys her paper down below, then walk up the back stairs each day to hand Mr. Teller his *Cape Cod Standard-Times*. He would thank me by inviting me in for a treat—usually Ho Hos or Ding Dongs.

Eventually, Mr. Teller wanted hugs, too. Long hugs, during which I might even finish the Ho Hos.

And then to the hugging he added rubbing his knuckle on my vulva.

I didn't know what he was doing, or why; in fact, I had no idea that it was bad *or even that there was anything at all private between my legs.*

One day, innocently enough, I was chatting with my mother in the kitchen as she washed dishes and I mentioned Mr. Teller's treats and hugs.

"But there's one thing I don't understand," I said. "Why does he do this?" and I reached out to her and did to her exactly what he'd been doing to me.

At my touch, she just about rocketed through the ceiling. It was beyond my understanding then, but I cannot imagine how my mom felt when faced with such a revelation, when all she wanted to do was protect me. The pan she'd been scouring was dropped into the sink; she banged through the front door and disappeared before I could fathom what was happening.

I watched her march right up the middle of the street to where Mr. Teller lived, and with confusion and fear, I saw her disappear behind the house.

I waited. I really can't tell you how long—I just stood frozen on the front porch. What was happening? What had I done? What had I said to have caused my usually serene, music-hall singing mother to lose her faculties and blaze up the street?

Eventually, I saw the unmistakable figure of my mother returning; she was now on the sidewalk instead of the middle of the road, thankfully. She stopped when she got to me.

"From now on," Mom said, "you leave the paper at the bottom of the stairs. You never go up there again." And then she went inside; I could hear her taking the pan out of the sink and going at it again.

What had once been secret was no longer secret; I didn't know yet what price this would cause me to pay.

And what of Teller? Not for us a trip to the police to report a sexual assault by an old creep; we were New Englanders: We sucked things up and kept them hidden. I had no idea I'd been molested; I just knew something very weird and shameful had happened.

Whatever it was, I had done something horrifically inappropriate, yet again. Yes, there were land mines everywhere, some so hidden you would never see them coming. To try to ease my stress, I took up repeating this sentence over and over to myself: "In ten years you won't even remember this." It didn't turn out to be true, but it certainly did a lot to ease my mind at the time.

. . .

From four years old on, my absolute best friend was Lucyann. She lived across the street, a couple of houses down, and we were inseparable. We played together almost every day, and her mom, Lucia, was like my second mother. (I had a third mother, too: Amy Kelly, my piano and flute teacher. I was blessed to have so many amazing women in my life.)

Lucia knew I was unable to speak up for myself—that if she invited me to stay for dinner, I would say no thank you—so she'd just call my mother up and say, "Lucille, Geena is staying for dinner, talk to you later," and hang up before my mom could say, "Oh no, don't trouble yourself. . . ." I loved Lucia so much. And I never had to worry about turning down something I really wanted. She would just force things on me, like her delicious oven-fried chicken with tons of garlic.

Lucyann and I would often watch TV with Lucia, and one night during Johnny Carson she proclaimed, "If you're ever on the Johnny Carson show, Geena, you know you've made it." I squirreled that little nugget away, right up until I finally was on Carson. She also often told me I was beautiful—"Just wait till you're grown up, Geena, you'll see," she'd say. I felt it would be much better if the other kids thought I was pretty right then, not just an adult thinking future-me would be attractive. But I still loved the compliment.

One of my and Lucyann's favorite things to do was save up our money and buy a quart of milk. Then, as one of us drank from the carton, the other would try to make the drinker laugh, the goal being to get the milk to come out of her nose.

She and I were always putting plays on in her basement, sometimes for just her mother, sometimes for mine, sometimes both. Those plays did not reveal a glimpse of future talent—in fact, they were just godawful—and our poor mothers suffered through so many of them. It wasn't as if they ever said, "Oh, yay, girls, another play!" but we were undeterred. We always had to be bewigged, usually with tights on our heads where the trailing legs would represent ponytails; when Lucyann got a set of plastic molded wigs for Christmas, we wore those instead.

But the most important things in our lives were our Wishniks, a brand of troll dolls—you know, with the super long hair. Most days I'd pack up my Wishniks and head to Lucyann's. She and I had created an elaborate fictional world featuring a series of trolls with incredibly complex lives. It was a soap opera that ran for many years.

My most important Wishnik was lavender-haired Kiki Kadoodle-hopper. She was a very famous actress, and she had a husband, Nick. You knew he was a man because I drew a mustache on him and cut his long red hair into a crew cut. For me, back then, defacing a doll was a deeply rebellious thing to do. Kiki had a plain, loyal, sweet sister named Amy, who always wore her green troll hair in a bun.

These were real characters to me, probably based on the characters of Ginger Grant and Mary Ann Summers in *Gilligan's Island*. (I watched every episode so many times that I can still remember the words to the songs in their musical version of *Hamlet*.) No one could guess how much my handful of Wishniks meant to me; they were my world. I have them all still, and the mounds of clothes I made for them. (Evening gowns for Kiki, of course.) I dove deeply into the minutiae of their lives.

In fact, Kiki/Ginger and Amy/Mary Ann were expressions of two sides of my own character: the proto-actress and the reserved, quiet girl people seemed to want me to be.

. . .

Bless you if you imagine I was inundated with suitors as a young woman. In fact, I had just one date in high school, with Eddie O'Melia, and he didn't ask me out for a second one. Over the years I've had multiple people come up to me and say, "My cousin/uncle/friend dated you in high school," and my reply is always "Is his name Eddie O'Melia? Because otherwise, not so much."

So it wasn't just the neighbors who felt I was a little peculiar. It was definitely boys, too. The Teen Youth Group at my church was led by our junior pastor, Wyatt, and as we sat in a circle at one meeting, he asked, "What would you look for in someone you may want to date?"

A very popular boy, Skip, went first.

"Well, I don't know *exactly*," Skip said, "all I know for sure is she wouldn't wear THOSE," pointing to my shoes. I didn't see that coming—that *I* would be the example of what was most undesirable in a girl.

On the sidewalk after church some months later, I was chatting with Junior Pastor Wyatt; I'd decided to seek his advice on how I could get boys to like me more. (Other than wearing different shoes.) At one point we lowered our voices to watch some squirrels play on a branch overhead, and Wyatt took this opportunity to say, "Why don't you try being like you are right now more often? You know, more *quiet*—not so *big* sometimes."

More training, then. It felt, once again, as if I'd stepped out of a lane I didn't know existed, but that was very obvious to everyone else. I couldn't know then that this would further stiffen my resolve to break out and become self-determining and entirely myself. No—as a teenager, this was traumatic and disheartening. I mean, look how well I remember every detail of these things! And I still have the shoes Skip hated!

. . .

When I was fourteen, I got a job babysitting for the neighbors two doors down, and they liked me enough to invite me to go to their church with them one evening. The Congregational church I grew up in was the very traditional, old-fashioned kind of Protestant church, but the one they took me to was positively *Pentecostal*; there were probably about five hundred people in this enormous tent. I remember the sermon was entitled "Fingertips on Glory." The minister explained that though we may have been righteous enough that we could just touch glory with our fingertips, we would have to fully turn our lives over to Jesus if we wanted to climb up and live in *actual* glory. He led a prayer at the end, and at one point he asked us to keep our eyes closed. If we loved Jesus, we were to raise our hand. He'd call out, "I see that hand . . ."

Eyes closed, I assumed everyone was raising their hands. This was a church, after all! I raised my hand too—no big deal; of course I loved Jesus, plus, no way was I going to risk standing out for *not* raising my hand. As soon as all eyes were open again, the pastor said that everyone who had raised their hand must come down front and turn themselves over to Jesus.

I was caught: I had raised my hand; I *had* to go down. The family I was with, who had entrusted the well-being of their young children to me, was thunderstruck to see me step out of the pew, but they didn't know I'd raised my hand. But there was no way of denying it now. As I made my way down the aisle, I realized that somehow, I had done something really terrible, certainly bad enough for the giant monster on the other side of the horizon to take another step toward me. Five hundred people were suddenly watching me. The only other person to go to the front, a woman ahead of me, had already collapsed, crying tears of joy; when I got there, I started crying, too, but in my case, it was because I was terrified and ashamed.

As I stood there, stricken, a woman came up and said, "Hi, Geena, I know your mom. . . ."

Ohhh, *perfect*. With that, the woman handed me a tissue and a New Age Bible and offered words of comfort . . . and then I had to return to my pew, to the family who now must have thought I was insane with religiosity. Or that they'd have to apologize to my parents for, like, converting me to a *different religion*. They drove me home and didn't say a word; I got out of the car and raced upstairs to hide that Bible under the mattress. I was panic-stricken that my parents would find out what I'd done—maybe I'd disgraced my whole church—so I kept it from them *forever*.

· · ·

In grade school I was used to getting straight As without even trying. In fact, my first-grade teacher would set me aside with some of the other kids to help them with reading. The only B that I ever got was in second grade, for Effort. My mom asked Mrs. Fearing what exactly she wanted me to put more effort into if I was already getting As. But things all changed when I started junior high. Suddenly, there were papers to write that would take several days, tests that required more than one night's study.

Things got serious fast: I was put on the National Honor Society, but that became a huge source of stress: Now I had to keep my grades to that level. If not, I'd be put on warning to bring them up again or be dropped from the society. I would inevitably self-sabotage and not be able to finish writing a report or to study for a big test, and then have one semester to claw my way back up, because if I ever got kicked out of the Honor Society, *that would be the end of my life*.

My dear mom really helped me out here because she knew that if

I faked being sick, there was probably a really good reason for it—usually because of not being ready for a test that day. So without admitting she knew I was faking, she'd let me stay home . . . and even make me the cinnamon toast reserved for when you were ill.

And then there were those days when Lucyann and I would head out to her backyard and pretend to be characters from a TV Western called *The Rifleman*, which we'd watch in reruns over and over. Because I was taller, I would be the father, Lucas McCain, a veteran of the Civil War, and she would be my son, Mark. The plots of the show quite often centered around Lucas having to save Mark by using his Model 1892 Winchester rifle. Lucas was certifiably badassy, and we played those roles with tremendous relish. In hindsight, it's interesting to realize that there weren't any female characters we wanted to play; instead, we chose a couple of the toughest male characters on TV. I was still the same little girl who had wanted a gun for Christmas.

Only now I had traded up—to a rifle.

Chapter Three
Lady Fatima's Town House for Young Ladies

People have matching furniture?

My family was oddball. Besides there being axes all over our house, the wallpaper was sixty years old; every chair at the dining table was different from the next; there was no shower; and the "guest room" was filled with one gigantic mound of stuff—old clothes, broken furniture, unfinished sewing or knitting projects, stacks of string-bound *National Geographic* magazines. To add to this pile, you would simply stand in the doorway and chuck whatever it was on top.

I wanted to host sleepovers but was embarrassed at the state of my house . . . so I decided I was going to do something about it. I wanted to start with the living room because that's where my friends and I would all sleep on the floor. By twelve years old I had saved up enough money from my paper route to order prepasted wallpaper and curtains from the Ward catalog, which I then picked up on my bike when they arrived at the package store. I stashed it all in my room, and one day, when my mom went off to her job as a teacher's aide, I wallpapered the whole living room, installed curtain rods, and hung the curtains by myself—all before she got home.

Mom was stunned beyond belief.

"What . . . how . . . what did you do?"

When my parents got over the shock, they really loved it. In hindsight, it was very strange that they didn't say, "Why didn't you consult with us!" I had changed their house! I was twelve! But I think they were just accepting of the way I was—perfectly capable of taking on big projects. And also knowing they would never have gotten around to it themselves.

There were a lot of projects. I was very, very busy. I built a high jump on the lawn behind the garage so I could practice at home; I made handbags and chokers out of leather to sell at the local flea market; and I spent a lot of time planning out what my talent portion would be when I eventually would try out for the Miss Wareham pageant. I never did go for Miss Wareham, but the talent would likely have involved me playing the flute while dancing around mannequins dressed in clothes I'd designed and made. I shudder to think.

. . .

By the time I reached high school, I was keenly aware that I was altogether too . . . *something* for the other kids around me. Too much? Too tall? Too oddball? I mean, I knew I was going to be an actor—that was never in question. Well, there was that one time when I thought another career might be even more appealing: a department store gift wrapper. At Christmas we would drive up to Boston to see the window displays, and this one year we bought gloves for my aunt Gloria at fancy Cherry's Department Store. We took them to the special present-wrapping department, and I watched in absolute awe as the workers tore off great sheets from giant rolls of wrapping paper and folded them around the boxes so very artfully. I physically craved to have that job, but my fixation wore off after that Christmas and I went back to my regular old movie star goal.

Anyway, I knew I didn't quite fit in. I had a general sense that my classmates rather liked me, but I had no success with that other kind of popular: *After School* Popular, where you would hang out with other kids, go to their houses, get invited to parties and such. The only real-life, outside-of-school friend I had was Lucyann; thankfully, we hung out nearly every day. But she wasn't in my grade, and I did so long to feel included.

A huge highlight of my high school career was when the most popular girl in my class, Sherry, asked if I'd like to walk to school with her in the mornings. I literally couldn't believe it. Why would she have suddenly thought of this? Had her mother perhaps put her up to it? I mean, we would both have said we were *friends*, but again not the hang-at-the-mall, have-sleepovers, walk-to-school-together kind.

Sherry dated one of the most popular guys in our class, Gary, through most of high school, and a call that Gary made to me in our junior year turned into one of the most significant calls in my life up until that point. He phoned at 9:00 p.m. on a Saturday to say that some classmates had gathered at his house for a party, and would I like to come join them? Well, this was it: the moment had finally arrived when my life would change forever, and I would become one of the kids who hung out together. I ran to ask my dad if I could take the car—and he said no. "Go out—at *this* time of night? No, it's too late to just be going out *now*." I could not make him see it my way: Even if I'd gone out at 7:00, I'd still be staying out until 11:00, so what difference did it make if I arrived late?? To this day I still wonder if my life would have changed if I could have gone to that party. Likely not. But an invitation like that never came along again.

There was a girl named Anna who moved to our town in junior high school, and from the moment she arrived I was obsessed with her. She was almost as tall as I was, but very comfortable in her body, and she became popular right away. I was in love with her. I really wanted to be her friend—and I did indeed successfully get her to befriend me. I even got to stay with her family when my folks had to go to Vermont for a funeral.

I was enthralled by how worldly she and her family seemed. Her parents used *cloth* napkins at dinner—and the whole family was from *somewhere else*, which made them automatically exotic. In high school, Anna would often talk about whatever new song she was obsessed with, and I would always say I loved it, too. Unfortunately, I couldn't honestly attest to the brilliance of the songs she loved. We didn't have a record player at home, and the radio in the kitchen was for news only. Should I tell her honestly that I didn't know the songs, but would love to hear them? No, I couldn't do that—how mortifying not to have a radio! So what I did was fall back on a highly risky, if understandable, ploy: I would simply gush about her choices, even if I'd never heard the actual songs.

One morning, Anna asked me if I also liked her new favorite song, "Golden Dreams."

"I love that song!" I said, wanting badly, so badly, to bond with her through any means possible. I'll never forget how her enthusiasm suddenly vanished.

"That isn't a song," Anna said, calmly, as though she laid this kind of tripwire for a living. "I made it up."

I needed to get out of Wareham, Mass. I needed to find a place where I could be someone else, where I could get a fresh start without everyone knowing how *gooney* I'd always been. Where the clothes I made might be appreciated, and no one had seen my giant platform shoes with the rainbow appliques on them. Where virtually the tallest person in the whole school—who mixed serious self-effacement with strange explosions of attention-grabbing behavior—could find a sense of belonging.

My brother, Dan, two years ahead of me, had been mercilessly bullied in high school. I can't even describe some of the unspeakable things his classmates did to him—including his teammates on the track team. Even the teachers would sometimes publicly bully him, if you can believe it: One of them, a woman, would hold his papers with a failing grade up for the class to see; another, male, teacher would only call him Dinny Dim Wit, and still two other teachers regularly called him Dumb Kid. Dan had an undiagnosed case of dyslexia, which people didn't really know about back then, and which caused him torment he didn't deserve, or even understand.

For Dan's junior year, he transferred to Bristol County Agricultural School—and the difference was dramatic and so gratifying. No one there knew he had been an object of bullying at his old high school; he was just the fun, likable new kid who fit right in and made friends easily. Thank God for that school, and my parents for taking the steps to put him there. Getting out made a world of difference for Dan, who got a degree in engineering and ran his own successful company in Las Vegas for many years.

. . .

Toward the end of my junior year, Wareham High announced that it was partnering with a foreign exchange student program. I was the only one to ask for an application. I prayed my parents would be able to afford it, because I *needed* to go—suddenly, miraculously, it looked like I could have a chance to try on a completely different life, just as Dan had.

Perhaps my parents sensed this; whatever the case, they promised they'd find the means to fund the trip. We signed me up to spend my whole senior year abroad, and I eagerly looked forward to seeing the list of countries I could choose from. But the entirety of the list turned out to be only one slot, with one family: in Sweden . . .

. . . where they spoke, I surmised, Swedish. It turned out I'd never given Sweden an ounce of my attention. I wasn't even clear about where it was. But now I was fully aware that there was a country almost four thousand miles away, across the Atlantic and into the vast, frozen north, and I would be going there. For a year. Where they spoke Swedish.

I. Could. Not. Wait.

A few weeks before I was to leave, some of my girlfriends from the track team and I went to a beach near the Massachusetts Maritime Academy at Buzzard's Bay, to have a farewell picnic.

I always felt so comfortable with my track friends—all of us were a little bit misfitty. Title IX had passed only very recently, and girl athletes were rather strange birds. The people who really, really wanted me to play sports were the members of the girls' basketball team—they would *beg* me to join. Terrified of having a whole gym full of people watch my gangly-ass self fail to score points, I'd always decline by pointing out that I didn't know how to play, at all.

"Then just *stand* there! You're the tallest girl in any town around here!" they said.

Nope, I was sure I was profoundly unathletic. On the track team I did the high jump, and the tactic I used to make up for lack of skill was to stand around looking as tall and confident as I could, hoping the other team would mess up simply from fear of what that giantess over there could do.

Anyway, there my track friends and I were, having our picnic, when a sailor in uniform a few years older than us ambled across the sand toward our group. We all stopped talking and stared at him; none of us had ever had an actual sort of grown-up man approach us to chat. He asked what we were doing, amiably, and my friends told him we were having a little going-away party for me. He asked us a few more questions, then turned to me and said, "Hey, can I talk to you for a minute?" We all looked at one another—*what's this about?* The other girls indicated discreetly that I should go, but there was no question that I wasn't going to go with him. I felt like I had to. He was an older man with a uniform on. I got up and walked with him a little ways from the group, and we leaned up against a low rock wall. He asked if I had a boyfriend, told me he thought I was pretty, and then started kissing me. Having once made out with Eddie O'Melia, I felt somewhat up to the task, but it was very odd to find myself suddenly kissing a stranger, a sailor, just out of the blue. (He was *in* blues). It didn't get hot and heavy; he eventually said goodbye and walked away, and I walked back to my friends.

We were all dumbfounded by what had happened. But what strikes me the most now was that we had all thought: *Of course if a guy asked one of us to go with him and make out, we were obliged to do so . . .* even if it meant leaving one's own going-away party. The wishes of a total stranger, a male, took precedence over doing right by close friends.

. . .

In late August 1973, with my senior year about to begin on another continent, my parents drove me to Logan Airport in Boston.

I couldn't say I'd thought any of this through terribly much, because as the plane was taxiing, I caught a glimpse of my parents waving from the departure lounge window. These were the days when you could accompany people to the very door of the plane, and when I saw them, this thought suddenly slammed into my head: *Hang on . . . So in other words, I'm not going to see another person I know—for a* year??

This was a colossal shock—though of course it *shouldn't* have been. I knew, even in that boggled state, that I would survive. I might even flourish. After all, this was to be the antidote to all of my not-fitting-in and "please-sit-down-you're-too-much." Stunned, I waved back at Mom and Dad, but I couldn't tell if they saw it, because we were speeding down the runway on our way to London, where I'd change planes to head north to Stockholm.

In Stockholm, a woman who worked for the exchange program met me at the plane and took me straight to the central train station. I had a million questions for her—*How on earth does this program work if I'm supposed to not see a single person I know for a year?*—but she hurried me along to catch a train. To my horror, she was not going to take me to my host family; instead, she found me a seat and asked a random woman sitting across the aisle to tell me when to get off the train. I assume that's what she said, anyway, because I couldn't speak *ett ord* of Swedish yet. And that was it: She was gone, and I was utterly alone in a foreign country, on a hundred-mile ride north to the town of Sandviken.

For a while we trundled through Stockholm and its environs, through vast railyards backing onto large Gothic buildings. The train picked up speed as it followed a sort of canal, then turned, heading out beyond the city. The streets gave way to fields, to low hills covered in evergreens; small villages raced by, with unpronounceable names punctuated with umlauts and overrings. Once in a while we'd pull into a station; I'd look expectantly at the stranger now charged with my welfare, and she'd shake her head. *Don't get off here.*

After about two hours, the train slowed once more, and my neighbor used a mixture of gestures and smiles to alert me to the fact that this was my stop. I had no idea how I was supposed to find the house; I had no address or even a phone number. (I didn't have any Swedish money for a pay phone, even if I'd had a number.) But from the platform I saw a lovely young woman of about twenty speed into the parking lot; she seemed confident that I was the person she was supposed to fetch. Really, I could have been anyone, and so could *she*, but perhaps I stood out as American? This was Ann-Katrin Sundelius, the daughter in the family that was hosting me. She welcomed me and introduced herself in very good English. I was utterly disoriented, confused, and a little terrified of what I'd gotten myself into, as well as suffering from a sore throat I'd somehow picked up on the plane. Ann-Katrin drove me the short distance to the house I was supposed to spend the next year in. There I met Karin, my host mother, and Rune, the father, as well as their son,

Lars, who was leaving the next day to fly to *my* hometown, in a true foreign exchange (though he didn't stay with my parents). I would get to know Lars well on the other end of this adventure.

After introductions, Karin took me upstairs to show me my new room—Lars's room, so very much a boy's territory. Karin stood in the doorway and perhaps intuited that the beer coasters and car posters covering the walls might not be exactly what a seventeen-year-old girl would be expecting.

To explain the discrepancy, she said, in English,

"We asked for a boy."

Before stepping out of the room, she added, "Don't change anything," and with that, closed the door.

Oh.

The rest of that first day I was in a fog, what with jet lag, a sore throat, and the instantaneous, overwhelming homesickness that had taken hold of me before the plane even left the ground. Eventually I changed my clothes and headed downstairs. The family was gathered in the back garden, where Karin handed me a tiny bowl containing a few yellow berries of some kind; politely, I ate them—only to look up from the now-empty bowl to see a smorgasbord of horrified expressions. I learned later that these were cloudberries, very special and rare because they mostly only grew in the wild—a Swedish delicacy. Turned out I was to have *shared* the minuscule bowl of berries, but I'd proceeded to gobble them all up. (*"So, those gluttonous Americans! It's true . . ."*)

For the rest of the afternoon, small groups of the family's friends would drop by to get a gander at the American Girl, and everyone talked about me in Swedish with great good humor. At some point in each visit, Karin would ask me to say what she'd taught me, the first words I would learn in Swedish: "Jag har ont in halsen" (I have a sore throat). Everyone would laugh delightedly. Thus far I had embarrassed myself with a bowl of berries, but redeemed myself by parroting my new phrase, so now I felt that it was a good time to ask for what I most wanted in the world at that moment: to call my parents. In theory, the call was to let them know I'd arrived safely, but now my real goal was to tell them that as lovely as my new family was, leaving everything I know for nearly a year was all a horrible, horrible mistake on my part and that I needed to come home on the very next plane.

In the morning, Karin set a very small glass of warm Coca-Cola in front of me, since she'd heard Americans liked Coke. I drank it, and evidently that was enough for her—I had proven that Americans *did* like Coke. I don't remember seeing it again after that. For breakfast that first morning, she'd made me an egg, sausages, potatoes, and porridge, *and* pancakes, and a *steak*, because she'd also heard that Americans ate huge breakfasts. It was extremely kind of her, so I ate as much as I could, wanting to do everything right. I didn't do everything right: The thing I did very *wrong* was to take the assumed hard-boiled egg out of the strange little holder it was in and smack it down on the table, to her utter astonishment. The soupy egg went splattering everywhere. There was no way she could make sense of what I'd just done; she didn't think: *Oh, Geena must have thought it was hard-boiled, and was just cracking the shell to peel it.* And I didn't even *try* to explain my behavior, because I'd never heard of soft-boiled eggs. I thought it was possible she'd given me an undercooked egg as a prank.

So began my first full day in Sweden. I was to be there for nearly a year.

. . .

Two days later, I was deposited at the Swedish equivalent of high school in Sandviken, where I met with the principal and got a list of my classes. He spoke English very well, so we had a brief chat before a student arrived to show me to my first class, which was history. And just as I hadn't realized I'd be alone for a year until I was *on the plane*, it was suddenly obvious that there was something else I hadn't thought about at all ahead of time: Swedish school was taught in SWEDISH. And unless the teacher was going to talk about the history of sore throats, I wouldn't understand a single word of this class. Again, I shouldn't have been surprised, but in fact I was stunned to realize that I was completely fucked. Where was that lady from the exchange-student service now, the one who had taken me to the train? Had anyone at her company put even a moment's thought into how this could possibly have worked?

After class, I sidled up to the teacher and said, in English, "Excuse me, but what am I supposed to *do*?"

The poor teacher admitted that she'd been wondering the same thing—after all, she couldn't very well teach the whole class in English just for me. She kindly showed me the seven pages I was supposed to read for the night's assignment, and we both completely skipped over the fact that the history book was, of course, also in Swedish.

That night, I read the seven pages by looking up *every single word* in a Swedish/English dictionary. What else could I do? I also wrote my third letter home out of probably a hundred letters I'd write in just the first few months. The gist of the letters was always the same: *This idea was a terrible mistake, I didn't realize what it would be like, I'm dying of homesickness, and I have to come home right away. Oh, and I'm so sorry you spent the money for me to come here, but maybe we can get a refund . . . when I come home, immediately.*

Mom would always write me back, of course, and tell me about things happening back home, how my dog, 99, was doing (she was named after a character on the TV show *Get Smart*); she'd say that they all missed me and were so proud of what I was doing . . . and not a single word about the only thing I'd written about, the coming-home thing. My letters became more and more impassioned: *Didn't you read what I wrote you, Mom? I really must come home! Maybe I can get my job back at Grant's Appliance Store to pay you back.* (I'd been hired to work in the credit department at only sixteen because they said I was the only applicant to ever know what a *"gross"* was.) But no, it was still "Thanks for your letter, Geena, so glad you're having a good time!" I tried amending my goal to see if I could get a different reaction: *Okay, I'm guessing you're probably thinking I should stick it out, learn from the experience . . . and I can see how that's important . . . so how about this: I stay until Christmas, and then come home. I will have gotten all the benefit out of being away for a long time, and I'd still be able to come back and not be home-sick and have the rest of my senior year in English. . . .*

But nothing worked. Mom responded to every letter as if I'd said none of that, as if I were writing about what a fabulous time I was having. Clearly, she wanted me to stick it out for the whole thing, and I would just have to accept that and make the best of it.

I started Swedish classes in the evenings as soon as I got there, and my host family spoke Swedish pretty much exclusively with me; this full immersion policy really worked. In a little over a month,

I could communicate and understand what I needed to get by, and by Christmas I was rather fluent. (And much less homesick, now that I could communicate *and* understand what the teachers said in school!) I'd already had five years of Latin, so in Latin class I could figure out what the Swedish words meant from knowing what the Latin words meant . . . a kind of reverse translation.

I was definitely feeling more at ease. For whatever reason, the kids at school had concluded that I was interesting and fashionable and, erm, *cool*. (Having landed from a different planet helped, of course.) My new classmates all assumed I'd been *very* popular with the boys back home. Apparently, they thought I was pretty, and dressed well. Hot dog! I wasn't about to disabuse them of these opinions because it seemed that I had successfully reinvented myself. Yes, I was tall; yes, I was quirky; and no, neither of those things disqualified me from being part of the in-crowd—in fact, I was right smack *in* the in-crowd.

Or maybe I was suddenly so popular because of the super dope cream-colored wool coat and super chic cream-colored beret my glamorous aunt Gloria bought for me for my trip.

A couple of months in I had a memorable conversation at the dinner table with Karin. There we were, Karin, Rune, Ann-Katrin, and I, chatting pleasantly over our Swedish meatballs, when out of nowhere Karin asked me why I never used the "bidé" in the bathroom.

"Varför använder du inte bidén?"

Why don't I use the *what now*?

Just as with Anna, who had tricked me with "Golden Dreams," I was faced with a dilemma: Did I admit that I had no idea what a "bidé" was, or did I bluff right back and assert myself?

"Jag använder det hela tiden!" I told her that I used it all the time—

since it was clearly a bad thing if I never used it. I assumed that since the thing she was talking about was something in the bathroom, it had to be that strange extra fixture in there that I'd never seen before. But I was utterly unclear about what it was supposed to be *for.*

"No, you don't, you've never even used it once," Karin said.

Never used it once, huh? And how did Karin know what I did or didn't do in the bathroom, anyhow? It was becoming clear that it was a very embarrassing not to use this thing.

"Well, I *do* use it, all the time. In fact, I feel like using it *right now.*" I promptly pushed my chair away from the table, stood up, and strode to the bathroom, locking the door behind me. And there it was, a low porcelain . . . foot bath? What was it about this thing that was so important to Karin that she needed to quiz me about it at the dinner table? Well, obviously it was important enough that I should prove immediately that I used it, a *lot.* So much so, in fact, that I just had to get up right in the middle of dinner to . . . wash my feet?

Honestly, if you'd never seen or heard of a bidet, would you have known what it was for? Keep in mind, I was a girl who had rather recently had to ask her parents what a tampon was. Accordingly, I turned on the water in the bidet and let it run for a while.

Oh, it's unbearable to imagine what the conversation at the table was like while I was gone, with me having suddenly gotten up from eating dinner to go in the bathroom and wash my ass.

. . .

During the summer before Sweden, I had spent a lot of time with Aunt Gloria, my mother's cousin, whom I adored. She was the only woman on either side of the family who drank, smoked, was divorced, and had a *career*—*so* exotic. She was classy, too—she wore a French twist in her hair and was very worldly and sophisticated. Also, she lived in Framingham, which was *almost* a city! I loved Gloria so much. She signaled to me that there was another world beyond the one I found myself in.

I think Aunt Gloria's sophistication and glamour engendered one of my childhood obsessions: fantasizing what I would be like on New Years' Eve 1999, when I would be forty-three. I pictured myself as being at a very elegant party, dressed chicly, holding a martini glass, and having a witty conversation with my gathered friends.

As a kid I visited Aunt Gloria and my cousin Tobey for the weekend now and then. During a visit when I was nine, Gloria had to work on Saturday morning, so she gave Tobey, then twelve, some money and left her in charge. Tobey suggested we go to the movies, so we went and got on a bus into the city *all by ourselves*. Now, at this age I wasn't even braiding my own hair, let alone going off with another kid anywhere we wanted to, with money. Tobey picked the movie, and I swear I lost my shit when it started. The movie was *Thunderball*, and the opening credits rolled over images of naked women swimming in silhouette through colored water. In amazement, I decided that I was going to have a very different life from what the rest of my extended family seemed to have. I was determined to have an *Aunt Gloria* kind of life.

When I was sixteen, Gloria took me to my very first play, at a dinner theater. I didn't know then that dinner theater was kind of cheeseball; I thought it was the height of elegance. The play was *Last of the Red Hot Lovers* starring Stubby Kaye (I still have the framed *Playbill* on my wall). Before the show started, Aunt Gloria ordered a glass of wine and lit up a cigarette, and my young mind could barely fathom such a sophisticated move.

As we ate our dinner before the play, she said: "When you're in college, we should go to the coast of Portugal. They have the best scuba diving there."

I couldn't believe my ears—first dinner theater, next scuba diving OFF THE COAST OF PORTUGAL? Where would it end?

That same night, Gloria also said, "You know, you're going to have to work on your laugh. Boys aren't going to like that, it's too loud."

Oh dear, there it was again—that stab. But what I didn't know then was that Aunt Gloria wouldn't be right about *every* boy. Matts would learn to love my laugh, especially after he did that thing to me that first made me laugh, then squirm, then not laugh *at all*—but in a good way.

. . .

Matts was a dreamboat whom I got to know on a school trip in February of my Swedish year. About twenty of us went to Amsterdam, and though I hadn't known Matts before this trip, one night at a restaurant he ordered calamari. I had never even heard of it, let alone tasted it. We bonded over my new love of fried squid and my first sip of beer, and we quickly became inseparable. Finally, and for the first time since fourth grade, I could say I had an actual boyfriend, and a gorgeous tall blond Swedish one, at that. I knew how to say "I love you" in Swedish, but now for the first time I could say it to a *boy*. Matts's parents were incredibly warm, loving people; they made it clear that I was a part of their family now, too. They even invited me to go along with them on a family trip and booked a hotel room for Matts and me TO SHARE—a thing so alien to me as to be almost unbelievable.

A whole new world—that of being in love—had opened itself to me, but there was still my inner New England church girl to contend with. Matts knew that I intended to stay a virgin, despite the shared room. Looking back, I would have made a fabulous Roman Catholic. But he showed me that that didn't mean we couldn't enjoy the full range of bliss afforded to human beings by mouths and hands and such.

One day, I decided I just had to tell Matts about the strange, inexplicable phenomenon that happened when he did that thing to me with his tongue:

"It starts out feeling good," I said (in Swedish of course, by now), "then it feels even better, then it's like amazing, and *then* it feels REALLY GREAT . . . and then it doesn't feel so good anymore after that."

And if that isn't the perfect description of an orgasm, something I had never even heard of, let alone experienced before, then . . . well that *is* the perfect description of an orgasm.

. . .

And then I was leaving Sweden—now fluent in a *couple* of new lingual things—to get back to Wareham, Massachussetts, in time for graduation. I brought home white clogs to wear with my white cap and gown, ye gods. When my parents picked me up at the airport, I had a hard time jumping right back into English. That might sound show-offy or made up, but I had really spoken only Swedish for ten months. I was now thinking exclusively in Swedish; even my dreams were in Swedish. Mom got a little teary on the car ride home from the airport because I sounded so funny.

One of the things I most eagerly looked forward to was seeing my Swedish "brother," Lars, he of the beer coasters and car posters. He was still there in my hometown, and his host family invited me to a barbecue at their house right after I got back. I couldn't wait to see him and have a conversation in his language and show him what I'd learned. (Swedes have often been amused to hear that I speak Swedish with the regional accent of the area where his folks lived, a *Sandviks dialekt*.)

I found Lars at the barbecue and launched happily into our now shared language, only to hear him say, "Oh, man, wait, I can't even . . . Dude! My brain isn't working that way now," in totally American-accented English, and, just like me, *he* now had a regional accent. He was speaking English with the same Cape Cod accent I always had. Rats, still out of sync—we'd traded languages! We've stayed in touch all these years, he's been a wonderful extra brother. He also got to know my parents and visited them while I was away.

About a decade after my time in Sweden, visiting my folks for Easter, I found an album my mom had put together of the letters I'd written home during that year away. Even the envelopes were in there—I guess because I often had more things to say after sealing them up. Things like, *"If you notice that some of the words are smeared in my letter, it's because my tears made the ink run."* It was a little horrifying to see them all collected like that, to be reminded of what I'd written at seventeen—my desperate attempts to get across how profoundly homesick I was. Mom came into the room and saw what I was looking at.

"Oh, those *letters*!" She sighed. "You can't imagine how hard it was to read them, knowing you couldn't come back."

"Well," I said, "you guys thought it was important for me to stay and see it through, I get that." I had come to realize that staying there had definitely been the right thing to do, no matter how hard it had seemed in the beginning.

"Oh, no," Mom said, "we would have been *fine* with letting you come home! But how *could* we? Lars might have thought you didn't want to stay with his parents!" Wait, *what*!? It *wasn't* about character building; it was all about not wanting *Lars* to wonder if it had something to do with his parents? Well. I had escaped Death by Politeness, but here I'd fallen victim to Excruciating Homesickness by Politeness, without even realizing that that infernal stoicism had caused my torment.

But the truth about Sweden is this: It delivered exactly what I had fantasized it would. I got to reinvent myself, but also to become more like the real me. My Swedish friends didn't know I was "the weird, tall kid." I would be immune for the rest of my life from homesickness, too. Being able to think in a different language also changed my neural pathways; the me who speaks fluent Swedish is a different person. My father always liked to refer to India as "the old country," because the experience had been so defining for him when he was stationed there for two years during World War II. And I guess I'd have to say that I think of Sweden as "the old country," too.

. . .

The other thing I most looked forward to after coming home was to see Lucyann—so I immediately gathered up all my Wishniks and ran across the street to her house to play. Yes, I was eighteen years old, but we needed to resume the soap opera of their troll lives after my Scandinavian absence. I couldn't wait to jump back into what was going on with the famous actress Kiki Kadoodlehopper, her husband, Nick, and of course Amy, Kiki's sweet plain sister. I had just been in a rom-com in Sweden, but to me the lives of Kiki, Nick, and Amy were almost as interesting as those of Geena, Matts, and Karin.

I was missing Matts terribly, despite the many cards and love letters we sent to each other. (I still have them all.) My parents invited him to visit us that summer, so Matts flew to Massachusetts to join us on our annual family vacation to Vermont. My brother and I picked him up from Logan Airport, and I spent the trip to Wareham informing Matts—in Swedish, of course, so Dan wouldn't know what we were talking about—that I'd changed my mind and we should have sex after all, right away. This caused the poor boy to turn a vivid cranberry color. He wondered if now was the perfect time to be discussing whether we should be making love—in front of my brother?

We were going to go camping in a homemade trailer my father *built himself.* The camper was essentially a flat-bed trailer with plywood sides: Dad attached wooden arches he'd fashioned at the top, then stretched a tarp over it all and tied it down with ropes. There were foldaway cots inside—and also my *parents!*—so this proposed lovemaking was going to have to wait. Fortunately, back in Wareham, my brother was working at the Ocean Spray bottling plant and had a rental house he shared with a friend. Matts's previously cranberry-hued visage now morphed into a postcoital cranberry-pink hue, in a little house afforded by virtue of the cranberry bogs of Massachusetts. After all, Wareham—besides naming itself "The Gateway to Cape Cod"—was also "The Cranberry Capital of the World."

. . .

I remember reading an article in *Reader's Digest* when I was twelve or thirteen entitled something like "Why Feminists Are Ruining the World." I'd never heard a thing about feminism before this, but the article convinced me that whoever these scary feminist people were, I was never going to be one of them. Ha!

The start of "Second Wave" feminism in the '60s ushered in an interesting phenomenon on TV: female characters with superpowers. *Bewitched* and *I Dream of Jeannie* were both hit shows that launched in 1964 and '65 respectively, and I watched both of them religiously. Female lead characters with special abilities signaled a lighthearted nod to the women's movement, as it were. But in hindsight, it's interesting that nearly every episode was about Samantha on the one show, and Jeanie on the other, being told to *sit* on their magical talents by the men in their lives. Sometimes Jeanie even had to be stoppered up in her bottle to prevent her from having free use of her powers. This happened in, like . . . several of my marriages.

Aunt Gloria had tipped me off about the potential male aversion to my laugh, and as I readied myself to go off to college, another relative—my mother's brother—decided to weigh in on my future during a drop in for coffee. Mom and I were in the kitchen, and Uncle Bill evidently thought nothing of having this conversation with Mom while I was sitting right there:

"Honest to God, Lucille," my uncle said, "I have no idea why you're sending a girl to college. That's just stupid. She'll just end up getting married and it'll have been a total waste of money."

I felt my heart race; I had never heard *anything* like this, and I was dumbstruck. I had somehow completely escaped exposure to the idea that college for girls was pointless. I also hadn't ever known it was okay to talk about girls as if they weren't even there. And this was dear Uncle Bill, who little me had once told my mother I was going to marry when I grew up!

"Well, she's going to go," Mom said. "It's already been decided." I knew she wouldn't want to get into an argument with him about it; I also knew there was no way in hell he or anyone else could talk her out of putting me through college. She was fiercely determined that I would have every opportunity possible to do what I wanted, I'm sure because she'd never had any chance whatsoever to do what she'd dreamed of. As I got older, she even urged me to put off having children for as long as possible, lest it hamper my career—the exact opposite of the typical mom yearning to be a grandmother. And I *did* put it off—all the way until I was forty-six, in fact.

. . .

My first day at Boston University included a sort of orientation for the roughly one hundred incoming freshmen in a small theater there. The professor talked about what the year would look like and all the exciting things we'd be doing now that we were theater majors.

About halfway in, he interrupted himself to say, "But I must tell you, you've chosen a very difficult profession. In fact, probably only about one percent of you will ever be able to earn your living as an actor." I was floored. What terrible odds! I quietly looked around the room at my new classmates and thought, *"Oh, these poor kids!"* Just part of my insane certainty that my future was predetermined.

This was actually the second time I was a college freshman. The first was a year earlier, at New England College in Henniker, New Hampshire, because there you could be an acting major without auditioning for it first. Being out of the country in Sweden meant I'd missed the required tryout for BU's acting program. But I ended up having a blast at NEC, in a tiny town where the college was really the only thing. It was so picturesque: for example, there was a quaint little covered bridge . . . which students thought was the perfect place to get high. The first time I ever smoked pot was on that very bridge, with my brother, who was *also* starting out as a freshman there. Even though he was two years ahead of me, he'd taken a few years' break between Bristol County Agricultural School and college. When he found out I was going off to New Hampshire, he decided he might as well start college, too, and why not go to the same place?

I remember so clearly that first time either of us got high. Someone handed us a joint, and we ended up laughing like idiots. The girl who'd shared her weed seemed to find the way we reacted embarrassing—*so* uncool. Fear of appearing uncool didn't seem to stop me from continuing . . . and even entering the occasional "Who Can Do the Most Hits from a Bong?" competition. Pot was soooooo much weaker back then, am I right?

Then there was the other time we "got high" together.

Dan had gotten his pilot license during our freshman year and wanted to take me for a ride. I told him I was terrified of the idea of flying in a small plane, but reluctantly agreed to go. No sooner had we taken off—and I'm talking about being ten feet in the air—than I started yelling,

"No, no, no, no, no, go down, go down, go down!"

Dan not unreasonably pointed out that it was too late—he'd been cleared for takeoff, and he couldn't instantly drop down again. I continued to scream until Dan was forced to ask for permission to land after an embarrassingly short amount of time.

I knew New Hampshire would be a one-year layover for me, though, because BU was my destiny.

As a kid, I didn't advertise my plan to become an actor. I kept it on the down low, even though in my yearbook under "Future Plans" I put *Go to the big city and become a star*. But in high school I didn't really think I should talk about it; I was weird enough already. Instead, in my junior year, I took aside my Madrigal Choir teacher, Mr. Peduzzi, and quietly asked, "Where should you go to college if you want to study acting?"

He immediately and very firmly said, "Oh, *Boston University*."

I figured when someone said something that confidently, you didn't need a second opinion.

BU thought so highly of its acting program that you had to start as a freshman even if you were a transfer . . . meaning you'd graduate when you were, in their eyes, a junior. And freshmen were not allowed to be in school plays—clearly because they thought you shouldn't be in plays if you hadn't had their super-good acting training yet. My fellow transfers and I found this maddening. We had all already *been* in college productions. Why, I'd already taken Acting I, II, and III at New England College! That meant we would only have four semesters to try to get cast in a school production. There were only two per semester, one in the small theater in the School of Fine Arts building with a student director, and the other on the big main stage at the Huntington Theater, directed by a faculty member.

The first time that I was eligible to audition I got cast in a small part in the musical *Knickerbocker Holiday*, as Mistress Schermerhorn, and I really wanted to land another play before graduating. When the plays for my last semester were announced . . . the student-directed one had only *two characters*. I was stunned. We were being robbed! I became very bold indeed and determined that we should organize a protest. That is, until *I* got cast in one of the two roles in the play, *Jesse and the Bandit Queen*. Then the fire behind my potentially super-badass protest scheme kind of fizzled out. Turns out I didn't see such a big need to strive for the greater good when I was the one getting the good.

When I was a student, BU's theater department didn't really offer any advice about how to get work as an actor after graduating. (Well, these were the "only one percent will succeed" people, so I guess that made sense. These days, they have fantastic programs to help students launch their careers.) Therefore, no one ever told me that if I wanted to be in movies instead of plays, I should go to LA, not New York. And I didn't think to call Mr. Peduzzi and ask him where acting majors should go to get cast in movies. I'll bet he would have said, very confidently, "Oh, *Los Angeles*."

As a result, I worked out my own genius plan for breaking into the movies, and this is how it went: I would become a famous model first, and then people would just *offer* me movies! Christie Brinkley had gotten in movies that way; so had Lauren Hutton. Because, you know, it's *so* much easier to become a supermodel than an actor. And the best place to become a model was New York City. That was why, when school was over, I went off to Manhattan with all my theater-bent classmates.

Oh, say, here's my opportunity at long last to clear up something about my college career: I didn't graduate. You'll find that Wikipedia says I have a BFA from BU, but I don't. What happened was, I didn't end up getting all the necessary credits. Mostly because I'd heard about something wondrous called "taking an incomplete," which meant I could put off writing the term papers or taking the finals as long as I wanted to. I ended up putting off completing my missing credits until . . . well, for about forty-five years now.

I also somehow managed to fail "movement" class my senior year, a seeming gut course if ever there was one. We had an assignment to create a stage fight scene that included three direct hits and two falls. I partnered with my close friend Joe Joyce, and we took our inspiration from the movie *Carrie*, then out in theaters. Joe introduced our performance as "a Brian DePalma film: *JOEY*." I pushed him down (first fall) then basically Joe would bug his eyes out like Sissy Spacek, and in response I would throw myself across the room and into the wall.

When we finished, the teacher said, "As usual, you two, it was amusing but it was not the assignment."

Even though we got an F on it, I still stand by the brilliance of our performance.

But hang on—there was still that pesky "can't ever do anything wrong in my parents' eyes" burden I'd shouldered forever. I decided the only way to save my folks the shame of failing to graduate was to bald-faced lie about the whole thing. And hope they just wouldn't notice I didn't invite them to my "graduation." Once my career took off and I started doing interviews, I still pretended I'd graduated in case my folks saw the article.

But now that they've both safely passed to where they can't be embarrassed, I can finally come clean to you. I should probably alert Wikipedia, too. And even though BU gave me an honorary doctorate in 1999—alongside Dr. Henry Kissinger ("Don't let yur Hollywood friends see dis picture of us togeder," he said)—I still fully intend to finish up those incompletes. At some point.

. . .

"Lady Fatima's Town House for Young Ladies" sounds like something out of a '50s nun movie, but it was where I lived when I first landed in New York City in the fall of 1978. Fresh out of college and having been forced by my favorite professor, Daisette McKelvey, to lose my thick Cape Cod accent, I was more than ready for this exciting new chapter of my life.

Lady Fatima's took up the entire top floor of the legendary Biltmore Hotel. It was thrilling to walk into the swanky lobby of this historic place, however dingy the room my classmate Maria Cuevas and I rented for fifty dollars a week each. Lady F's "town house" was on the floor with what used to be the maids' quarters. The Biltmore had been built in the air rights above Grand Central Station; you could get off your Pullman and wander straight into the hotel. And in 1970, feminists protested its men-only bar—it was actually *called* the "Men's Bar"—leading to Mayor John Lindsay's backing of a bill that banned sexual discrimination in public places.

Little did anyone know that just three years later, the beautiful H-shaped hotel, filled as it was with so much New York history, would be razed overnight and a Bank of America building—all glass and no soul—would be raised in its place. And little did I know that on my first full day in New York I'd meet one man I'd have to run away from, and another I'd marry three years later.

Chapter Four
It Has Hair on Its Arms

I was determined to make it there because if I did, I was pretty sure I could make it anywhere. It was up to me.

On my very first full day in New York City, I got dressed up to the nines and hit the streets, hoping to land a quick salesgirl job while I figured out how to become a model. Almost immediately, a man miraculously stopped me on the street—*and asked me if I was a model*.

"Not yet," I said, "but I *want* to be!"

"I think you could be," he said, "and I should know—I'm a model agent." He pointed to a gleaming forty-story office building behind him. "My office is right over there. Want to come up and talk about it?"

"Well, yes," I said, hardly believing my luck. It looked like I was going to become a model *on my first day in the city*!

The man's office was on the twenty-third floor; when we arrived, he muttered something about his assistant being out, and then, ". . . but come in, take a seat, let's chat!" The conversation started out very businesslike—he asked for my name and phone number and was eager to hear what my goals were. I told him about Christie Brinkley and Lauren Hutton and my plan to follow in their footsteps as a model-turned-actor.

"Great idea!" he said, reaching into his office drawer, from which he fished out a stack of old-looking magazines and proceeded to show me pictures of supermodels before they became famous, all naked. He said the only way to become a model was to do nude pictures and "be accommodating" at a lot of parties, which he would arrange.

"This is how everyone starts," he said. "It's the classic way to break in. The biggest stars? They all did it!"

Somehow, I still thought we were having a serious discussion about ways to launch a modeling career, so I said, "Oh, no, no—I'm not going to do it that way. I'd prefer to just do it the regular way."

"But this is the *only* way you'll make it! This is how it works, doll!"

We went back and forth, and he was becoming rather adamant about it, so I knew I needed to stop him. I said that I'd just rather not be a model if that's what was required, and he glowered and spluttered at me.

"Well, then, you just don't have any sense!" he barked. *"In fact, you should be on the other side of this desk right now making me the happiest man in the world!"*

Okay, then, crystal clear, got it. My typically timid nature was nowhere to be seen as I skedaddled out the door.

The positive part of this was that my shy, don't-make-trouble Massachusetts self was already a little tougher, and on my first day in the metropolis!

Back at Lady Fatima's that night, my roommate, Maria, exploded when she saw me.

"Thanks a lot!" she yelled.

"What did I do?" I said, imagining all kinds of transgressions.

"You gave our phone number to some creep," she said. "He called and said he was a friend of yours, and asked if I wanted to be a model, too, so I went to see him . . ." Maria, with her no-bullshit personality, probably cracked him upside the head when he pulled that stunt on her.

So that was the first man I met in New York City. The next one I met, I married.

• • •

There was a brief time in the early 1980s when each Saturday afternoon a crowd would form outside the Ann Taylor window on Fifth Avenue at Fifty-Seventh Street in Manhattan.

It was all my fault.

I had gotten a job as a salesperson that very first day in New York. I'd basically gone from the fake model agent's office to Ann Taylor and bam! Job secured. I loved it. It felt sophisticated and fun, and I got all dressed up every day.

I don't know what possessed me do this: One Saturday afternoon, during a lull on the sales floor, I was checking out the new window display. It had two mannequins at a café table, sitting down to a lunch of fake food. For some reason there was also an empty chair at the table, as if they were waiting for their mannequin friend to show up.

I said to one of the other girls, "Dare me to go sit there?"

"Do it!" she said.

So I did. All made up and dressed nicely, I stepped up into the window and sat down on the extra chair. A few people who were walking by just then saw me get in the window and stopped to see what I was going to do. Ah, right—I hadn't thought about what I would do once I was there. So, I just froze, you know, *like a mannequin.*

Turns out I have an uncanny ability for motionlessness . . . and to *not blink,* either. (Good to know, now that I suddenly found myself pretending to be a mannequin.) A crowd started to form, like this: New people asked the first group what they were staring at—I could hear them talking through the window—and the first ones kindly didn't give the game away, simply saying, "Just wait." Now more and more passersby wanted to know why everyone was looking at a bunch of mannequins and waited to find out what the secret was. When I finally moved and blinked, everyone got what the deal was and cheered happily. At which point, I froze again.

After a while the noise outside brought the manager over, who was horrified.

"Geena! Get out of the window!" she scolded. But seeing the size of the crowd that had gathered gave her pause. She said, "Actually—*stay in the window!*"

This was much more fun than putting clothes in the dressing rooms away, so I kept it up. About an hour in, a handsome waiter whom I'd never met arrived and gallantly entered the window with some *real* lunch for me—he worked in the Soho Charcuterie restaurant at the top of the building—and the crowd cheered for him, too.

My masquerade was a hit. After that first time, the manager hired me to be a fake mannequin in the window every Saturday. The large crowds were translating into increased foot traffic in the actual store, and I was having a great time, while refining my technique. I learned the best way to keep my eyes from moving was to focus on a single speck of dust on the glass. I figured out how to breathe without moving my chest. I perfected the art of judging when to move: I'd wait just until I sensed people were about to walk away, and then they'd be hooked again when one of the "mannequins" moved.

I was determined to look as much like the other mannequins as possible. I got some shiny makeup to help me appear plastic, and a very synthetic-looking wig, like they wore. I even came up with the idea of tying a dark thread around my wrists to make it look as though my hands were attached. I could hear everything the people outside were saying, and that gave me helpful pointers, too: one day someone said, "Hang on—it's not a mannequin, it's got hair on its arms!" (The next time, it *didn't*.) Another time, I heard a guy say, "How can it be mechanical? It's not plugged in." So I took the most subtle electrical cord I could find and ran it down one of my legs, placing the other end out of sight. I enjoyed it immensely when a sharp-eyed observer would say, "Look, it IS fake—it's plugged in!"

The window wasn't the only good thing about the store. For a start, we got generous employee discounts, so when we had a sale, I could afford to buy a few Ann Taylor clothes. Each day I'd don my latest Ann Taylor getup, get fully made up and coiffed, and head from the subway to work, feeling like an actor in a montage scene as the music plays and my character strides down Fifth Avenue, determined and young and with their whole life ahead of them.

One day, the actual CEO of Ann Taylor came in, and the manager introduced me to her as an example of the employees at the flagship store. To my delight, the CEO remarked that I looked "*just* like an Ann Taylor girl—you're such a great image for us!" This was high praise indeed, and I jumped on the opportunity it presented. As a preteen I would pore over the Sears catalogs that came to our house. I even wrote to Sears once, asking to be in the catalog, and they'd sent back a sweet note telling me that they shot their photos in New York, so it wouldn't be possible. But here I was *in* New York, in the presence of the Ann Taylor CEO . . .

"Thank you," I said. "I'm glad you think so, because I would very much like to be in the Ann Taylor catalog, please."

The woman was completely taken aback.

"Oh! well," she said, ending our little encounter as fast as possible, "it doesn't really work like that." Ah well, at least I had tried.

On another landmark day, to my amazement, Didi Conn—who had recently played Frenchy in *Grease*, my all-time favorite movie at that time, which I'd seen in the theater literally two dozen times—came into the store, and I raced over to make sure I'd be the one to wait on her. She urgently needed five different blouses to go shoot an appearance on *The $25,000 Pyramid*. I took this task as seriously as a heart attack and had her all set up lickety-split. At the time, I thought it was a terrific achievement to be able to watch the show and see her wearing what I had helped her pick out.

One Monday, I was straightening racks in Ann Taylor when that handsome waiter who'd brought me lunch in the window called out to me.

"Hey, Big Girl, go for coffee?" he said, in a thick Brooklyn accent.

I froze. I didn't know him at all—I had seen him only that one time in the window . . . and a couple of times on the stairs as he passed by me on his way up to the restaurant—and I didn't know what to do. I'd never been asked to go out with someone I'd never even officially met. But since I was pretty much genetically incapable of saying no to anything or anyone, *at any time*, I said yes. I figured that before the actual coffee date on the upcoming Thursday, I'd think of some excuse why I couldn't go. Alas, the day arrived—and I had forgotten to inform the handsome waiter that I couldn't go! So when he said, "Okay, ready?" I had to oblige.

His name was Richard Emmolo, an Italian-American waiter from Brooklyn. It turned out that he was very charming, and incredibly smart, and I felt him to be *so* exotic. He was cool, and older; he wore a cashmere coat and smoked cigars. I thought he was the most unique person I'd ever met—not realizing yet that there were, I don't know, thousands of Italian-American waiters from Brooklyn in New York City.

Richard had fantastic taste, too, very adult (he was ten years older than me). The first present he bought me was a gorgeous pair of maroon suede spike-heeled shoes with an ankle strap; although I had some decent Ann Taylor clothes, my only shoes were a pair of worn-out flats. These high heels cost two hundred fifty dollars, an unfathomably large sum back in the late '70s. (It's not nothing *now*.)

I was incredibly self-conscious around Richard in the beginning; he was so sophisticated and worldly, and for our first real date he took me out to a fancy restaurant. When the salad he'd suggested I order arrived, I was suddenly in a quandary: Somewhere I'd read that it was bad table manners to use a knife when eating a salad (yes, I had in fact studied up on how to be even *more* polite), and the pieces of lettuce were huge. Either I could break that lettuce-cutting taboo, and thereby prove myself a hick to this sophisticated man who was ten years older than I was (a full-on adult!). *Or* I would have to try to jam great huge, uncut bites of salad into my mouth. I couldn't *not* eat it; that would have been the rudest choice of all. As it was, I waited until he wasn't looking and folded up each big lettuce piece as best I could. Idiot.

From the start Richard was so solicitous of me. Once I'd moved in with him, he ironed all my clothes, and did all the cooking and cleaning. He made sure the Italian guys in the social club at the bottom of our SoHo building looked out for me on the nights I worked late. I got a second job as a cocktail waitress at the WPA restaurant in SoHo, and as I walked back home at 2 a.m., I'd hear deep voices say, "G'night, Geena," from each of the street corners I passed.

Neither of us was making that much money, but we'd still go out at least once a week and have dinner with a nice bottle of wine and all the courses. Speaking of wine, Richard once asked, "BD [Baby Doll now, instead of Big Girl], do you think you can work your way up to *half* a bottle?"

. . .

Even though I worried about bringing Richard to Wareham, with our funky old house and pile of axes under the dining room table, he fell in love with my parents right away. He loved that they seemed like a throwback to another century; my father would take him out chopping wood, the whole bit. Richard started calling me his Yankee Doodle Sweetheart after he saw what my folks were like. His admiration for my mother may not have been entirely mutual, though.

Some of the things he said just rubbed Mom the wrong way. He had a tendency to say things to me like, "You must be cold. Don't you want to put a sweater on?" which drove her NUTS, even though that's the exact kind of thing she would say to me all the time. He'd also say, for fun, "If we get married, we're going to have eight strapping boys!!" and she'd just about fall over.

Mom was very invested in my career and was worried about anything that might derail it. She said things to me like, "I'll pay for it if you want to have that mole on your cheek removed," or "Should you dye your hair blond; I read that they get more roles?" Whenever I visited my parents with Richard, Mom would sit across from him at the dinner table and give me eye rolls and sidelong glances at some of the things he said.

One time, during a visit home, Richard peeked in his sandwich when I opened mine, only to find the desiccated corpse of a spider right there on his slice of ham. It had probably floated down from some undusted corner. Undeterred, he simply lifted it out of the sandwich, closed the bread, and tucked in; my heart swelled.

I urge you to find a partner who won't bat an eye at a dead spider in his food. I knew then that I would never have to be worried about my folks' messy house.

This, despite the fact that Richard was the neatest person I've ever known. He kept his small apartment meticulously clean. Even if he was drunk after friends had been over, he would hold himself up by the mop handle and scrub the floor (he scrubbed so hard he wore the pattern off the linoleum).

The apartment was like a carefully packed ship's compartment, too, and he knew exactly where every item was. One Christmas I wanted to buy Richard curtains for the bedroom to match the bedspread, but the bedspread was an odd color. I came up with the idea of finding a book with the same color on its cover—Richard owned

Richard was so entertaining, I decided I wanted to create a cartoon strip about him and me, called "Imogene and Tony." This one is about forty-five years old.

hundreds of books—and bringing it to the store with me for comparison's sake. Richard came home from work the day I had swiped that book, a novel bound in imitation Moroccan leather, glanced at the bookshelves, which covered a *whole wall* in the apartment, and within seconds said,

"Where's the Booth Tarkington?"

. . .

Once a week, on Sundays, when the phone rates were cheapest, my parents would call to see how I was doing. "How I was doing" was that I was living with Richard, and they could *never know* *that*. To make sure that only I would answer their weekly call, I had a red Batphone installed in Richard's apartment that only they had the number to, and every time it rang, I'd pretend I was still at Lady Fatima's. Problem was, they knew I had a roommate, and they knew her name was Maria, and they seemed to get suspicious as to why a) she never answered the phone, and b) she never seemed to be home. That girl slept a lot and worked a lot!

Accordingly, my mother became somewhat obsessed with speaking to her.

"I just want to say hi," Mom would plead. "Can you put her on the line?"

"Oh, no, Mom, she's still sleeping," I'd lie groggily, often a little worse for wear after a Saturday night hanging with Richard and his friends. Clearly my mother had suspicions, as she started calling in the middle of the day ("Aw rats, she's at lunch!") or later ("Oh no, she went out with friends") and back to very early ("Sleeping in again!").

I dreaded every Sunday. I felt like I was getting an ulcer from the constant stress of waiting for that stupid red phone to ring and having to make up endless reasons why Maria couldn't come to the phone. I started not answering if they called in the mornings, since I didn't want to have to spring to alertness to ward off Maria inquiries. I had to come up with some excuse to explain why I didn't answer in the mornings, so I told her I'd started going to church. I added a little fun fact by saying it was a cute Swedish church I had happened upon, and that I was now attending. (I did *see* one, once.) One Sunday, I answered the second time Mom called, and I repeated that I'd been at church earlier.

Mom said, "Well, I called the Swedish church to find you and they said you weren't there, and they'd never seen you."

Who would do that—call a church to track you down? This was all too much. Believe it or not, my breasts and sexual organs had started aching. I was clearly guilty that I was having sex, and Mom and Dad had to be prevented at all costs from knowing. Now, brother *Dan* lived with his girlfriend, Marilyn, and had started smoking cigarettes and drinking alcohol—just like I had—but he had told the folks about it right up front (very much unlike me). He complained that I was spared all the grief he was getting from Bill and Lucille because I was hiding everything from them. (Years later, I also hid from them that the reason I called them at 3 a.m. to tell them that I loved them was because I had taken ecstasy.) Dan didn't realize I was doing a truly bang-up job of giving *myself* grief—so much so that I couldn't take the crushing guilt anymore . . . and Richard and I decided to get married.

Don't get me wrong: We would have gotten married anyway—we were very much in love—but the Batphone and my phantom pains and stress levels definitely made it happen sooner.

The ceremony took place in the church where I grew up, the First Congregational Church of Wareham, where my parents had also been married. As I was getting dressed that morning, my mother helpfully pointed out, "It's still not too late to change your mind." My dad walked me down the aisle, and we invited the whole congregation to the wedding, just as my parents had done thirty years earlier. The reception was in the Fellowship Hall next to the church, which had a very strict rule of no alcohol except for wedding receptions, where one flute of champagne per person was permitted. Later, we drove down to Connecticut to celebrate with some New York friends, where my new husband managed to leave my suitcases on the sidewalk outside a bar. When I realized this, all the way back in New York, I'm ashamed to admit I said, "If I had a knife right now, I'd stab you in the heart."

A single glass of champagne and a death threat: This was the start of my first marriage.

. . .

Even though I'd now developed a significant side hustle with the window mannequin thing—you could also find me in the window of a cute boutique in Soho on Sundays, with my shiny makeup, shaved arms, and plugged-in-automaton bit—my focus was still on becoming a model as my way into acting. But I had yet to find myself a modeling agency.

I'd made a list of the top five agencies in New York at that time and was picking them off one by one, in order of their status. I started with the premier Ford Modeling Agency, run by the legendary Eileen Ford. She was the top talent scout in the business and had discovered everyone from Christy Turlington to Christie Brinkley. I showed up for an open day where you could just come by with your portfolio of photographs. A female agent walked by each of us tryouts, lined up with our portfolios and hopeful expressions. She hadn't said much of anything to the others, but upon reaching me she stopped and stared at me, then looked very intently at my photos, then back to me, looking penetratingly all the while. . . .

"Come with me," she said, and took me into an adjacent room. This was it, gold, struck: the Ford Modeling Agency! Onetime home to Jean Shrimpton, Ali MacGraw, Candice Bergen, Jerry Hall, Lauren Hutton—the list went on and on. I waited, breath bated, until the agent reappeared—with Eileen Ford herself! Without saying a word to me, Ms. Ford enacted the same little performance: She looked at me sharply, then microscopically at my photos, then me, then my photos . . . before slamming shut the portfolio, turning to the agent, and announcing, "Yes, you're right. Her jaw *is* too big to be disguised by makeup."

Back out on the street, great crowds of New Yorkers charged by.

I wasn't completely undone by what had just happened, not at all; this had just been the first stop.

At the number two agency, Wilhelmina Models—established by Wilhelmina Cooper, who had once been ordered to lose twenty pounds by none other than Eileen Ford—I was told I was both too tall and too old to make it, at six feet and twenty-two years old. At that time, the tallest a model was supposed to be was five-ten, I later learned, because the sample sizes were made for models between five-eight and five-ten. So, at the next agency I went to, I had miraculously lost a half inch and a year; same for the next one, and still I was hearing I was too tall and too old. By the time I hit the Zoli Agency, I was five-ten and just eighteen years old, and they found me just about all right enough to sign me on.

So now I was an actual model. Things had moved so fast; little did I know they would soon move even faster. But before they could, I had to learn how to be the body parts of various other models in New York City.

. . .

My career as a model was, shall we say, unorthodox, but like the Ann Taylor job, I adored it. There was something wonderful about walking through those New York streets knowing I was making decent money as a Zoli model; I guess I should have garnered real confidence about my body image from it, but still, I just couldn't accept any kind of compliment. I mean, come on, who the fuck should feel good about their body if not a frickin' model, fer Chrissakes? Instead, I decided I must have figured out a way to *trick* people into thinking I had a good body: I just knew how to stand, it was all in my deportment . . .

whatever I could come up with to avoid the lure of believing my body was all that. The internal logic was such that I would go from the set of a lingerie shoot—a set upon which I posed in skimpy thongs and the like—and return to the dressing room to put back on my giant granny panties, which by rights I should have been wearing. I *did* figure out how to trick people regarding my height, though: I took to wearing high heels everywhere, so if someone was worried that I might be too tall, I could simply blame the shoes.

To my great excitement, I landed the cover of a magazine—the *#1 marker of success*! It was the YAY SUMMER! summer issue of *New Jersey Monthly*, that bastion of all things fashionable. I was posed on the sand in a one-piece bathing suit and giant hat—which completely covered my face. But otherwise, cover girl! I was making enough money to, somewhat sadly, leave Ann Taylor behind. Being too tall for the clothes sometimes, I tended to be hired for panty-hose or bathing suit or lingerie ads, where height didn't matter. And despite my fervent conviction that my body wasn't attractive, I was regularly cast as a body *for other models*, meaning a beautiful model had been chosen for her face, but her body would be replaced by mine. This still made no dent in my self-regard, by the way.

The body-double gigs caused me to end up in numerous bizarre scenarios. In a commercial for a new shower spray called "Savvy," someone else was cast for the face, while I was cast as her body in the shower. For this, they put body makeup all over me, and then I waited for ten hours while the face model did her part, which consisted of her singing a song:

> *"I'd cover myself in diamonds,*
> *Eat caviar every day.*

But I'm no millionairess,
So I lavish Savvy body spray!"

I make no apologies for falling asleep on the couch during those ten hours of *that* song—who wouldn't?—and I don't think it was my fault that they'd given me a ribbed chenille bathrobe to wear while waiting, which left huge lines across my body as I snoozed. But I *am* sorry that the body makeup artist then had to frantically rub my legs to try to get rid of the lines so they could shoot me. That was probably not in her original job description.

Before shooting photos for my first Victoria's Secret catalog in San Francisco, I was asked to dye my pubic hair blond, so it didn't show through the sheer underwear. Which, of course, I did—I wasn't about to argue with anyone, let alone Victoria's Secret. Later, the more experienced model with whom I was assigned to share a hotel room told me about this same request they'd made of her: "They told me to dye my bush blond. But I said, *no fucking way!* I told them, 'I have a life, you know.'"

That kind of response—saying *no fucking way*—had never entered my head. I had a life, too, but it only meant anything if I was making everyone happy. Hence, platinum bush.

· · ·

My hands had their own career back then. In a L'Oréal TV commercial for their makeup line, the on-camera model was to be filmed applying makeup, but I was crouched behind her, looking at her in a mirror as *my* hands applied the makeup to her eyes! For a L'Oréal nail polish commercial, perfectly manicured model's hands would be playing the piano. On the go-see, there was a piano and the sheet music to the L'Oréal theme song right there, so I sat down and played it, which landed me the gig. I was thrilled. On the day of the shoot, they did my full hair and makeup *and* dressed me in a gorgeous gown, in case they decided to use more of me than just my hands. I sat at the piano, feeling beautiful, and when they called action, I started to play the song.

The director immediately started shouting.

"Don't play the keys up *there*—play the keys *here*."

"Well, you see, that's not where the tune is played," I said.

"I don't give a fuck where it's played!" he yelled. "Who told you to play the actual fucking tune anyway?"

I was so embarrassed. I moved my hands to where he wanted them and pretended to play.

"Keep your head out of my shot!" he barked.

I could feel tears forming as I craned my neck back, back; they fell when he began pushing on the backs of my hands.

"Flatten them out!" he screamed. "I can't [push] see [push] your [push] nails!"

There can be a lot of indignity in modeling, especially in the lower rungs where I was finding work. One time, I auditioned for a commercial in which a woman would be sprayed with beautiful, rainbow-inflected water. At the go-see, they wanted to splash water on us and take a Polaroid at that instant so they could see what we'd look like when it happened in the ad.

"You're having a fabulous vacation! You're very happy and loving it, big smile!" the director shouted as a huge bucket of ice-cold water was hurled at my head. Sadly, the look of horror on my face when this happened wasn't quite what they'd asked for. Flash! "You didn't smile!" the director said with surprise, and I skulked off to the bathroom with a wad of paper towels.

Another time, I was sent to an audition for a jeans ad. There were three people sitting behind a desk in a small room, and I was told to turn my butt toward them, pull down my jeans, and then hop around happily pulling my jeans back up again over my presumably fabulous derriere. Alas, the jeans I had on that day were super-tight, and it took just an inordinate amount of hopping around to try and yank them back up while seeming happy about it. When I finally had them back up again, I turned around, to find three rather stunned-looking faces. There was really no need for anyone to say anything; I simply left the room.

It must be said that my lack of experience could sometimes make things complicated for the people trying to employ me.

At one go-see I was surprised to see a bathtub sitting in the studio, so me being me (*see under:* Ann Taylor window) I just got in it. The clients at the audition thought this was highly amusing; my chances of getting the job only increased when it turned out that the photos for bathroom fixtures would include the model in a fog-filled bathroom playing the flute.

"Well, it turns out I play the flute!" I announced from the bathtub, garnering more oohs and laughter . . . and the actual gig, right there on the spot. That never happens.

Next day, I came back to the set, only this day I had my hair all twisted into knots to make curls, and had left myself un-made-up, figuring the hair and makeup folks on set would be handling that. When I arrived, another shoot was happening over yonder, and I meekly waved hello. The ad people looked up and waved me toward a lounge. As time wore on, occasionally someone would come and peek in, not say anything, and go away again. Eventually, someone came in looking very somber.

"I just hate to tell you this," the woman said, "but the agency sent the *wrong girl*. The curly-haired girl who came yesterday was funny and charming, and she plays the flute . . ."

"But that was me!" I exclaimed.

"What?!" the woman said, doing a cartoonlike double take. "Who told you to come like *this*?"

"I thought I was supposed to come without makeup," I said, my voice trailing away as I suddenly saw myself—twisty knots and all—through her eyes.

"Oh, dear, put some makeup on immediately!" the woman sputtered, and went off to tell everyone the flute-playing charmer was here after all. Later, my flute playing went the same way as my piano playing had, even though those talents had landed me the jobs in the first place. I was in a beautiful Grecian gown, with wind blowing, fog drifting, and doves flying, playing the flute near a bathtub . . . when the photographer suddenly said, annoyed, "What are you doing with your face? Your lips look all funny."

"Well, I'm playing the flute. That's how you play."

"Who told you that you should actually *play*? Stop doing that, it looks terrible!"

But there were plenty of cool, creative things that I got to do, too. I shot a really fun shoe commercial—well, really, it was a Swedish candy bar commercial, but the candy bar name, SKOR, means "shoe" in Swedish. (*Skör* means "brittle," but Americans didn't know from umlauts—Häagen-Dazs hadn't taken off yet—so the candy bar name left off the dots.)

In the commercial, eating the brittle/shoe candy bar was to turn me into a Swede. I started the ad speaking with my American accent, but each bite gave me more of a Swedish lilt, until I was finally in ecstasy over the candy bar, speaking fully in Swedish. The late '70s/early '80s were the height of "Sweden is sexy" time around the world, hence the inner logic of the ad. *Whatever it takes*, I thought—and I had the unique challenge of doing half a commercial in another language.

But despite getting work, my modeling career hadn't *really* taken off. I wasn't being asked to appear in the fashion magazines, or ads for products much more upscale than bathroom fixtures. My agency suggested I head off to Italy, where I would have another chance at being "discovered," and perhaps come back as a new sensation. So, off I went to Milan. I had just enough money to stay for six weeks; my hope was that I would become the next big thing really, really fast.

I stayed in a youth hostel while I was there and had a little picture of Richard on my bedside table. My roommate picked it up one day, and noticed that it had kiss marks on it—she gave me plenty of shit for that.

While there, my local agents taught me how to phonetically pronounce the lines for an ad for Mon Savon soap in Italian. In the commercial, I would need to look into the camera and say confidently, in Italian, "Come close . . . closer . . . even closer."

Then the script had me say, "The word I use to describe my skin is . . ." and then a male voice off-camera would interrupt and say, *"Splendida!"*

I really got that script down and can still say it word for word today. The only problem was, at the audition, I simply could not bear for someone to call my skin "splendid," even in a commercial in Italian. So, every time the man said *"Splendida!"* I would look down as if to say, "Who, me? Oh golly, don't be silly!" The woman casting the commercial thought I was perfect, and the job was mine—IF I could stop looking embarrassed when the man spoke and just *take the compliment*. But I simply could not yet break out of my training: my self-effacement was so ingrained that I found it impossible to be any other way, even if it lost me a gig. The woman was very sad to say I wouldn't be getting the job. So much for being an actor—I couldn't manage to simply *act* like I thought I had good skin.

So I struggled in Italy; then, near the very end of my sojourn there, I lucked into a hand-modeling job for Italian *Vogue*, for eight pages of watches. *At least I will have had one important job*, I thought, even if it's only my hands. When I arrived for the shoot, the *Vogue* editor thought my nails were a bit too long, so she asked the manicurist to trim them and redo my manicure. Very unfortunately, she cut them so severely that there was no way they could show my nails. With no chance of finding another hand model in time they shot just my *wrists*.

What to do? I was returning from Italy with nothing to show for it. I decided that nobody Stateside needed to know that my "eight-page *Vogue* shoot" was just stumpy shots of my wrists. So, when I went back to my usual routine of go-sees, and people would ask how things had gone in Italy, I could honestly say, "I have an eight-page spread coming out in Italian *Vogue*." Naturally people were extremely impressed with that, and I started to get more jobs, and of a higher caliber than before—after all, I was about to be *very* famous! Occasionally someone might ask if I had the pictures yet, and I'd just tell them that the magazine still hadn't come out. "Can you believe it? Europe, huh?"

On I went, building a career modeling, inventing all kind of wiles to finagle jobs—all the time with one and a half eyes on my real future as an actor. One time I was sent on a go-see for a Western-themed fashion show in New York City, and when I was there, I blurted out, "I happen to know how to twirl guns!" My agent was absolutely stunned that I landed the job.

"They said you're going to be the last one to go out! What did you say to them?" she asked, pointing out that *all* the other models booked were actual *supermodels*.

"I told them I twirl guns!" I said.

"You twirl guns?!" she said, hardly believing her, or my, luck.

"Well . . . kind of?"

In fairness, I *had* played the role of Belle Star, an outlaw, in a play in college, and I had indeed learned how to spin a gun into a holster for the show. But now it was time to see if I could learn to fully twirl a gun in a week, and sadly, all I really managed to do was take the skin off my finger practicing (which just showed how seriously I took it). Out on the runway, with a bandaged finger, I just waved the fake guns around a bit and pretended to shoot them in the air, saying, "Pew pew!"

Mercifully, the fashion show people didn't even notice that I hadn't put on a gun-twirling exhibition. They'd been too focused on not being able to jam the cowboy hat on my big-ass head.

• • •

One day, my commercials agent at Zoli got a call from a casting agent looking for models who could act. My agent, of course, knew that that was my goal, and said, "We have one!" For the first time, I was going to get to audition for a part *in a movie*. Amazing, and it had come through my modeling agency—my plan all along! I was told to wear a bikini under my clothes just in case, because the role called for some scenes in underwear, and they would want to see me in a bathing suit if the audition went well. Off I went to an office in Midtown, where my audition was videotaped. After I read, the casting assistant didn't ask to see my bathing suit, though, so I pretty much instantly put the audition out of my mind. They were only going to want to see me in a bikini if I read well, so obviously I hadn't.

And what were the odds I'd land a part in my first movie audition anyway? My mind turned elsewhere. Now I was heading to Paris for the first time, to walk the collections. I'd even taken runway-walking lessons in New York before this trip—you know, where you learn to sashay and place each foot right in front of the other just so—the kind of walking one only ever sees on a catwalk. I was in Paris, thrilled to be hired for a few shows, when I got a message to urgently call my Zoli agent. I found a pay phone in the Paris Metro and called.

"YOU GOT THE PART," he said when we were finally connected.

"What?" I shouted as the 10 train to Gare d'Austerlitz rattled by.

"It's amazing, you got the part!" he shouted back.

"What part?" I asked, confused. I had truly put the bikini audition out of mind.

The director of the movie and the casting director—the great Lynn Stalmaster—had apparently really liked my audition tape, and the lead actor had especially loved my *Brooklyn* accent. There was one line in the audition scene that I said this way:

"If I just frown, he loses his hawd-awn," referring to the unfortunate detumescence of the character's boyfriend. The Boston accent

I'd worked so hard/haad to lose had been replaced almost immediately with the one I heard every day from Richard.

Turns out the lack of footage of me in a bikini had been a mistake on the part of the casting assistant, and when the director responded so strongly to my audition, he was really put out by this oversight.

"Well, get her back in so we can see her in a bathing suit!" the casting director said, only to be informed that I was in Paris just then. They asked my agents if they had any photos of me in a bathing suit, and wouldn't you know, lucky me, they were able to send over a couple of Victoria's Secret catalogs, where I had been windblown, airbrushed, perfectly lit—and with no pubic hair showing through the sheer panties, either. (Lord knows what photos of me in that dingy, fluorescent-lit room in Midtown would have looked like.)

Yowza. Either way, deal done. I got the part. Richard was over the moon for me. He believed in me right from the start; he'd tell everyone that I was going to be in movies someday, and now it was actually happening.

I headed back to New York immediately, even though I was told there was no rush. Perhaps, once you hear what the movie was and who the principals were, you'll be amused to learn that to this day I still harbor a nagging regret that I didn't stay and walk the runways in Paris. I've wanted to experience everything this planet has to offer, and that would have been bucket-list-y for sure.

But it was not to be. Instead, I came back to New York, only a model no more, to work with the director Sydney Pollack and the star Dustin Hoffman.

The movie?

That would be *Tootsie*.

Chapter Five
Never Sleep with Your Costars

I t was beyond my wildest imaginings that I would get the first movie role I auditioned for. What were the odds? It's hard to overestimate how fortunate I was: I'd be doing scenes with Dustin Hoffman, directed by Sydney Pollack. I was flabbergasted that such a thing could happen so fast. Or was I? Because part of me felt like—well, this was exactly what was *supposed* to happen.

Before I started work on the movie, I was a little worried about my lack of experience. Surely there were some secret "movie" acting techniques no one had ever taught me, and they might expect me to know about them. My trepidation only deepened the first morning on set as I was led past Sydney Pollack talking to some extras; they were playing actresses waiting for an audition to be on the soap *Southwest General*. (I would later learn that it was extremely unusual for the director himself to be talking to extras; usually the first assistant director conveys the director's wishes to them.)

Sydney seemed exasperated. He was saying, "Be more authentic! Don't try to just *show* me you're nervous—*feel* it."

Oh no. What if he says something like that to me? I mean, I wouldn't blame him—this is my first-ever movie set, and I genuinely don't know what to do—but still, how terrible it would be if . . .

My whole life I couldn't bear the idea that I'd be caught out not knowing how to do something. In many, many cases I've just pretended like I already knew how to do something in case it was shameful to not know how to do whatever it was. I had to avoid being in a position where I might be yelled at or put down, no matter what. So I'd fake knowing how to do things until I figured out how to *actually* do them. In a way this was kind of like an acting exercise. I was living that "fake it till you make it" concept long before I ever heard the term.

When I was at BU, I had a work/study job where I got to design signs and posters for the campus, and it was a blast. There was a big book of examples of different fonts, and I would pore over it to find the most interesting ones for my projects, then hand-letter the text, looking at the examples in the book for reference. One day I was told that the lead graphic artist in this department wanted to meet me; he'd been impressed with my work. I went to his desk and waited there while he finished up something he was working on . . . and saw what he was doing: He was pulling transparent sheets of lettering out of drawers and *rubbing on* the letters from the sheets. I was about as shocked as I'd ever been. THAT was what the book I'd been looking at was: It wasn't examples of fonts you could get inspiration from; it was a catalog of the types of rub-on letters you could *buy*! And big surprise—I didn't tell him I'd been hand-lettering my work. It would have been admitting I wasn't doing it the way he did it, and it would show that I was too dumb to ask someone how I should make the posters in the first place. They hadn't ever noticed that I'd go off and take hours to make a "Class Meeting

Here" sign, when with the premade letters, it would have taken a couple of minutes.

And so now here I was again, only this time on the set of a major motion picture, and I could not let myself ask how things worked on the set. I mean, everyone *knew* it was my first movie! What harm would there have been in simply going with that, and asking questions? As the biggest example of this, I didn't know you were supposed to come to set only when you were in the scenes being shot. I just assumed everyone was expected to come every day. So I did. Every day, 6:00 a.m., there I was. I did notice that some days they put makeup on me and some days they didn't . . .

This is not how it works, obviously—you're only called to set on days you're shooting something. But I never asked, and no one ever explained it to me. I think they assumed I just *wanted* to be there every day—and I did!

I needn't have worried about Sydney. He was incredibly welcoming to me, and always treated me with great respect, as if I were a seasoned pro. Sydney loved actors; he was one himself, of course, and *Tootsie* was the first time in years he'd acted. Dustin Hoffman had convinced him to take the role of his character's agent, whom he played brilliantly.

The first scene I shot was the one that necessitated all that wear-a-bathing-suit-under-your-clothes business for the audition. My character, April, is in the dressing room that she'll be sharing with Dustin's character Michael's fake persona, "Dorothy." April is hanging out in her underwear when Dorothy walks in, forcing Michael to try to keep it together under these unusual circumstances.

And so there we are, shooting my first scene. We do a couple of takes, and then we shoot another one where Dustin unexpect-

edly walks into the door; I ad-libbed, "How you doin', you okay?"
Sydney liked that take; that was the one used in the movie.

After we cut, Sydney called me over.

"Why aren't you nervous?" he said. I think he was asking not
because my ad lib was anything at all special; I suspect it was
because I had calmly gone with it when Dustin Hoffman changed
things up.

"Well," I said, confused, "should I be?"

"Well, *yes!*" Sydney said, similarly confused. "This is your first
movie. In fact, this is your first day on your first movie. That man over
there? That's Dustin Hoffman. And you're in your underwear . . ."

He was right: I wasn't the least bit nervous. Was that because
this was exactly what I'd planned for since I was three years old . . .
a destiny fulfilled kind of thing? (Also, I had no trouble hanging
around in underwear—I'd done so many lingerie shoots as a model
that underwear was kind of my jam.)

My confidence only grew as we went along, and a lot of it had to
do with Dustin.

Dustin mentored me throughout the shoot and gave me all kinds
of advice for the future career he seemed sure I would have. One
of the most important lessons he gave me was on my second day; at
lunch, he took me with him to watch the dailies. Dailies are when
the director, heads of departments, and others gather to assess the
footage shot the day before. Most people go to dailies to check their
work on the technical end of things: Was it in focus, was the sound
clean, did they get all the angles needed?

Let's be clear: The people who *don't* go to dailies include actors
on their first movie in supporting roles.

But Dustin brought me with him because he wanted to teach

me *how* to watch them; he felt that reviewing what you'd shot could be a very valuable tool for an actor. Let's say there was some facet of the character that you were trying to reveal, but you see that it didn't quite come across. If that was the case, you could potentially have a chance to make up for it in another scene. Since then, I've watched dailies on every movie I've worked on (bar one), and it *has* been invaluable. Maybe that's why I really enjoy watching my own movies: I have no problem watching myself, because I'm really used to it. Some actors don't like to watch themselves on screen, and some have never seen the movies they've made. Anything is good if it works for you.

In movies, I'd quickly discover, you have one shot at getting a scene right—the day you shoot it. It's not like the theater, where there's another performance the next night. Over the years I would come to realize it would always be the case that if I'd shot the scene again the next day, I would've done a better job. But I learned that it's all right to do the best I can *at that time*. I'll do better next time. This would end up being incredibly freeing for someone who tended toward the hyper-self-critical. The realization that I would always do better if I had it to do over again meant that what I was doing in the moment was my absolute best.

I can't tell you how liberating that feeling would come to be, in every aspect of my life: "I'm doing the best I can *today*" . . . and it all stemmed from that moment of generosity from Dustin Hoffman toward a beginner on her first movie.

Not all of Dustin's advice was so weighty; the days were full of little tips and tidbits. Another piece of advice was regarding male actors: "Never sleep with your costars," he said. "It's just a bad idea. It complicates everything. Here's what you say if they hit on you: 'Oh, I would love to—you're *very* attractive—but I don't want to ruin the sexual tension between us.'"

I squirreled that one away.

When I showed up on set—every single day—I would go get a director's chair out of a closet, pull it up right next to Sydney, and there I'd stay. Nobody ever said, "You really *shouldn't* sit next to the director," and I never picked up on the fact that there weren't any other actors sitting near him. People might have thought I had some nerve sitting next to the director while he was working, but Sydney, for his part, must have just assumed I wanted to learn. So there I was, in the most valuable seat in town.

What I didn't know at the time was that there's a distinct hierarchy on a movie set, and everyone stays strictly in their own lane. The props department puts the directors' chairs out where they're supposed to go: Director and producer(s) sit here, actors over here. When an actor has a certain status in the cast, a chair with their name on the back is set out, but I didn't know any of that. There was no chair with my name on it . . . but what I did notice was that my *character*—radiologist April Page—had a chair with her name on it, because she's a star in the fictional soap opera. I also noted the closet where the chairs were kept, so I'd just go in there and take out my character's chair.

Only later, of course, did I get the cold sweats: *"Oh God, you don't get your own chair . . . and that was actually a prop for the set! And you don't put it where the director and producers are sitting . . ."* But despite the cringeworthy aspect of it, I was happy I did it, and Sydney didn't seem to mind at all. Filmmaking can be a stressful endeavor and some days he'd put his head in his hands and say, "Nobody's going to want to see this movie."

I'd find myself saying, "It's going to be *great*—you as director and Dustin as the star? Guaranteed to be a huge hit!" (It was.)

Sydney would turn to me, smile, and say gently, "Aw, sunshine, that's what I got you here for."

Late in the movie, Sydney uses a number of reaction shots for the big moment when "Dorothy" walks down the stairs to reveal she's a he. Because it took so long to turn Dustin into Dorothy, Sydney could use the waiting time to shoot these reverse shots without Dustin being there. When it was my turn to shoot reaction shots, Sydney himself walked down the stairs so he could direct me at the same time.

"He's coming down the stairs and he says . . . something *shocking* [I react]. And now it's something . . . even *more* shocking [reaction]. And now he says something strange and confusing [reaction]. Now you're not sure you heard him right [reaction]. Now he does something really REALLY SHOCKING [reaction]!"

Oh, how I loved being in a movie. I am a certified night owl, but those six weeks were the only time in my life that I sprang out of bed every morning. I could not wait to get to the set. Turns out that that whole experience was a masterclass in filmmaking, and from two industry geniuses—Sydney Pollack and Dustin Hoffman. I would never have to walk on a movie set again feeling like I didn't know what to do and pretend like I did. And there I'd been, in all my naivete: ensconced next to the great Sydney Pollack in a chair that read "April Page" on the back.

It's the best job in the world.

And some of that advice from Dustin turned out to be helpful almost right away. . . .

. . .

Right after we wrapped *Tootsie*, the head of my modeling agency—the eponymous Zoli—thought it would be a good idea to take me and a couple of other models/actors to Los Angeles to make the rounds and meet casting directors. Now that a few of his models had gotten acting jobs, he was thinking that perhaps the agency could expand to represent actors as well as models. I was all for going to Hollywood; I was already realizing that although I'd lucked into a film being shot in New York, the bulk of screen acting work would probably be out there.

Zoli just so happened to be great pals with Jack Nicholson. (This was Jack at his peak—in the previous couple of years he'd starred in *The Shining*, *The Postman Always Rings Twice*, and *Reds*, and the following year he'd star in *Terms of Endearment*.) So, *every night* for the entire week we were there, we three models and Zoli had dinner with Jack Nicholson. (Oh, Warren Beatty showed up at one of the dinners, too.) One day, Jack even invited us girls over for lunch. He sent a limo, and when we arrived, we watched him swim laps in his pool for a while; then he made us tuna sandwiches with a glass of milk, like we were all fifteen years old.

A day after that, I got home from our meetings to find a message under the hotel room door—"Please call Jack Nicholson"—and his number. I showed the message to Barbara, the friend I was sharing the room with, saying, "I am going to keep this note forever! Look—'To: Geena Davis. Please call Jack Nicholson!'"

Which I did.

"Hello, Mr. Nicholson," I said. "This is Geena . . . the, uh, the model . . . I understand that you called me."

Jack said, "Sooo, Geeeena . . . whenzit gonna *haaappen?*"

Uh-oh. Well, come on—I should have known that was what this would be about!

"Oh, Mr. Nicholson, I'm afraid you've gotten the wrong idea . . ."

"Aw c'mon," he said, "I'll send a car over." How could I get out of this without offending him? And then it suddenly occurred to me that I knew *exactly* what to say:

"Well, that's very flattering, Mr., uh, Jack—but you see, I have a feeling we're going to end up working together someday," I said, "and, well, I'd hate to have ruined the sexual tension between us."

Jack didn't skip a beat.

"Aw, man, who told you to say *that*?"

I revealed nothing. Many years later I'd tell that story at an event honoring Dustin that Jack attended, and he roared with laughter. I have no idea if he berated Dustin for the advice afterward.

. . .

The week before Christmas 1982, *Tootsie* hit movie screens and was an instant smash. Only *E.T.* filled more theater seats in 1982. By the following spring it had beaten *Close Encounters of the Third Kind* as Columbia's biggest ever domestic success.

Unfortunately, there were two moviegoers who weren't *entirely* delighted by *Tootsie*—Bill and Lucille Davis.

The movie wasn't the first time I'd acted in my underwear. When I'd been at college in New Hampshire before transferring to BU, I was in a faculty-directed production of Stephen Sondheim's *Company*, and because I was to appear in my underwear in *that* role (my first play—and a character also named April!), I didn't invite my parents to come up and see it. My teacher was shocked that I hadn't invited them and took it upon himself to secretly do so—rats! They were *not* happy.

Yet now, a few years later, I was home for Christmas—and as *Tootsie* had just come out, I was taking my folks, and Dan, and his wife, Marilyn, out to Dartmouth, about a half hour away, to see me in my underwear again. No one else was in the theater in the daytime, so there was no way for them to judge how "normal people" would react. After the lights came up, we all walked to the car, and Dan said he thought it was great. Otherwise, not a single word from the parents . . . In the car? Still nothing. We'd been driving back to Wareham for about twenty minutes when, finally, the silence was broken.

"Well!" Mom said. "What'll we have for dinner?"

Keep in mind, I didn't say, "So, what'd you think?" when we came out of the theater, either. None of us knew how to behave—except my brother. It was just a little surreal for all of us.

But overall, the folks were happy for me that I was in a movie. They just seemed a little muted about it.

But a few days later, when Lucyann's mother, Lucia, came over to visit my mom, I found out why: "Nobody can believe this!" Lucia said, fit to burst. "Somebody from Wareham is in a *movie*! It's just unbelievable!"

My mom just looked at her blankly for a beat.

"Well," Mom said, "she studied acting in *college*."

Exactly! What else was supposed to happen? No wonder my folks didn't blink when I said I wanted to major in acting. We didn't have a clue that in all likelihood it would never work out.

. . .

My next job, amazingly, came along with little effort.

Dabney Coleman had played the chauvinistic TV director of

Southwest General (the soap opera in *Tootsie*), and we'd gotten to know each other on set in New York. Dabney—whom I came to adore, one of the funniest people on the planet—was heading back to Los Angeles to star in a sitcom called *Buffalo Bill* for NBC. The show was about an immoral, narcissistic guy who is the host of a daytime talk show on a fictional station called WBFL-TV which takes place in, you guessed it, Buffalo, New York.

Dabney recommended me for the role of Wendy, the naïve, idealistic intern in *Buffalo Bill*, and my audition was good enough that I was able to decamp to Hollywood already with a paying job. The pilot was subsequently picked up for a run of thirteen episodes, so when I moved to LA full-time, Richard came with me.

But LA just wasn't Richard's kind of town; he was a New Yorker through and through and didn't really settle. One day, I gently suggested that he head home for now . . . and though there was no great drama, it became clear we were going to move along with our lives apart. Thankfully, we remain very close to this day.

When I told my folks the sad news that we were getting divorced, my mom said: "Well, all I can say is I never said ONE WORD against him, not one." So all those times she looked at me and then jutted her chin at him, that didn't count as communication, I guess? But Richard still talks about them all the time, and considered them to be the salt of the earth.

. . .

I had thought I would never love a place as much as I loved NYC, but I think I'd been fantasizing about LA since I was a kid, without realizing it. I was always drawing pictures of what my "adult life" would look like, and one favorite activity was designing my future house. I didn't know they were tiles when I drew them, but every house that I drew had little red humps on the roof. When I got to LA, I realized that all the fantasy houses I'd drawn had such roofs.

In LA I felt, for the first time, that this was exactly where I was supposed to be. It hadn't been Wareham; as a kid I often thought Cape Cod was wasted on me—that I was taking up the space of a kid who would have loved everything about it. I didn't like seafood, and I was afraid of the beaches there and couldn't swim. I was terrified of the ocean because as I was about to go in the water one day, my mom had said, "Be sure to look out for any Portuguese Man of War: They look like a balloon floating on the surface, and they have very, *very* long tentacles, so even if they're really far out, they can still sting you." As you can imagine, that was enough for *me*, so while all the other kids were splashing about freely in the water, I was standing only calf-deep, squinting at the horizon. I couldn't ever put my head underwater because then I wouldn't be able to see the floating balloon. But I loved everything about California—the weather, the scenery, the houses . . . and I got to drive everywhere again, which I realized I'd missed.

When I first moved to LA, my parents came to visit me, and they had an extra checked bag with them that had only food in it. My mother brought a pot roast in a suitcase. There were potatoes and vegetables, a jar of rhubarb pie filling, and a wrapped-up ball of dough. The first night, Mom made the pie and served the whole dinner. When my parents were heading home a week later, they saw bananas in a store that were three cents a pound less than at home, so they filled the now-empty suitcase with bananas.

While they'd been in LA, I'd told my dad that I was going to write an episode of *Buffalo Bill*, which caused him to say, "Be sure to give good parts to the other people, too."

The episode aired on February 9, 1984. That's the only script I've ever written, by the way. I've always wished I could be like Sylvester Stallone and write my own *Rocky*, but I'm convinced writing a movie script would take more focused attention than I have.

But now that I've written a frickin' BOOK, maybe it's time to rethink that.

. . .

I was now firmly ensconced in Los Angeles, and my résumé boasted a hit movie and a beloved sitcom. I really felt like the stars were aligning . . . but we didn't know if *Buffalo Bill* was going to be picked up for another season. In fact, there ended up being a whole year between the two seasons—and it turned into a dark time for me. I was running out of money, so I fell back on modeling. The LA scene was very different from New York—very little work—and I was only able to secure gigs like a full-page ad for Macy's housedresses in the *LA Times* Sunday paper. I got calls from a few people on *Buffalo Bill* wondering if that was actually me. I was so embarrassed, and it hit me: *How am I now a housedress model?*

The weight of this question drove me to depression. I had a cute little one-room apartment near Toluca Lake, and a rescue kitten—Kierdy Haird (a silly, sort-of Swedish pronunciation of "Kitty Head")—but realized I was no longer showering or getting fully dressed every day. I'd simply lie on the bed, Kierdy Haird lying on my feet, and stare at the ceiling.

Depression Tip

Teach yourself to sleep as much as possible. As you know, sleep is very healthy. And it certainly helps to pass the time.

It was Dabney Coleman who recommended a therapist to me. I'd never seen a therapist before, and I rather looked forward to my weekly sessions, if nothing else. As time went on, my therapist was very bothered by how depressed I continued to be, but her concern soon grew to be a problem in and of itself. She started making me sandwiches when I came (fortunately not tuna ones like Jack Nicholson, but still), and got all caretaker-y, which is inappropriate for a therapist.

About a year in, she told me she felt I was getting more depressed, not less, and said, "I think you need to see someone else. I think you should see my husband instead."

Yes, folks, I was fired by my therapist, and her idea for treatment was to start therapy with the man she lived with. But boy howdy, it worked. It was such a completely ridiculous suggestion—not to mention just this side of dodgy—that it sort of sobered me up.

Eventually, *Buffalo Bill* returned, and I was back in the swing. But long-term it was not to be; the second season was its last. Brandon Tartikoff, then head of NBC, later wrote in his memoir that canceling the show was his biggest regret.

After *Buffalo Bill* I did several guest-star spots on various shows. I had no idea about the nature of guest-starring roles; I was naïve enough to assume that the reason it was called guest *star* was because they considered you a "star" they were bringing on to enhance their show.

Yeah, that wasn't quite right.

. . .

My first guest-starring role was on an episode of *Knight Rider*. For those of you too young or perhaps too cultured, *Knight Rider* was the show that made David Hasselhoff famous (at least in the United States; he was already huge in Germany, as I was about to find out). David played Michael Knight, the owner of a 1982 Pontiac Firebird Trans Am that could talk to him, in a faintly superior-sounding voice.

I was playing Grace Fallon, a sexy secret cat burglar. In one scene, my character was to seduce Michael Knight—"I'm not the cat; kisses don't lie"—and it seemed that David Hasselhoff's longstanding policy was to have the makeup person spray both him and the woman he was kissing with breath freshener ahead of any face sucking. Nothing says sexual tension like having your tonsils hosed down with peppermint. I'll admit I was trepidatious when David invited me to his trailer at lunchtime. Fortunately, all he wanted to do was have me page through the voluminous collection of clippings he'd scrapbooked that detailed his superstardom as a singer in Germany.

Eventually, Hasselhoff chases the mysterious cat burglar across a rooftop, knocking him/her down and ripping off the balaclava to reveal . . . well, a sexy cat burglar who kind of *wasn't*. My hair was smashed to my head in clumpy lumps, rather than cascading down, hot-librarian style. The director was deeply annoyed at this, feeling I was at fault for not having hair like a waterfall, so we had to fix my hair up again, and do a fake reveal where David had to *pretend* to rip the hood off to reveal the perfectly coiffed "guest star."

Things could only get better?

If you're too young to remember *Fantasy Island*, well, God bless you. *Fantasy Island* was a phenomenon in the late 1970s and early '80s. Its basic premise was that you could go to this magical island and have your fantasies come true. The place was run by Mr. Roarke (played, suavely, by the Mexican actor Ricardo Montalbán). Each week, a plane filled with guest stars would arrive on the islet; it was just one side of a fake plane. Each episode was shot—listen, I hate to burst your bubble—not on a beautiful island in the middle of a pristine ocean, but on a lot behind the Queen Ann Cottage in the middle of LA County's Arboretum, just south of the 210.

I was on an episode called "Don Juan's Last Affair." When I deboarded the half plane, I was handed a cocktail in a coconut, the show's traditional welcome—but they'd put so much lip gloss on me that when Mr. Roarke toasted my arrival, the straw in my drink ended up continually sticking to my bottom lip. (This director thought I was messing everything up, too.) Despite the glamourous makeup, my name in that episode was the decidedly bland "Pat," and "Pat" had a fantasy: She needed to experience the joys of romance. Presto! "Don Juan" comes back from the dead, in the form of hunky Argentinian actor Alejandro Rey, to teach her the art of love. Only thing was, there was a height difference between "Don Juan" and "Pat" that couldn't be easily masked.

This was a problem only because there was a scene that called for me and Alejandro to take a romantic walk together, holding hands . . . and the Hollywood formula has always been that the man must be taller than the woman, unless it's for comic effect. (I was cast opposite both Dustin Hoffman *and* Michael J. Fox for that very reason.) Fortunately, the crew was able to scout a nice grassy slope. Alejandro strolled partway up it, while I walked at its base—and all was well: Pat and Don Juan looked perfectly matched, and Alejandro got to deliver this smooth line:

"Ah, *Patreezia*—how anger flushes your cheek . . . like the peach's blush!"

While we're on height, it's certainly come up a number of times over the years, what with me being so tall—but a lot of actors *are* tall, contrary to the common myth that most actors are short. Chevy Chase, William Hurt, Jeff Goldblum, Andy Garcia, Brad Pitt, Tom Hanks, and more of my costars? All tall. In cases when the male actor was just a bit shorter than I was, I've come up with a no-fuss way of shrinking: No need to ask a guy to stand on something to make him seem a little taller! Instead, if our legs don't show in the shot, I can stand with my knees together, then splay out my feet to either side. Depending how much shorter I need to be, I can just reverse-plié deeper. I'll admit, I don't really care right now about trying to fix the notion that men should always be taller than women in romantic movies. There are enough seriously underrepresented groups of people that I can't handle trying to add another one.

I wasn't done with guest-starring on TV shows; they really saved me financially, and I was grateful for the jobs. And some of the roles were fun and weird, like when I played a practical-joke-loving nymphomaniacal oceanographer named Melba Bozinski on an episode of *Riptide*.

But these experiences so clearly demonstrated the almost militaristic hierarchy of sets: Being a guest star basically meant you were a rather low-totem-pole interloper. I didn't care about the size of the roles when guesting—thus far I'd only had very small parts—but I think I'd become spoiled by never being treated somewhat like a second-class citizen before. And forget about the poor extras, who were even made to eat from a different craft services table, as if they couldn't be allowed to touch our food. This means that when I'm in the main cast of a show or movie, I always try to make sure everyone feels valued and seen; I hope the people I've worked with can attest to that. Because of course I also want to win an award for "Nicest Person to Work With, Ever."

...

By the mid 1980s, the sitcom *Family Ties* was as big as it got. It was what used to be called "appointment TV," where people would hurry to finish dinner or to get home from work in time to sit in front of an actual television set and stay put for thirty minutes or an hour to watch their favorite shows. This sounds like a prehistoric idea when said out loud now, in the world of streaming, downloads, and watching TV on your computer, but back then? There was a reason more than 100 million people tuned in to the final episode of *M*A*S*H* in 1983. It was because if you missed it, you *missed* it. Television back then was a communal thing. You watched it with your family or friends, all sitting around and laughing at the same jokes at the same time, crying at the sad parts along with everyone else in the room.

Family Ties was a signature part of that tradition. The show made a superstar of Michael J. Fox and ran for most of the 1980s. It concerned a Republican son (Fox as Alex P. Keaton) of liberal parents (played by Michael Gross and Meredith Baxter) and was very much of its time. The 1980s saw capitalism go wild, and Republican values suddenly became de rigueur. It was the time of Reagan and Bush Sr. and the explosion of Wall Street excess.

My guest star spot in 1985 ran across two episodes. I played Karen Nicholson, a wildly incompetent (and short-lived, although not short) housekeeper in the Keaton home, and a passing love interest for Alex P. Keaton. He announces he needs someone "beautiful, sensuous, and intelligent" to help him get into a fraternity, and whoops, there I stood, emptying groceries on the kitchen counter!

I worked plenty in 1985: I made *Secret Weapons*, a height-of-the-Cold-War-inspired TV movie starring Linda Hamilton. I was Tamara Reshevsky, a Russian agent; we were recruited to pass as Americans so we could trick unsuspecting American men into giving us secrets by sleeping with them. The whole thing was summed up in the tagline: "Enter the secret world of the Soviet school for sex spies!" It was an upgrade from a nymphomaniacal oceanographer, I suppose, but not by much. In the classroom in which we learned to be Americans, I fake-Russian-accented my way through exchanges like:

Teacher: What do you know about Americans?'

Tamara Reshevsky: Dey oll wear blue jeans, even the presidyent!

That same year I found myself in an episode of *Remington Steele* with Stephanie Zimbalist and Pierce Brosnan. I was a tennis teacher called Sandy Dalrymple this time, a name so memorable that some thirty years later I bumped into Pierce, and he exclaimed, "Miss Dalrymple!" (Note: He was doing one show per week, I was no one, and decades later he could remember my character's name? Isn't that amazing?) But despite his terrific memory, the specter of the hierarchy stalked me back then; Pierce loved to sing on set in between takes, and me being me, I liked to join in, until after a few songs he not unreasonably asked, "Must you sing, too?"

Aw, rats—I had stepped out of my own shadow and paid a (very small) price, yet again. Growing to deal with this would prove to be crucial in the coming years, but in the meantime, I just went on trying—and failing—to figure out where the land mines were.

Many years later, the fabulous Polly Bergen would play my mother in the series *Commander in Chief*, and I was stunned to hear her liberally dropping the F-bomb on set and making very racy comments. I asked her about it, and she said, "Oh, honey, when you get old, you just don't give a fuck anymore."

I'm trying to not give a fuck before I'm old-old, but I can see that she's right. I'm pretty sure I'll be one salty old broad when I get there.

. . .

On the back of my guest appearance on *Family Ties*, the producers told me they wanted to make me my *own show*, and so was born *Sara*, created entirely with me in mind. I was over the moon.

I couldn't believe how lucky I was—that these insanely talented, successful people were going to create a new show for *me* . . . which they then didn't cast me in.

They'd decided I wasn't "conventionally" pretty enough or if this big goofy gal with a giant head of curls would appeal to everyone, so they decided instead to cast someone whose hair, presumably, would do the sexy librarian thing when *her* balaclava was removed.

That is, until a little while later, when my phone rang.

"Geena, the pilot of *Sara* didn't go as we'd hoped, so we'd like you to play Sara after all."

"Hot dog!" I said, the whole created-for-me-in-the-first-place business instantly erased from my mind. Now I was going to have my very own sitcom on NBC. It seemed that I wasn't going back to modeling anytime soon.

NBC was styling *Sara* as "the new *Mary Tyler Moore Show*," so when it got picked up, I headed over to the writers' room to introduce myself, assuming they'd want to meet me and get a feel for my sense of humor. But my stepping up led to me getting my toes trodden on big time.

They didn't even invite me into the room.

"That's okay, we're good," one of the writers said. "We got this. We created *Family Ties*, so obviously we know how to do this."

Oh, no: There I was, playing the title character, feeling my oats, bouncing over to introduce myself, and it was as if I were laughing too loud once again, and I'd better bring it right down. I had assumed that they'd want to get to know me and incorporate things about me into the character, but clearly not.

The show was funny, even so: Sara McKenna, my character, was a defense lawyer in a legal aid office, and *Sara* also featured a young

Alfre Woodard playing my BFF, Rozalyn Dupree, as well as Bill Maher playing a sexist character called Marty Lang who always referred to Sara as "kitten" and complimented her on her "getaway sticks."

After the showrunning was turned over to the head writer partway through, a concern suddenly arose that perhaps I was "too pretty" to be relatable to the audience—the solution to which, it was decided, became that from then on I should be dressed in plain clothes (gray or beige), wear no makeup.

I couldn't win for losing: first, not conventionally pretty enough; then, too pretty to be relatable.

Despite thinking this was a horrible idea, I went along with it and shot the next episode in a gray suit, sans makeup. I could only get through it because at the dress rehearsal one of the male writers took me to one side and said, "Don't worry, you look beautiful on camera this way . . ."

I believed him. The very first time I realized that I might be pretty had been when I saw myself on video in college for the first time. I remember thinking, "Wait just a second here—maybe I AM pretty . . . but only if it's on camera!"

But when I watched the episode on TV . . .

"OH MY GOD! OH MY GOD! OH MY GOD!"

Kierdy Haird the kitten head just looked at me as if to say, "Yup, gray is not your color."

Next morning, it seemed that NBC agreed with my cat. The edict came down that I was never to be purposely made to look like a plain Jane again.

In the end, the show went along, but for me, not feeling like part of the team made it feel less than joyful. Despite my being the title character, no one thought I should be included in the process.

Given that NBC wanted me to become the new Mary Tyler Moore, I figured I should take the big boss—the then-head of the network, Brandon Tartikoff—to lunch to talk the whole thing through.

In hindsight, I suppose to go over the showrunner's head to talk to the head of the network was quite a ballsy move. But I didn't know it was, only four years into the business. I figured, *I'm the star of one of Tartikoff's shows, so why wouldn't he want to talk to me?* Fortunately, Brandon not only accepted my lunch request, but was very interested to hear what I had to say.

I didn't beat around the bush.

"In my opinion, I'm not being utilized in the way that I could, and the show needs to be great, or else why are we doing it?"

The way I thought things might go was that Brandon would either talk to the producers and make some changes, or not pick it up for any more episodes—and he opted for the second fix.

Making *Sara* was not a horrible experience by any stretch of the imagination. We had a lot of fun on set, and I loved the directors and my castmates and the crew on the show. We finished up our final episodes and had a very nice wrap party. Champagne was poured, and at one point I heard someone call out, "To Sara!" I turned with a big smile to join in and saw that the writers were all toasting one another—not a single one looked my way.

That was *Sara* in a nutshell. I wasn't Sara to them—never was, and never would be.

. . .

Fletch was a movie starring Chevy Chase in which Fletch, Chevy's *Los Angeles Times* undercover reporter character, is on the trail of a man who for some reason wants Fletch to kill him. (It's complicated, okay?) I managed to get an audition for the female lead, but though the producers really liked me—"You're so funny; we love you"—they *also* said, "You're just not conventionally pretty. You don't look like the girl you'd expect a lead character to fall in love with." To still have me in the movie somehow, the producers turned the role of the newspaper morgue chief, "Larry," into a female so I could play it. I liked the name so much I told them not to change it. I had gone from Pat in *Fantasy Island* to a woman called Larry, via one Dr. Melba Bozinsky and an unforgettable Miss Dalrymple.

I could feel something percolating; my phone was ringing regularly. Off-screen, things were looking up, too. *Sara* had given me enough cash to buy my first house. Ronnie Claire Edwards, who played our secretary on the show, told me that Los Feliz was a fabulous neighborhood, so without a second of research I headed straight there and bought a 1926 Victorian-style place with a big rounded window in the living room and a tiny round swimming pool in the back. Oh, and there were ninety steps from the carport to the front door, which kept me fit (and yes, of course I counted them—many times).

Turns out I bought that house *twice* and managed to move into it and out of it four times. When I got cast in a movie called *Transylvania 6-5000*, starring Jeff Goldblum, well, I fell in love with Jeff, and sold the house to buy a house with him. I then bought it back after Jeff and I split up; I kept it through two more relationships, moving in and out. I figured my neighbors on the street could assess the state of my love life by the number of times they saw a moving truck outside.

• • •

It was around this time I found out that Mom was laminating articles and reviews. If I'd wanted a big supply of placemats with my face on them, I was all set. She told me delightedly that people seemed to enjoy the way my name was spelled.

I said, "Yeah, I tell them you didn't know how to spell Gina the right way."

"Oh no, that's not true," she said. "I lived in a neighborhood full of Italians for a time. I knew very well how to spell 'Gina.'"

"Then why didn't you spell it G-I-N-A?"

"I didn't want anyone to think it was pronounced 'gina.' As in *va*-gina."

Here I'd thought my name was misspelled for a sweet, funny reason, but it turned out my entire identity was based on the fear of vaginas.

Chapter Six
My Bug Phase

I was rather dazzled from the beginning.

We were in Zagreb, Yugoslavia (now Croatia), to begin shooting a movie called *Transylvania 6-5000*. Our mutual friend, Ed Begley Jr., brought me over to meet Jeff Goldblum, and I could immediately see from the sly smile playing on the lips of this insanely charismatic person that I was in trouble. What I didn't realize was that I was about to embark on a whole new chapter of my life, and that Jeff would be with me for all of it, and me with him.

By that point in his career, Jeff had done some very cool stuff. He was in *Invasion of the Body Snatchers* and *Silverado*, and he played Michael in *The Big Chill*, among many other things; he'd also appeared as "Jeffrey" in an episode of *Laverne and Shirley*, in which he kissed my future director Penny Marshall, while spouting French to her.

In *Transylvania 6-5000*, a totally goofy-ass movie, Jeff and Ed play a pair of reporters heading to Transylvania to investigate Frankenstein sightings; along the way they come across a number of other archetypal ghouls and monsters. (Rumor has it that this may have been one of the tallest casts ever assembled in a film: Jeff, Ed Begley Jr., Michael Richards, Jeffrey Jones, and I all averaged out to six-three.) I play Odette, a nymphomaniacal vampire. Hey, from nymphomaniacal oceanographer to nymphomaniacal vampire in just one year—surely if I kept this up I could one day play a nymphomaniacal astronaut!

The director, Rudy De Luca, had been described to me by one of the producers thusly before I met him: "This guy, I'm telling you, he's never directed before, but he's a genius! In fact, he might be the most *genial* man I know!" (I would later use that pleasing malapropism for the name of my production company, Genial Pictures.)

As it turned out, it wasn't entirely clear to us on set that Rudy was the most "genial" man. For one thing, despite having written the script, he seemed profoundly unfamiliar with it. There was a scene in which the evil Dr. Malavaqua, played by Joseph Bologna, is draining Ed Begley's character's blood, for some reason; Ed is supposed to wake up, very weak from the ordeal: "What's happened to me?" Accordingly, the makeup artist used pale makeup to make Ed look like he'd lost a lot of blood, but during rehearsal for the scene, Rudy suddenly yelled:

"My God, look at Ed, he's all pale! Get a doctor!" Yeah. Even though he was the writer, we weren't entirely convinced he'd ever *read* the script.

Another day we shot a scene where my vampire character has flown up to a bedroom window as a bat (naturally), then turned back into a vampire. I'm standing by to make my entrance; Ed and Jeff are in the scene and there as well, but the first shot will be of just the window. Rudy asks for the gauzy curtains to move a bit to show that the window is open, so Repetza, our Yugoslavian props guy, waves a hand fan on them lightly.

The director says, "I don't see nothing, there's no wind."

Repetza kicks the fan up a notch—the curtains are certainly fluttering now.

"More wind!" again . . . And then *again* he calls out: "More wind! I don't see nothing!"

Now the curtains are flapping madly; Ed, Jeff, and I are wondering, "What the hell, is there supposed to be a hurricane out there?!" Finally, we realize, *he's looking at the wrong window.* He's on the other side of the room looking at a window where there is no crew, no Arriflex BL camera, and no lights.

In the end, the whole shoot was so unhinged we nearly turned to anarchy. We fantasized about trying to shoot scenes without Rudy there. As it was, Rudy would sometimes fall asleep while we were shooting, and the camera would keep rolling. One time he fell asleep, and at the end of the scene the first assistant director nudged him awake. Rudy bolted up in his chair and yelled, "ACTION!"

The first AD said, dryly, "No, the other one."

"CUT!" Rudy yelled.

When I auditioned for the part, it was my first experience with sexual harassment in the industry; it left me with shame and humiliation that was hard to get past and made me realize how vulnerable I really was. The number of times over the years where I would be in the position of "didn't want to do it, got bullied into it anyways," would come to be staggering.

Only as time went on did I understand how rampant sexual harassment was in my business, and the extremity of what so many of my peers were suffering. Up until then, it had somehow never crossed my mind that I might be sexually exploited at work. This may have been because I'd been treated with such respect when I started out, or because I didn't learn what to look out for after being molested as a child on my paper route many years before. (I'd also always been incredibly naïve—I remember as a model telling my agent, Susan, how shocked I was that a photographer had propositioned me in exchange for work. She looked at me bemusedly and said, "So you mean you're *not* sleeping with photographers?")

Back to my audition: There's a scene in the movie in which I sit on Ed Begley Jr.'s lap and press his face into my breasts as I try to seduce him. It's silly and over-the-top, but makes sense in the context of the movie. The director wanted me to act out that scene for my audition . . . with *him*—actually sitting on *his* lap and shoving *his* face into my breasts. I tried to laugh it off as a joke, but he insisted. There was another man in the room, the producer, I think, and I looked to him to help me out, but he just chuckled and shrugged, like this was all great fun. I ended up doing it. I didn't feel like I had a choice, though of course I did.

This would be the first in a series of such incidents in my career that made me realize that the mistreatment of female actors was everywhere and plentiful and so, so disheartening. It was clear to me that acting out this scene in the audition was simply and only for the director's jollies, and I didn't yet have either the experience or confidence to tell him where to shove it.

You tell yourself, *I'll never let that happen again*, and though you're ready for it now and know what you'd do differently, nothing exactly like that does happen again. Something *else* will happen, something you didn't see coming or anticipate ever happening, and you will suddenly find yourself unequipped to handle that, too.

Becoming my authentic self and protecting that person was hardly a linear endeavor. As with many things in life, it tended to be two steps forward, one back. I'd been forced to compromise myself in an audition, but I was determined to get past it; my tougher self was slowly growing in me through such pains, through such slights.

Here's a sampling of the glowing audience reviews of *Transylvania 6-5000* from Rotten Tomatoes:

"Barely legal to even watch because of its shittyness."

"What you should know about it going in, is that it's beyond stupid—it's so far beyond stupid."

"I like Geena Davis' chest and legs."

"Oh, Jeff Goldblum and Genna [*sic*] Davis, I'm so glad your careers were not ruined by this hideously unfunny film."

"Watch this with a few baked friends and you will have a great evening."

What the movie lacked in quality, it more than made up for on a personal level. By the end of filming it was clear that Jeff and I were going to be together. Our mutual interest had grown into romance, and back in the States, we eventually moved in together.

I wish the start of our relationship was as simple as I've just described, but I'm afraid it wasn't. When I left for the movie, I was living with—and engaged to—one of the most wonderful men I've ever known, the actor Christopher McDonald. He was and is a truly beautiful person . . . and I broke his heart to be with Jeff, I'm ashamed to say. He didn't deserve that at all, and this dear man eventually forgave me, for which I will always be grateful. And to my great delight, we even got to work together a few years later.

. . .

If *Transylvania 6-5000* had been a silly, weird-ass reentry into moviemaking, my next project was the complete opposite, and a big, big deal: My first ever lead movie role, as the journalist Veronica Quaife in David Cronenberg's *The Fly*.

Cronenberg is a masterful writer and director. His tastes are incredibly eclectic; among many others, he cites both William S. Burroughs and *Bambi* as strong influences on his aesthetic, which makes sense when you see *The Fly*, a movie that manages to be simultaneously tender, poignant, completely nauseating, gross, and terrifying. David saw the movie as an operatic, tragic love story, in which Jeff's character faces the ravages of his transformation into a fly in the same way the rest of us must face the onslaught of age and physical decay. (In fact, there was a subsequent opera made based on the movie!) Later viewers also saw a metaphor for the AIDS crisis that was then ravaging the world in the mid-'80s, but to David, the movie was more about the universal horror we all contemplated the older we got.

Enter Jeff . . . and then, enter me.

There was initially great wariness about having me involved in *The Fly*. Once he was cast, Jeff recommended me for the role of Veronica, and the creative team liked my audition a lot: Jeff and I, perhaps not surprisingly, had tremendous chemistry. But the producers were concerned that Jeff and I might split up during the making of the movie, and that, of course, would spell disaster for the project. A few years later, Dave Letterman asked me on *The Late Show* if there was friction in our marriage because we were both actors. I countered with "No, no, because we're rarely up for the same parts."

There was no chance of our splitting on *The Fly*: We lived and breathed that movie; it was about as intense a creative experience as you could hope to have. We were obsessed with the script and worked on it tirelessly together, and even as we did so, I recall understanding what an incredible opportunity it was to be able to work so intensely with a costar. We were also fortunate in that David Cronenberg was at the top of his game.

The script was so well written that it needed no alterations, but David welcomed the few suggestions we made. A small scene in which Jeff's character, Seth Brundle, buys Veronica a heart-shaped locket—she admits at the start of the movie that she never wears jewelry—was a moment we suggested. Jeff contributed some genius Goldblumian dialogue, enrichening a performance that was easily good enough to get him an Academy Award nomination, which was widely predicted. Unfortunately, the precedent held: very few actors had ever been nominated for a horror role. As for me, well, I got to utter a line that's now entered the culture, though most people don't remember that I first said it in *The Fly*:

"Be afraid. Be very afraid."

The Fly was a once-in-a-lifetime experience; I rewatched it recently, and the love story still strikes me as powerful and tragic. It's the stuff of *King Kong* or the *Beauty and the Beast*, and I think you really feel for Veronica when it becomes clear the man she loves is no longer even a man. *The Fly* was actually a remake of a movie of the same name that came out in 1958, and which was also successful. In that one, the scientist and the fly trade *heads*, and the end scene shows a fly on a spiderweb with a tiny human head crying, "Help me, help me!"

For my first lead movie role, I couldn't have asked for a better experience; what a blessing to be so welcomed and appreciated yet again by a true auteur, this time David Cronenberg. This was how I wanted to feel—strong and confident, not compromised by a lecherous supposed "genius." *Cronenberg* is a genius, and I got to make a movie with him and with the man I loved, too.

When *The Fly* came out, Jeff and I snuck into the back of a huge

Times Square theater on opening night, eager to see how a really big crowd would react. Turns out it was perfect. People were yelling at the screen throughout: "Don't go in there!! He's a *fly!*" At one point a man came up the aisle to where we were standing in the back of the theater, pulling along his assumed girlfriend; he turned her head to look at each of us, then said, "See? I *told* you!"

There's a scene later in the movie where my character visits Seth when he's very far gone toward becoming a fly—so far gone, in fact, that as we're talking, his right ear falls off. When we shot the scene, we thought it was one of the most emotional ones in the film, where, despite the horror of what's happening to him, my character finds the strength to comfort the man she loves by hugging him. What we *didn't* realize was the reaction it would get when I hug him on the *same side* where his ear fell off. At that moment in the theater, when I smushed my face right where Seth's ear used to be, a great roar of horror arose from the audience. The screams and shouts of disgust went on so long that you couldn't hear any of the dialogue in the next two scenes.

To our delight, the movie was a hit. . . .

Back in Wareham, though, to the locals my star seemed to have dimmed tragically. As I was no longer regularly on their TVs in *Buffalo Bill* or *Sara*, some churchgoers on Sundays went as far as to take me to one side and whisper sadly, "Oh, Geena, what *happened?* We thought you were going to be famous. . . ."

As for the two most important people in Wareham, well, *The Fly* didn't signal a rise in my stature to them, either. My folks were visiting my brother, Dan, and his wife, Marilyn, in New Hampshire, when the movie came out, and it being a big deal they duly traipsed off to see it on the opening weekend. Knowing they were going to be watching, I eagerly awaited their call.

Silence.

In the end I couldn't stand it and called my brother.

"Well?" I said, impatiently.

"Marilyn and I loved it, that was awesome!" Dan said, and I could tell he meant it. Then there was a pause.

"Thanks, Dan. . . . What about Mom and Dad?" I asked.

More silence.

"Dan, put them on," I said.

My mother came on the line.

"Hullo?" she said, shakily, as though someone in the family had died and she had to tell me the bad news.

"Mom, are you okay?" I said.

"Uh-huh," she croaked out.

"Mom, what's wrong?"

In the background I heard my father call out, "You're gonna have to make better movies than that if you want me to watch 'em!"

"Well," Mom said with a still-quivering voice, "there's something about that movie we didn't like . . ."

"Well, what was it?"

"You know."

"No, I honestly don't," I said.

Silence on the other end.

"Mom, I *don't* know what you're talking about, there are so many possibilities. Was it when the baboon turned inside out? Was it when Jeff pulled his fingernails off?"

I was getting a little peeved that the movie I loved had brought on this reaction, even though, yes, it was extremely gory. "Or when I give birth to a giant maggot? Come on, Mom, what?"

There was a long silence, and then she whispered, "The . . . sex."

. . .

I always fall in love with my characters and never want to stop being them, so I've wanted to do a sequel to nearly every movie I've been in—except *Thelma & Louise*, because duh. You can't imagine how many people have asked me if there was going to be a sequel to that movie. "We thought maybe you got away somehow." No, we did not. We're pancakes at the bottom of the Grand Canyon.

A couple of years later I got a call from one of the producers of *The Fly* saying that they were going to be making a sequel with *me* (Cronenberg was not involved), and he was very excited to send the script right over. I was over the moon! I assumed Jeff would be in it too, in flashbacks. *The Fly* ends with me still pregnant, so I was obviously going to carry on our story! I got the script and cracked it open immediately; it started with a *very* gory birth scene (of course), which continued onto page two, where my character . . . dies. Bleeds out and dies on the delivery table. I frantically flipped through the rest of the pages and yup, that's all I do: die gruesomely in the first two minutes. Kinda like . . . Bambi's mom.

So, for that particular sequel I let someone else in a Geena wig bleed out on the delivery table instead.

A few years later, I pitched an *alternative* sequel *to The Fly* to the head of Fox Studio, then Joe Roth. I said it could only work if we ignored that *The Fly II* had ever came out, and Joe said, "No problem there: No one saw it."

He loved my idea, so we hired a writer. Unfortunately, we never got the script right. I'm still bummed about that. The story was that Veronica gives birth to *twins*, who seem normal in every way at first—although she's totally paranoid they'll, you know, bug out.

As they grow, things that should be completely expected take on ominous meanings to her: They love sugary cereal? Uh-oh. They're always climbing up on things? Holy shit.

But when they reach puberty, something unmistakable does start happening. Instead of peach fuzz, they start growing little fly hairs. Then it becomes a race to see if she can get the fly out of them before they're too far gone; ultimately, the computer says there's not enough human genetic material to separate out the fly, so I program it to use the material from *both* of them to make one boy. At the end I'm on trial for killing one of my boys, because I can't produce him.

Cool story, right? They can make you look young now with CGI—maybe I can still make that sequel.

Oh, and it's called *Flies*.

. . .

While we were making *The Fly*, I read a book I was crazy about. There was a *lot* of time on set in Toronto for reading. As you can imagine if you've seen the movie, Jeff was in the makeup chair for hours on end. So I spent the downtime reading novels. This related to another piece of advice Dustin Hoffman had given to me during *Tootsie*: Always be on the lookout for books that would make good movies, and if you like one, buy the rights.

One author I'd always loved was Anne Tyler, so when her newest, *The Accidental Tourist*, came out, I immediately picked it up, and just plain adored it. Most important, it had a female character in it that I wanted to play from the moment she first appeared. I called my agent to ask how you buy the rights to a book. I had no idea how much such a thing would cost but learned that the movie rights to great books often got sold before the book ever came out. That was the case here; the rights were long gone. I was crushed and decided that I hated whoever was going to get to play Muriel Pritchett.

I shook it off and moved on: another bug was crawling up the walls of my career.

• • •

Fresh off the success of *Pee-wee's Big Adventure*, Tim Burton was a hot new director, and *Beetlejuice* was his next big project. I got cast as Barbara Maitland, and though I die seven minutes after my name appears in the opening credits, this was no *The Fly II*. In this one, dying wasn't a hindrance to still being in the movie.

I got cast in *Beetlejuice* after a meeting with Tim Burton, no audition this time. During our meeting, Tim showed me drawings he'd made of what the movie was going to look like. He had pinned them up all over the walls; I was ecstatic and told him so.

"I just want you to know, I *get* this movie, I *really get it*," I said. Later, he would tell me that one of the reasons he cast me was because he wasn't sure *he* really got the movie, so it might be handy to have someone around who was very sure they knew what it was all about.

I'd realized by now that I really didn't want to play the kind of typical female roles I was seeing. I wasn't conventionally pretty enough to be cast as eye candy, and I didn't want to just be the *girlfriend* of the guy who goes off to do something cool; *I* wanted to have cool challenges, too. That's why I chose these unusual films, like *The Fly* and *Beetlejuice* (and pretty much every movie after those two), because they gave me challenging and unusual things to *do*.

It was only as time went on that I realized there was a unifying theme to what I was inexorably drawn to: These were women who were taking charge of their own destiny. I wanted to act out characters who were bold and self-possessed, probably because I felt myself to be so far removed from those qualities. And these roles would work in the opposite direction, too, teaching me how to configure my own fate in my life off screen. What this all meant was that in the '80s I found myself in what people might describe as "offbeat" films, but to me they were opportunities to try on what it would be like to be a more confident and assertive person than I was.

I probably thought of myself as somewhat eccentric, which could explain these offbeat choices, but what's notable is that in many films at this time, I tended to play the character who brought reality to the extraordinary. I'm not the crazy one in these situations! I'm not Beetlejuice; I'm just a normal (albeit dead) gal, in an extraordinary situation. In *The Fly* I'm a working journalist who is facing the horror of my boyfriend becoming an insect. (And this dynamic would continue in the next movie I made with Jeff, *Earth Girls Are Easy.* More on that in a moment.) It's often been my job to make the audience believe in an alternate reality; to normalize it.

Like Sydney Pollack and David Cronenberg, Tim Burton is a true auteur, and had very colorful ways of describing what he wanted that were eminently actable. In one scene, we're stuck for ages in a waiting room in the afterlife, and there's a man sitting next to me with a shrunken head. He turns his shriveled little noggin' to me, and Tim said, "Just pretend it's somebody a little bit weird who has chosen to sit next to you on the subway. You know, it's really not that big a deal, but also, 'What are you looking at?'" This was a genius thing to say; it absolutely nailed the moment for me.

I'd gotten quite good at picking the parts I wanted to play—and of course you can only pick from the roles you're offered—but I was having a terrific time with all of these colorful characters. But often the most enthusiastic offers were for quite bland, one-dimensional characters. Why were they so often thinking of me for those roles?

I eventually figured out why: People were assuming that the characters I was playing were colorful because *I* made them colorful; therefore, if they cast me in the boring, one-dimensional female role in their movie, I would be able to just magically make the part interesting. But I *couldn't*; it had to be in a script already. I was just good at choosing colorful parts.

I'd found that making the female supporting character(s) more interesting was not high on the list for many filmmakers. Those characters were often there just to perform a function that didn't rely on them being fully developed. I remember when I was going to meet the great Martin Scorsese about his new movie, *Cape Fear*, in the early '90s: I knew he thought I might be too young to play Nick Nolte's wife (a role that eventually went to Jessica Lange), so I came up with a pitch about why it would make the story even more interesting if there were a reason Nick Nolte's character married someone so young, and the impact her personality had on their screwed-up relationship. Mr. Scorsese seemed dumbstruck by my suggestion. Fair enough; he's a frickin' *genius*, and I should have realized he wasn't someone you suggested changes to! But I often wondered if the idea of making female characters more dimensional is just something male writers and directors don't see as necessary.

• • •

Beetlejuice was the first set my parents visited. We filmed in New Hampshire, and being Vermonters, they felt right at home, it being next door and all. They were so at home, in fact, that they brought their new, not-homemade camper—a secondhand Airstream trailer—to stay in. As for me, well, I was a ball of stress the entire time they were there, worrying if they were doing okay—because I knew they wouldn't ask anyone if they needed anything, and would no doubt refuse food or drink or even a chair the whole time. Fortunately, the assistant director kept them busy by making them extras in a couple of scenes, which gave them something to do and eased my worries a little. At one point in the movie a gaggle of locals watch as the crazy old house is being remodeled, and there's Dad in his obligatory panama hat, standing behind Mom as they watch the goings-on. Dad was delighted that they each got a very small check for being extras; he asked them to make his out to "Will Davis," not Bill Davis. I asked him why, and he said, "That's my stage name."

But my mom's greatest contribution to *Beetlejuice*—at least if you asked the crew—was the giant box of baked goods she'd brought with her to share around set. (She was too shy to hand them out herself, so I did it for her.) Lucille was a genius at baking, although when you pointed that out, she'd always say the true talent in the family was *her* mother, who'd used only her cupped hand for measuring and still managed to produce perfect pastries. From then on, Mom would always bring or send baked goods for the crew on my sets, to the point where, when I'd start a new movie, inevitably someone would have worked with me before and would knock on my trailer door wondering if she had delivered any apricot squares.

. . .

I was mad about Jeff—I felt so in sync with him. I have to say we delighted in each other. He didn't want me to suppress my quirkier tendencies like so many others in my life had; rather, we celebrated in, and brought out, the quirkiness in each other. We were a couple who seriously considered installing bumper cars in the hallway to get from the bedroom to the kitchen when remodeling the house we bought. We dubbed my bathroom in the new house Weddingland. The walls came covered floor to ceiling in crazy over-the-top flowered tiles, so we just went with it: I put AstroTurf on the floor, and a picket fence around a fake flower garden; the whole thing was decked out with Styrofoam wedding bells and countless bride and groom cake toppers. In fact, maybe Weddingland was to make up for the very unflowery and cake-topperless wedding ceremony we actually had.

Jeff and I had been together for about two and a half years when we decided to go for a weekend in Vegas to do silly Vegas stuff. (We'd never been there before.) It was Halloween night 1987, and we'd invited Ed Begley and his then wife, Ingrid, to come with us. Ed had recently turned thirty-eight, and we wanted to celebrate. We had dinner at a weird restaurant in Caesars Palace, which had examples of all the cuts of meat stuck to a platter. The waiter poked each one with his ballpoint pen when describing them. Dinner over, it was time to decide what next—a show, maybe, or we could lose our shirts on the tables . . .

Ed said, "It's getting late; have you already picked where you're going to do this?"

It turned out Ed and Ingrid assumed we'd invited them on this trip to be witnesses to our marriage.

It had been the furthest thing from our minds, honestly, but Jeff said how about we go ahead and do just that, since the idea was now on the table. I froze. It was so unexpected; there was no time to even think about whether this was the way I wanted us to get married. I knew I wanted to marry him, no question about that, but still. So Jeff and I went and sat on the curb in front of Caesars Palace to discuss it.

I was teary, and Jeff tried to make me feel better.

"It's fine," he said. "We'll just plan for something else . . ."

"But I think I *do* want to do it tonight!" I sniffled.

"Okay, then we'll do it tonight!" Jeff said.

"Well, now I've ruined it by crying!" I said.

Jeff, ever patient and loving, put me at ease about that, too. So we called one of those goofy all-night chapels, which sent a white limo to pick us all up. It was 3 a.m.; Elvis didn't officiate, I'm sorry to say, but a certain Reverend Sandy did, bedecked in a red robe. (I'm pretty certain she was not a vampire, despite her clothing and the late hour.) In fact, she was profoundly serious about the whole thing, admonishing us at great length about the profundity of the step we were taking before God . . . something I think an Elvis minister would have rather glossed over.

We all piled into the car to head back to Caesars Palace and as soon as we started to drive away, we burst out screaming and laughing. The first hint of light was edging along Las Vegas Boulevard; it was November 1, 1987, and I had just married my soul mate.

. . .

Beetlejuice turned out to be a huge hit; I was on a roll. Now it was time to work with Jeff for the *third* time, in a movie called *Earth Girls Are Easy*, in which I was a Valley Girl and he was an alien.

(The other two aliens were Jim Carrey and Damon Wayans, so how much fun was *that* movie!)

Now, as someone who's made a point of speaking out about the quality of roles available to women, being in a movie called *Earth Girls Are Easy* might seem a little problematic. But I am anything but precious; I don't give a shit what people think. It's just meant to be a goof. (Anytime someone has wanted to compliment me on that movie, they typically say, "You know, I actually LIKED *Earth Girls Are Easy!*") The script was penned by the actor and comedian Julie Brown. My character, Valerie Gail, gets knocked out when a spaceship lands in her swimming pool. Three fur-covered aliens emerge: Jeff is the blue one; Jim Carrey is red; and Damon Wayans yellow. When I come to, I realize they're nice and introduce them to spray cheese. My friend decides they need a makeover and shaves them, and they emerge as attractive, human-looking creatures, so much so that we head to a nightclub and a whole series of aliens-abroad-in-a-strange-land scenes ensue. Eventually they want to return to their planet, and I leave with them.

Earth Girls Are Easy is also a musical; I get to lip-sync to an '80s banger, "The Ground You Walk On." At the time, Julien Temple, the director, had only made music videos. He brought his own eccentricity and creative mind to the shoot, to the point where we'd be walking to set and he'd see something weird and say, "Ooh, that looks cool, let's shoot that!" Directors who come out of that world tend to have a more seat-of-the-pants, guerrilla-filmmaking style. If the movie had super-serious intentions this approach might have been frustrating, but on *Earth Girls* . . . it added to the freewheeling sense of fun. For some reason I had recently bought a giant four-foot princess telephone, and for some other reason brought it to set to show Julien. He promptly put it in the movie in a nightmare I'm having in which I'm trying to call somebody.

And then something really weird happened.

About ten days in, Julien took me aside.

"Can I ask you something?" he said.

"Of course," I said.

"Are you . . . being as *funny* as you can be?"

This I was not expecting.

"Um . . . HUH?"

"Well, I don't know," Julien said. "That was a question from the producers . . . is there any way she could be, you know, *funnier*?"

"Okay, sure," I said, absolutely deadpan. "I'll be funnier." This was so bizarre—what the hell? Though I was thrown by the producers' comment, I made a decision: I was not going to change a thing. I felt like I was doing the role the right way, so I just carried on the way I had been. I got my girlfriend Sarah Zinsser to come to set as my "acting coach," so she could watch what I was doing and give me honest feedback. She thought I was doing fine, so on I went.

Three days later, with me not having changed a thing in my approach to the character, Julien took me to the side once again.

"I don't know what you're doing differently," he said, "but everyone is THRILLED! It's terrific. They say it's *so* much funnier!"

. . .

Lawrence Kasdan had directed Jeff in *The Big Chill*, and they were good friends, so I got to become friends with Larry and his wife, Meg, as well, both of whom I adored. It turned out that the Anne

Tyler novel I loved so much, *The Accidental Tourist* . . . well, Larry became the writer and director of the movie adaptation.

I was sick just thinking about it. Now my friend was going to make a movie of the book I adored, and I couldn't help thinking that this was bad for my chances of getting the part. I mean, I knew by then how to fight for a part, but that had always been with people I didn't know. This time, I feared that my insane need to be liked would make it impossible to push for the role with an actual friend. I couldn't risk the possibility that Larry might pull away if I made him uncomfortable.

But the bigger risk was not to tell him how much I wanted to play that part. So I did, on a night when Jeff and I were over at Larry and Meg's for dinner. Thank *God* I brought it up, because it turns out I don't think he would have thought of me for the role. When I shared how passionate I was about it, he seemed surprised.

"Really? Huh . . . I don't know, you have that sort of patrician background. I can't picture you in such a blue-collar role."

Larry knew I had grown up on Cape Cod, so he had the idea my family must have been like, you know, the Kennedys—playing football on the beach behind our estate and such. I assured him that this was profoundly not the case, that I had grown up in the nobody-would-vacation-there part of the Cape . . . the not-even-really-*on*–Cape Cod part of the Cape.

So I lobbied hard for the part. I told him I planned to become thin as a rail for the role because that's how the character was described in the book. That intrigued him.

I ended up being one of four women who were asked to do a screen test for the role of Muriel Pritchett, a dog trainer. I'd never done a screen test, which—as you may know, or can imagine—is when the person auditioning is on a set being filmed, playing opposite whoever is already cast in the movie, to check for chemistry, etc. In this case, that actor being William Hurt. The four of us women each had a trailer near the soundstage, just like you would if you were really making the movie—and I was just a basket of nerves. I'd never wanted something so much in my life.

The screen test itself consisted of two scenes.

The first was a long monologue I would give to William Hurt, playing the lead, Macon Leary, a grieving writer whose child has died. I worried about how to deliver it without making it too speechy or ponderous. Fortunately, Jeff gave me a great idea: He suggested that I should balance a stick on my finger as I walked along with Bill Hurt, so that my attention would be distracted by the effort of keeping the stick in place, and that way the words would just flow more naturally.

It was a genius idea; later, Larry admitted he loved how I'd managed to make the speech less precious than it could have been, and the stick was what did it.

The second scene was incredibly emotional; the character was enraged, broken down, so when it was my turn, I had to really prepare for shooting it. I was doing all my sense memory stuff behind the set and was told it would be one minute—good! I felt ready, I really had my emotions flowing . . . and then the AD came back and said,

"Sorry, Geena, we blew a light, it's going to be more like ten."

WHAT! How would I ever get back to that emotional place?!

So here's what happened:

After I finished filming *Tootsie*, I started taking acting classes with Jack Waltzer in New York, whom Dustin Hoffman recommended. Something Jack worked on with us was instead of trying to manufacture emotions, you could work with what you were *already feeling*. You missed the bus, you're late for this audition? Use that emotion. You had a fight with your roommate, but the audition is for a comedy? Well, add that layer underneath the humor. It will make it richer.

This suddenly all clicked in for me the day of the screen test. I'd been in the "just right" emotional state to do the scene the way I wanted when it got delayed. Disaster. I lost the feeling almost instantly, and frantically tried to get it back . . . but it wasn't coming. I was furious—*Why did they screw this up for me?*—and then the lightbulb came on. *Wait a second, I am enraged and broken down! Fantastic!* It was an incredible aha moment—what Jack had tried to teach us back in New York now fully kicked in.

The AD appeared again.

"Couple of seconds and we'll go!"

Great—I'm ready, I'm so ready . . . The hairdresser came over to give me a little touch-up and managed to accidentally poke me in the eye with the tail of her comb. I didn't say anything. All I could think was: *"You just ruined my life—now I'll never get that anger back again . . ."*

Or hang on . . . *I'm mad and upset all over again!*

And then, eye tearing but not a hair out of place, I went out and nailed the screen test, and Larry Kasdan called me a few days later to say I had the part of Muriel Pritchett.

It was a role that would change my life.

Chapter Seven
Eyes Like Navel Oranges

Anne Tyler's novel is about a recently separated travel writer named Macon Leary, a buttoned-up man whose young son has been murdered. His life is changed by meeting an offbeat dog trainer, Muriel Pritchett, with whom he becomes entangled.

The book was an invaluable resource for playing the character, so I made lists of all the ways she was described, the adjectives and adverbs used . . . and one of the most striking things about Muriel was how thin she was described to be. Variously, Anne Tyler mentions that she is "a thin young woman in a ruffled peasant blouse," that her "ankle was about the thickness of a pencil," that her legs are like "toothpicks," "her face a thin triangle." Another character describes her as "a flamenco dancer with galloping consumption."

So all I had to do now was become a toothpick. I knew how to be thin—I'd blessedly been thin my whole life, which my mother somehow attributed to whose genes I'd "chosen" to inherit. Her side of the family all struggled with their weight, and it tortured my mom to the extent that she was in an endless cycle of losing and regaining weight her whole life. One time as we were doing the dishes, she cast an appraising eye at skinny me and said, "Hmf. You're a *Davis*."

Now that I'd landed my dream role, I wanted to do everything I could to do right by it. My last experience on a set—"Can you be funnier?"—had left me with some lingering self-doubt, so I decided I wanted to get an acting coach for the first time. And to my great good fortune, I was able to engage the services of the now-late Roy London.

Roy London was a force of nature. The list of actors he tutored is long and illustrious. *I* found him by asking Garry Shandling, for a recommendation, and he said, "Roy is *the* guy." I'd never worked with a private coach before, and I didn't know if it would help, but it turned out to be one of the best decisions of my life.

Roy and I would meet every day for a couple of hours and go over every line, every scene, every underlying motivation of the character, day in, day out. Before we started, Roy had gone through the script with a fine-tooth comb, then shared his ideas about the character's subtext with me in great detail. The difference between what people say and what they mean by it can, on screen, be an incredibly affecting mismatch. The audience will unconsciously pick up on the hidden emotions, which might even be *The last thing in the world I want is the thing that I'm saying right now.*

For *The Accidental Tourist* I made thousands and thousands of notes on what we discussed; my script became covered with them. The one thing Roy never had me do was to act out anything for him, which surprised me; he was only about deep preparation, so I could fully inhabit Muriel Pritchett. He said the fun for him would be to see how I'd interpret what we talked about.

. . .

John Malkovich was the person who had bought the rights to *The Accidental Tourist* before it came out, and he may have done so thinking he would take the role of Macon (though I don't know). John would have given a fascinating performance—darker, maybe, quirkier?—but in Bill Hurt, the movie found its perfect Macon Leary. He was a brilliant actor who could portray a deep well of emotion behind his eyes. Actually, scratch that—I have no business trying to explain why Bill was so brilliant. He was just one of the best we've ever had.

It turned out that Bill could seem to be in a dark place sometimes, but it's possible he might have wanted to come across that way so that people would leave him alone. For example, when Bill entered the makeup trailer in the morning, if someone said, "Good morning, Bill," his answer might be, *"Good??"*

On one of the first days of rehearsals, I picked up on the extent of this potential problem.

Bill was chatting with me about how great the script was, and he was eloquently describing how delicate, how ethereal and fragile the foundation was upon which the story was built. I wanted to voice my agreement, so I said, "Yes—it's like . . . it's made out of balsa wood or something."

Big pause.

"You don't get it at all! What are you even talking about?"

Okay, noted. Avoid the sand traps.

...

Early in the process, we were lucky enough to get a visit from Anne Tyler herself. We were shooting in Baltimore, where the book takes place and where she lives, and during rehearsals, Larry invited her to come by to meet us. We were all such incredible fans of hers and weren't disappointed. She seemed like a very lovely, beautiful, serene kind of person. She literally glided in that day, and for some reason we all spontaneously introduced ourselves as our characters. It was kind of magical and I could see that she found it affecting.

"Hello, I'm Macon Leary," Bill said.

"Pleasure—I'm Sarah Leary," Kathleen Turner said.

"I'm Muriel Pritchett," I said, and she continued down the line, meeting the people who had only existed in her mind until now.

I was in awe of Kathleen Turner, who was playing Macon's ex-wife. She'd already starred in *Body Heat* with Bill, and the hilarious *The Man with Two Brains* with Steve Martin, as well as *Romancing the Stone*, *Prizzi's Honor*, and *Peggy Sue Got Married*. Her résumé was ridiculous. Knowing she'd worked with Bill and was clearly a very self-possessed person—not to mention just too incredibly glamorous for words—I figured I should invite her out for a drink to see if she might have any advice on how to work with Bill, whom I could sense might be difficult to get close to.

I'd never invited anybody like superstar Kathleen Turner out for a drink before, but she was game. She showed up in full movie star mode, including a luxurious fur coat, and as we settled ourselves, she ordered a shot of bourbon, lit up a cigarette, tossed her hair, and said,

"So, what's on your mind?"

"Well, you've, uh, worked with Bill before . . . obviously! And, well, this being my first experience—you know, one can already see, uh, potential . . ." I was feeling around for how to say it best.

I eventually blurted out, "I just wondered if you have any advice basically on how to work with Bill?"

Kathleen picked up her glass, and said in her unmistakable deep voice, "Just tell him to go fuck himself."

She threw back the shot and slammed the glass down on the bar. Bad. Ass.

. . .

When I first started to work with Roy London, he said he'd heard that William Hurt could be somewhat unreadable, which sometimes threw his costars off—so Roy put *a lot* of time into preparing me for that. He had a brilliant idea, which would turn out to be incredibly effective.

Roy said, "You're going to throw *him* off instead. You're going to stand too close to Bill, invade his space. If you're starting to feel insecure around him, you're going to laugh and tell him a joke."

This was as much an acting challenge as a personal one; Muriel gives Macon no ground in the script, so it made sense that I do the same with Bill, off-camera.

"If you say, 'How are you, Bill?'" Roy said, "and Bill replies, 'You wouldn't understand how I'm feeling,' your answer will be, 'Oh, okay—see ya on set!' You are to never get sucked in to doubting yourself. Muriel never does, so neither will you."

This was one of the signal moments in my career in which a role

I was playing was leading me to personal growth in my off-screen life. Bill's take on the world was Bill's; that didn't mean I had to mold myself in order to fit into it. This was an astonishing revelation to me; I'd spent my entire life trying to massage everyone's feelings, walking on eggshells, subjugating my own wishes to keep the peace. I was far too interested in pleasing other people, in keeping them happy, and trying to figure out continually what way they'd like me to be.

My self-effacement was bone-deep, so without Roy's counsel things almost certainly would have gone very differently. At the least, given that Bill did sometimes seem to skirt the edges of a dark world, I can easily imagine that every day I might have thought, "Oh no, Bill seems to be in a mood—did I do something wrong? How can I fix this?" That had *always* been my way, but not on *The Accidental Tourist*, and continuingly less so in my life moving forward. I was determined to nail this relationship, and with it, the role.

But there were other things I needed to do in preparing for this role. Anne Tyler has a masterly way of describing characters, and I made a list just of the ways Muriel walked:

Her angular, sashaying walk broken by the jolt of her sharp heels. . . . she clicked off toward a car that was parked down the street . . . Muriel came tapping down the stairs . . . Her arms were full of parcels, her hair was flying out, and her spike-heeled shoes were clipping along.

"Angular," "jolt," "sharp heels," "clicked," "tapping," "clipping"—the sharpness of Muriel as she walked, the very music of her step, felt like a key to her character. The eccentricity of Muriel could be found in those sharp footfalls, and from what she chose to wear. The costume designer Ruth Myers put together an extraordinary and very limited wardrobe of clothes to create outfits for Muriel from—reflecting both Muriel's constrained economic means and her deep eccentricities.

Larry Kasdan has the highest emotional intelligence of any director I've ever worked with. He did his own perceptive and moving adaptation of the novel when he came on board; Larry is simply a brilliant director who deeply values acting and actors.

But he was also my pal. At one point during filming, Larry said he didn't like what I'd done on a take, and to try it this other way instead.

I said, "Sorry, do you think you could just leave off the part about how you didn't like what I did, and just tell me the 'let's try it this other way' part?"

Larry paused and rolled his eyes.

"Oh, my God, you actors are so *sensitive*!" he whined comically.

We had a wonderful rapport and friendship. In fact, I don't think I've ever told him this, but of everyone I've ever known, he's the person I've most liked to make laugh. There was something about the way he delighted in my sense of humor that made me feel like I was funnier than I realized—and made me want to make him laugh even more.

. . .

My efforts to remain unaffected by working with a big star like William Hurt were perhaps working a little too well. One day, a couple of weeks in, he'd had enough.

"Can we all go talk, please?" Bill said to Larry and me.

The three of us convened in Larry's trailer.

"You don't understand what it's like, Larry. She's ruining everything," Bill said. "She's just talking all the time, or tap dancing . . . or telling jokes!" (["Muriel] talked so much—almost ceaselessly; while Macon was the kind of man to whom silence was better than music." —from *The Accidental Tourist*.)

Bill paused, letting the full horror of my behavior sink in. Then he went on:

"I can't work like this, Larry. She's driving me insane. You've got to tell her to stop."

Oh, no! What would Larry say? The old pressures were swirling— maybe I should have tried to read Bill's moods after all . . .

And then Larry spoke.

"Well, Bill, I don't know what to say to you. When it comes time to shoot, Geena's ready. And you're not. I'm sorry, but I don't know how I tell her to stop being ready."

Something must have happened in that meeting to smooth out the bumps a bit. Things started to go along very well; I was already in awe of Bill's extraordinary acting ability, but now I felt like he'd taken me on as a partner. It ended up being one of the most fulfilling working relationships I've ever had, and Bill had very kind things to say about my performance when it all ended.

It turned out some people agreed.

. . .

I was in Japan with Jeff when the news came through.

We turned on the TV at 8 p.m. just in case, and when we saw the news, we jumped around like crazy people. Larry Kasdan had been nominated for an Academy Award, for both best picture and best screenplay (along with Frank Galati, who'd written the original adaptation); John Williams had been nominated for his score.

And I was nominated for Best Supporting Actress. I had to let those words sink in; I was thirty-two years old, and this was my first nomination for anything. A year earlier I'd been told I wasn't funny enough on the set of *Earth Girls Are Easy*. Now I'd have to find something to wear to the Oscars.

But before I could even imagine what dress I might don, I got a telegram. It read, "CONGRATULATIONS, YOU DESERVE IT. YOUR PAL, BRUCE WILLIS."

I had never met Bruce Willis; never ever ever. We had no mutual friends, nothing. At the time, he was one of the biggest movie stars in the world. And he had taken the time to send a *telegram* congratulating me? How fantastic is that? (I put the telegram in the box with the message from Jack Nicholson.)

My parents were absolutely thrilled when I got nominated, and an added bonus for them was the movie was rated PG, meaning they could talk about it with their church friends and not have to worry about their reactions.

The six weeks between the announcement of the nomination and the award ceremony were a whirlwind of excitement. You do a lot of press, and they keep you plenty busy. But the gown issue was troubling me. I had a vision in mind, but I couldn't find it. Back then, it was nothing like the machine it is today, where most people borrow directly from designers. I didn't even know about stylists. I was going to stores and looking at dresses and asking the salespeople if I could borrow something, and of course I was turned down. Even though they recognized me (usually after having to mention *Beetle-*

juice), a retail store wouldn't have been able to loan me a dress off the rack—I would have to had gone directly to the designer to borrow something, but I didn't know that. What was I going to do? Fortunately, Ruth Myers, the brilliant costume designer on the movie, said she'd help, and collaborating with Bill Hargate, we designed the dress I wore—custom-made, a shimmering dream in pale blue, with a huge bouffant train at the back.

That year the Oscar ceremony producer, Alan Carr, decided that it would be fun for Hollywood couples to present the awards, and Jeff and I were included. At rehearsal the day before the ceremony, we practiced it two ways: first, a voice intoned:

"Please welcome Jeff Goldblum and Academy Award nominee Geena Davis"; and the second time it was, "Please welcome Jeff Goldblum and Academy Award winner Geena Davis," to which Jeff whispered, "It's going to be the second one," and I have to say that sounded pretty good.

Then, before you know it, it's Wednesday, March 29, 1989, the day of the ceremony, and you wake up early, and your skin is breaking out in hives!

At least I thought that's what it was. I was getting all splotchy and frantically called my publicist, Susan Geller, who said, "You need an Epsom salts bath," but I was too hyper to lie in a bathtub, so I just wet my skin and shook Epsom salts on myself. Eventually, I calmed down enough to get my hair and makeup done, and my gown on. But there was still time until Jeff and I had to get in the car at around 2 p.m. (it takes hours to get there, with all the traffic), so I figured I should eat something. Accordingly, I covered myself in a big sheet and scarfed down a huge plate of spaghetti, and while I ate, I turned on *The Oprah Winfrey Show*.

Well, it seemed not everyone agreed with Bruce Willis!

Oprah had a panel of five film critics on the show to discuss the nominations, and at the exact moment I tuned in they were on the supporting actress category. One by one, every single critic said I was the only one with no chance of winning. One even said, "I think she was miscast. She's too pretty for the part," to which Rex Reed responded, "Too pretty, are you kidding me? She's too *ugly*. She has eyes like big navel oranges."

And with that, my nerves went away; I had zero chance of winning, so what was the point of being nervous? And anyway, the other nominees were so good: Joan Cusack and Sigourney Weaver, both for *Working Girl*; Frances McDormand for *Mississippi Burning*; and Michelle Pfeiffer for *Dangerous Liaisons*. And Rex Reed had said I had eyes like navel oranges, so that was that. Surely no one with eyes like oranges ever wins anything.

Now we're at the actual show, and it turns out Best Actress in a Supporting Role is the first award presented. Out walk Melanie Griffith and Don Johnson to present the award—then very much the It Couple, replete with matching blond highlights. They go back and forth with some comedy bits—"Why don't you just take a couple of deep breaths and try and relax and pretend you're in Lamaze class or something?" Don says, and "It's particularly appropriate the award is for supporting actress because well, let's face it, I have supported one or two actresses in the past"—and Melanie comes back with, "And one or two have supported you," which was nice.

Then they read out the names.

And then they read my name out again, right after the words, "And the Oscar goes to . . ."

Everything turned into slow motion. I kissed Jeff, but I don't remember walking up the stairs . . . I do remember Melanie kissing me on the cheek with her bright red lipstick, and as I drifted over to the podium, I worried that I must have a big kiss mark on my cheek; that was why I held my hand up to my face during my acceptance speech as though I were the most bashful person alive; I was trying to hide it. I gave my speech in a quivering voice, and then I was Academy Award winner Geena Davis, and with that out of the way for the rest of my life, I thoroughly enjoyed the rest of the evening. I didn't get back to my seat for about forty-five minutes— they took me to a press room for interviews and photos, still in a daze—but eventually I was back in the auditorium and nothing would ever be the same.

After the show, Larry Kasdan found me and said, "Hey, you had the right idea: Get nominated . . . and then *win!*"

Five years later, during the Northridge earthquake, the Oscar fell off my mantelpiece, and now it leans forward, like a skier going down the ski jump. When I asked if it could be fixed, I was told no, but that they could give me a different one. I demurred. I wanted to keep the real one. And it's fun to have an unusual-looking Oscar, a little off-kilter, like me.

Roy London called the day after the awards, of course: "I got a hundred and forty messages on my answering machine, and then it broke!" he said.

"Yeah, oh, I got lots, too," I said. I had actually gotten eleven. But! What I also got were bouquets of flowers—at least forty, which Jeff and I arranged on our back lawn. I sat amid them, holding the bunny he'd bought me for Easter while he took a photo.

I called my folks right after the ceremony, and they were beside themselves. My dad's voice sounded hoarse—I think he must have been yelling when I won.

The morning after the Oscars, the school staff where my mom was an assistant teacher had a surprise: They held their own Oscar ceremony for *her*. The faculty all dressed up for the occasion, with the principal presenting a little award to her for "Best Mother of an Oscar Winner." Brilliantly playing along, my hammy mom delivered her acceptance speech, perfectly imitating the way I had delivered mine, replete with palming her own cheek.

. . .

On the back of the Oscar win I became a superstar . . . in Wareham.

I was asked to be the parade marshal for the town's semiquincentennial—250th year anniversary—in 1989. My parents and I rode in a convertible in the parade, wearing costumes from that period. My dad had grown out muttonchop sideburns for a *year* in anticipation of the anniversary.

For parts of the parade, there were no observers at all except the people living in the house we were passing, so there'd be maybe a couple sitting in lawn chairs out front. When we came into view, they'd say, in a perfectly normal, conversational tone, "Hi, Geena, nice to see you." The car would creep awkwardly along until finally they'd say, "Bye, Geena, take care now."

. . .

Once you win an Oscar everything works out perfectly, right? Well, no, obviously—I still had plenty of challenges that forced me to realize I hadn't yet become my authentic self. Life has a way of reminding you that the universe doesn't offer a simple straight line to fulfillment; there are setbacks, and it's how you grow from them that increases your ability to kick some ass.

In 1989, I made a movie called *Quick Change*, directed by Howard Franklin—and Bill Murray, who also starred in it.

But I probably should have bolted right after the meeting for the role. Or better, *during* the meeting.

It took place in a hotel suite (which wouldn't be allowed today, not after Me Too), and as soon as I walked in the door—before I could even meet the other people in the room—Bill Murray came up to me excitedly and said, "Have you ever tried the Thumper?"

The what now? He pointed toward the bedroom of the suite, and sitting on the bed was a largish contraption with big handles on it.

"It's amazing, you have to try it!" This was so weird. When Murray said I had to try it I assumed he was joking and said no thanks, laughing, and headed toward the area where two other men were sitting, to introduce myself.

But Murray wouldn't have it. He insisted, still smiling and excited, that I lie on the bed and experience this strange kind of massage device. Pretty quickly, it was clear that this was a nonnegotiable thing. I said no multiple times, but he wouldn't relent. I would have had to yell at him and cause a scene if I was to get him to give up trying to force me to do it; the other men in the room did nothing to make it stop. I realized with a profound sadness that I didn't yet have the ability to withstand this onslaught—or to simply walk out. I ended up sort of perching across the corner of the bed while Murray placed the thing on my back for a total of about two seconds. Strangely, he never asked anything about if I'd liked it after all that. He just introduced me to everyone and went on with the meeting.

Yes, I got the part. And it turned out that the Thumper was the reason. I later learned it was a test—to find out if I was going to be easy to work with; be *compliant*. I had just won the Oscar and Murray thought I might have gotten a swelled head from that.

I had no idea about all that at the time. I prepared for the role and didn't see Murray until the first day of shooting *Quick Change* in New York City.

• • •

Quick Change is a comedy caper about three bank robbers who hatch a perfect scheme to pull off a heist in broad daylight; then all they have to do is get to the airport to get away. But New York being New York, they just can't get there. They try everything: cabs, subway, cars, bicycles, even walking—you name it. Murray does the robbery in full clown costume and makeup; he then takes it all off before the police arrive, thereby blending in with the hostages, and fooling the cops who are looking, naturally enough, for a clown.

I play the bank robber's girlfriend, Phyllis, and the movie is really funny. It had a stellar cast that included Jason Robards, Randy Quaid, Tony Shalhoub, Stanley Tucci, Phil Hartman, and a host of others.

I was helped yet again by Roy London. Here's just a tiny example of the kind of great ideas he gave me: As the gang is finally approaching the airport, they see a plane taking off, and Randy

Quaid's character moans that, given their luck that day, it's probably the plane they were all supposed to be on. Phyllis's response is, "No, if it was our plane it'd be crashing." My instinct was to say my line also as a complaint about our situation, but Roy suggested I say it as a way to *comfort* Randy's character.

Once again, that's genius. It goes against how you might think to play it, and it's funny as hell. But before I would ever get to that scene, I had a lot more to deal with than a line reading.

. . .

I was in the makeup trailer parked on a street in Manhattan on the morning of the first day of shooting when the second assistant director came into the trailer to let me know they were ready for me on set. I told him that the wardrobe department had just asked me to wait for a second while they got a belt, and he said, "Okay, then, just come after they bring it."

Mere seconds went by before affable, everybody-loves-him Bill Murray came raging into the trailer, violently banging the door open.

"WHAT THE FUCK ARE YOU DOING?" he bellowed. "Are you fucking kidding me?! Get the fuck OUT THERE!" And with that, he got behind me and roared in my ears, out of the trailer, onto the street, "Move! Move! Move!" By now we were getting close to where everything was set up: It was a big outdoor scene at an intersection, and between the cast, crew, extras, *and* spectators, there were easily more than three hundred people there—and Murray was still screaming at me, for all to see and hear.

"STAND THERE," Murray shouted, pointing at a piece of tape on the asphalt. Then, still shouting: "ROLL IT!"

What in the very fuck??

Fortunately, it was a scene where I didn't have any lines, because I couldn't have gotten them out anyway. I was shaking all over, dying from shame. We did two or three or four takes, I can't remember, and at some point, he nudged me with his elbow and said, all innocent and butter-wouldn't-melt-y, "What's with you, you good?"

The point of this story is not to reveal that Bill Murray has a very dark side; that's hardly news. And it's not to admit that when I had lunch with my manager and my agent *that same day*, I didn't tell them what had happened because I was so ashamed (I never told anyone). And it's not to admit that I would later find out that the screaming performance was all an act to make sure I knew my place. And it's not even to point out that he had been raging at me in full clown getup: the makeup, the shoes, the whole nine yards.

No—I tell this story because sometime later we appeared together on *The Arsenio Hall Show* to publicize the movie. You can look it up on YouTube. Watch how Bill flirts with me and paws at me and even pulls down the strap of my dress; take note of Hall's grotesque enjoyment of all this while you're at it. For that matter, notice how I giggle and go along with it, as if we're great pals; as if the raging hadn't happened, as if the way they're both objectifying me is really fun. Like so many women in a situation like that, I didn't know how to avoid being treated that way; I shut up and played along.

But then, one year later, I met my "Louise," in the form of Susan Sarandon. And everything changed.

Chapter Eight
The Blond One

Back in 1987, Jeff made a movie called *Vibes*. Its director was Ken Kwapis, and he and Jeff became friends. And thank God they did, because something Ken said ended up profoundly changing my life, my career, and even my way of looking at the world.

All from mentioning a script he'd read called *Thelma & Louise*.

"Every actress in town is after it," Ken said. "You gotta read it. It's the best script ever." My agent got ahold of a copy for me, and Ken was right—this was the best script I'd ever read. It was smart, funny, *and* dark, and very moving—written by a woman, about women, with two—TWO!—strong female leads.

Its author was Callie Khouri, then a line producer for music videos, whose close pal Amanda Temple just so happened to be married to Julien Temple, who had directed me in *Earth Girls Are Easy*.

The backstory to the movie was almost as compelling as the script itself. Both Callie and another friend, Pam Tillis, had been mugged one night; and Callie had clearly had no luck, as before that unfortunate incident with Pam, she'd also been mugged at gunpoint while being escorted to her car by Larry David, of all people. The idea for the story subsequently came to Callie while she was driving to work: "Out of nowhere I thought, *Two women go on a crime spree*. That one sentence!" she later told *Vanity Fair*. Once she'd finished the script, she shared it with Amanda, with the idea that Amanda would produce it and Callie would direct. What they initially thought would be an inexpensive indie movie hadn't attracted funding, but it eventually landed in the hands of Ridley Scott, who, together with his producing partner, Mimi Polk, bought the rights from Callie for half a million dollars.

Ridley had directed some huge movies by that point in his career—*Alien* and *Blade Runner*, to name but two. But in trying to hire a director to make *Thelma & Louise*, Ridley came up against some entrenched preconceptions about the movie, and about women. Ridley told *Vanity Fair* that one director he spoke to said, "Listen, dude, it's two bitches in a car," to which Ridley said, "Why are they bitches? Because they have a voice?" In trying to sell the movie to other directors, Ridley realized he was "talking [himself] into it" and he decided to just make the damn thing himself.

Ridley saw the movie as an epic odyssey ("It's their last journey, so the last journey should be epic," he said in a later interview). Susan Sarandon appreciated what he'd done: "Ridley took this little thing and placed it in this heroic landscape," she told *Vanity Fair*. "He put it against John Wayne's backdrop."

Ridley understood that the movie was a major statement of female empowerment. "Women's equality has never been a question for me," Ridley said. "Women are my equal, and some of them are smarter than me. I still didn't fully understand the grotesque nature the male can be to the female. Grotesque not just physically but attitudinally. I read the script and would ask Callie—who knew every inch and consonant—'*Does this really happen?*'"

The roles of Thelma and Louise were already cast by the time I read it: Holly Hunter and Frances McDormand had been the T and L choice of Callie Khouri when she was going to direct her own script, and after she sold the rights to Ridley and Mimi to produce, Jodie Foster and Michelle Pfeiffer became the next pairing. The timing didn't work out on that one, as Jodie went off to do an obscure little thing called *The Silence of the Lambs* and Michelle shot *Love Field*. Goldie Hawn and Meryl Streep were also in talks to do *Thelma & Louise*, but Meryl thought one of the two main characters should survive, and that pairing also faced scheduling issues.

As for me, well, I had my agent call Ridley's office approximately fifty-two times (that is, every week, for a *year*), to remind him that I was available and interested. I knew an important script when I read one and wasn't above pressing my case tirelessly. During that year of weekly phone calls, I even met with my acting coach, Roy London, many times, to work on the script. In other words, I was preparing for a movie *other actors had already been cast in*—that's how insanely fixated I was on it. Roy convinced me that I was ready to go for the more jaded, more mature character, Louise. Surely, it was time for me to play a role like this; I was nearing my mid-thirties!

When Ridley decided he would direct the movie himself, he knew all about my longtime obsession with the film because of the many phone calls and agreed to meet with me. So, in late 1989, I had tea with him at the Four Seasons in Los Angeles—and until the Darjeeling was cold and the tiny cucumber sandwiches had dried up, I laid out all my stored-up, passionate arguments for why

I absolutely *had* to be in the movie, playing Louise. Ridley listened thoughtfully, then sat back in his chair.

"So, in other words," he said, "you *wouldn't* play Thelma?"

I had to think quick. Had I just argued myself out of this film by passionately advocating for the wrong role?

The pause was only very brief before I said, "Well, what's so *interesting* is, while I've been talking, I've been *listening* to myself, and all the reasons why I should play Louise, and you know what, Ridley?"

Ridley looked at me, apparently not knowing what.

"It just doesn't sound *right*," I said.

Then I just made shit up about why I absolutely *had* to be Thelma.

. . .

In the end, Ridley Scott cast me as neither Thelma nor Louise: I was loosely attached to the film for quite a while, but there came a time—while Ridley was on a long and exhaustive search for the perfect person to play the *other* role—when I received an offer to play the lead in a very funny Carl Reiner comedy, and my agent told Ridley that I would have to sign on to *that* movie unless *Thelma & Louise* was locked down by the end of one particular week. I was taking a HUGE risk making an ultimatum like that, but it had to be done, and just before 5:00 p.m. that Friday, I inked a deal to play *either* Thelma *or* Louise. Ridley would choose which one depending on who the other actor was. I was beyond thrilled—and I was still pretty sure I could pull off the Louise or Thelma roles equally well . . . that is, until Ridley cast Susan Sarandon as Louise.

. . .

Here's a multiple-choice quiz that perfectly describes who I was before I met Susan Sarandon:

The male model with whom I'm doing a romance-themed photo shoot for *Cosmopolitan* magazine has terrible breath. Do I:

a. Tell him, discreetly?
b. Offer him a mint, pretending I'm just sharing?
c. Ask someone else to give him a mint?

Answer: Suffer silently through the entire four-hour shoot.

It's not overstating it to say that Susan has changed my life more than anyone I've ever known. The second I met her, I saw she was so obviously Louise—what had I been *thinking*?—and I was delighted to be Thelma.

Once Susan was cast, Ridley asked us to meet with him to go over the script and bring up any ideas we might have for tweaks. In preparation, I'd found a few bits of dialogue I wanted to adjust, then I sat down to plan out the *girliest* possible way—the least challenging, most inoffensive route—to present my trifling requests to Ridley Scott. This had nothing to do with Ridley. I'd only met him once at the Four Seasons and I had no concept of what he would say or how he would react. No, this was all about my standard operating philosophy: the single point of life is to make sure no one has reason to find you troublesome.

Here are some of the techniques I planned to employ to bring up my ideas:

Humor: If I present this one as a joke, maybe Ridley will think, "Ha, that's funny! But also, hmm . . . Good point!"

Transference: See if I can figure out a way to make Ridley think that he thought of this change himself!

Defer: For this tweak, I'll wait until we're on set because no one in their right mind would bring up five things in one sitting!

This was where I was at as I was preparing for a role in what would come to be one of the greatest feminist films of the last thirty years.

This was *not* where Susan Sarandon was at.

As we sat down to discuss the script that first day, I swear it was, like, on page one that Susan said, "So, my first line here, I think we should cut it. We don't need it . . . or, I suppose we could put it on page two . . ."

My jaw hit the floor. Susan went through each scene with confidence and ease. Ridley was completely unfazed, of course. Why I had assumed ahead of time that I'd need to whip out the girly tropes, I have no idea, but there it was. Ridley engaged with Susan on every point, and when she pitched a whole new *scene* she thought was necessary, Ridley agreed.

I knew in that meeting that I was now on another planet, a new, exciting, powerful planet, and Susan Sarandon was the Queen Alien. How had I *never* been exposed to a woman like this, a woman who very simply and clearly said what she thought? How could she possibly have sat there expressing opinions that didn't start with, "This is probably a stupid idea," or "I don't know what you'll think, but . . ." I was so long conditioned to think it shameful to be seen and heard, to think it was impolite to sort of, well, exist.

Susan was a revelation. Somehow, I'd reached my mid-thirties without being able to speak up for myself . . . even when I was one of the leads in a movie—about strong women! Clearly something was up, and this was going to be a whole new experience for me. But now the movie needed the rest of the cast, and I *was* bold enough to make a suggestion.

I recommended my former fiancé, Christopher McDonald, for the role of my husband, Darryl Dickinson. Apparently, Chris showed up at the audition already in costume—a costume he'd put together to best portray a blowhard carpet salesman, replete with a new-grown mustache—and absolutely nailed it. Chris is an incredibly talented actor, and one of the funniest people you'd ever meet (which was one of the reasons I'd fallen in love with him back when); there were many times he cracked the other actors up when the cameras were rolling. This was especially true with Harvey Keitel, who'd been brilliantly cast as the one cop on our side.

Harvey had to do a bunch of scenes with Chris, and it turned out he just couldn't *not* laugh. During one scene in the garden during a rainstorm, Harvey asks Chris if he has a good relationship with Thelma, "Are you . . . *close* with her?" Harvey says, clearly trying to carefully refer to their sex life.

Chris says, "I'm about as close as I can be to a *nutcase* like that," and the way he says "*nutcase* like that" while throwing his eyes to the rainy skies is totally hilarious, and Harvey just bursts out laughing. Ridley kept it in . . . because he really didn't have a choice; Harvey cracked up in every take.

Chris's ability to improvise is second to none, too. There's a scene early in the movie in which he slips and falls in the driveway and then berates a workman standing nearby. That wasn't in the script. Chris just happened to fall and decided to blame the worker, giving this nonspeaking character a name: Homer.

With Chris and Harvey in place, and Michael Madsen chosen to be Louise's romantic partner, all that was left was to cast the drifter role, J.D., the charming guy who sleeps with Thelma and steals all their money—but also, and crucially, teaches Thelma how to commit armed robbery. Billy Baldwin had originally been cast but dropped out to do the very cool movie *Backdraft*.

Ridley and the casting director wanted me to read with four candidates who were up for the role at their auditions. One by one, they came into the room where Ridley, the casting director, Louis DiGiaimo, and I waited. I read with the first three (whom I later came to think of as "the brunettes"), and all of them were very talented, handsome, and perfect for the role. At that point I had no preference. I would have been happy with any one of them.

Finally, the last auditioner walked in. Roy London had mentioned to me the name of a student of his whom he thought would be terrific for the role, and now here he was at the auditions. Pretty much from the second I clapped eyes on him I knew, too, that there was something very special about him. Besides being stunningly gorgeous he was an insanely talented actor. We launched into the first audition scene. All the potential J.D.s had memorized the scenes, but I hadn't. I was holding the pages.

And this is how it went:

Actor says his line. I just stare at him, wondering how someone could be so charismatic . . .

Then: "Oops, sorry . . ." and I say my line.

Actor then says his next line, and I'm thinking, "Wow, he's such a natural . . ." Then I come to, and scramble to find my response on the page.

Terribly embarrassed, I quietly murmur, "Oh, my God, I'm so *sorry*, I'm ruining your audition!"

Actor just grins and says, "'S awright."

Eventually we finish the read and he leaves. Ridley and Louis huddle together, discussing the candidates one by one, as I'm packing my things—really slowly, so I can eavesdrop on what they're saying—and as they hadn't yet gotten to the last one, the charismatic guy whose audition I'd nearly messed up, I couldn't resist butting in.

"Would it be at all helpful if I shared my impression?" I ask.

"Oh, absolutely—yes, yes, please, please," Ridley and Louis say. "What did you think?"

It seemed so obvious to me I couldn't help being incredulous that I had to say it out loud.

"The *blond* one?!"

I'm sure Ridley would have chosen Brad Pitt without my two cents. You could just tell he was crazy about him during the shoot.

Fast-forward to a few years later, and I was boarding a flight from Geneva to LAX. As I walked down the gangway, a group of flight attendants seemed to be waiting for me at the airplane door. When I got close, one of them said, "*Guess* who you're sitting next to?! George Clooney!"

For *once in my life* accomplishing the feat of saying the perfect thing at the perfect time, I replied, "Guess who *he's* sitting next to?"

Sure enough, there was George Clooney, nibbling on his nuts, and he was just as warm and friendly as you'd hope him to be. We chatted for quite a while, until suddenly he said, "You know what, I hate that Brad Pitt."

I laughed and said, "No, you don't. Isn't he, like, your best friend?"

"No, no, I *hate* him," George said. "He got the part in *Thelma & Louise*."

"Oh, I see! Did you want that part?"

"Well, yes—couldn't you tell when I auditioned with you?"

Ah, no, I could *not* tell. I didn't recognize any of the guys at the auditions, though all had been working on various shows and movies. I didn't think, "Hey, look, it's George Clooney!" when George walked into the room. *ER* was still a couple of years away. Back on the plane, I *could* have laughed and said, "Oh my God, were *you* one of the guys with brown hair? I don't remember you at all!" but I didn't, even though I'm sure he would have cracked up at that.

Nope, too *polite* still.

Instead, I said, "Oh yes, I *could tell*. You were so *great*."

Wimp.

For the record, the four candidates for J.D. were, in no particular order, George Clooney, Mark Ruffalo, Grant Show, and Brad Pitt. Quite an amazing lineup.

. . .

Talking of love, if you've seen the movie, you'll know that I share a love scene with Brad Pitt. I was uncomfortable with the projected extent of skin I was being asked to show—unlike in *Tootsie*, there wasn't going to be any underwear—so Ridley Scott found himself interviewing a slew of body doubles who were more used to flashing the flesh than I was. A line of them snaked through the lot where we were filming, right past my trailer door, and I couldn't stand it any longer—I'd worked as a model, after all—so I told Ridley I'd do it.

I needn't have worried. Ridley seemed much more concerned about how *Brad* looked than I did in that scene, making sure the lighting was just so, and even personally spraying Brad's abs with Evian.

"So, Ridley . . ." I called out. "I must already look good, I'm guessing!"

Brad, for his part, couldn't have cared less about all the fuss over his looks. He was just embarrassed about a tiny little pimple on his butt that the makeup gal recovered after each take.

· · ·

On a day when we were filming driving shots, we broke for lunch. As I was walking to catering, Ridley caught up with me and said, "Hey, Geena, you know the scene this afternoon when you and Susan are driving in the car, and you're both feeling so great, so free? What if you were to sit up on the back of the car seat and just take your T-shirt off?"

Unable to come up with anything at all to say—even a simple "Nah, maybe not"—I stammered, "Uh . . . so . . . they want me to eat lunch *right away*, so . . ." and ran off to find Susan, who was already eating.

"Susan," I said, "guess what! In the scene this afternoon, Ridley wants me to take my top off!"

Susan looked up at me for a second and said, "Oh, for heaven's sake."

With that, Susan simply dropped her silverware onto her plate, stood up, and walked over to where Ridley was now sitting.

"Ridley," Susan said, "Geena's not taking her *top off*," and then she calmly turned around and sauntered back, sat back down, took up her knife and fork, and dug back into her lunch.

Every day was like that—a kind of reprogramming for me. Just to observe Susan moving through the world was like learning a new language or something. She was just who she was at all times. Susan was perfectly fantastic to work with . . . and she was also able to say exactly what she thought or needed; it was enlightening to me just how normal this was perceived to be.

Aside from my daily badass tutoring with Susan, we had tremendous fun together making that movie. She and I had lessons in stunt driving, which we loved. When we went to the shooting range to practice firing guns, we bonded over how black our snot was when we blew our noses afterward. For the bar scene, before Louise kills the would-be rapist, the production found a country-western honky-tonk in Bakersfield, California, and hired the regulars as extras for the scene. In between setups, they would line dance, just for fun; Susan and I asked them to teach us how to do it, and when Ridley saw us all going at it, he added a line dance sequence to the scene.

Also, for the part of the scene in which we're sitting drinking at a table, we quietly asked the props guys to put just a little taste of booze in each shot we drank, to help make it feel a little more realistic. After shooting the scene . . . Susan and I realized we were drunk. We giggled and quietly asked props just how much we'd drunk, and he said, "Oh, probably a third of a shot each," which sobered us up pretty damn quickly.

There was a part of the bar scene in which my character was

really hammered, and Susan taught me a super technique for act-ing drunk: Spin around enough to make yourself dizzy; when you stop, you'll sway and falter in the way you do if you're drunk . . . and the more you spin, the "drunker" you'll seem.

Speaking of getting drunk—for a scene when we're driving through what looks like Arches National Park, Thelma is supposed to start laughing hysterically about the murder, until Louise cuts her off and says it's not funny. I wasn't sure how I was going to spon-taneously laugh hysterically—even if I could think of the funniest thing in the world this was going to be hard to pull off, especially on multiple takes! So I decided to secretly get drunk, hoping that would help. The props guys put some beers and a bottle of vodka in my trailer, and I really pounded it all; when we got in the car to shoot the scene, I leaned over to tell Susan, but I just started laughing so hard that I couldn't stop. Yay, it had worked! The only problem was that once the scene was shot, I had to take my drunk ass to bed for the rest of the day. Fortunately, Ridley didn't care; the scene is still one of the most powerful in the movie.

Meanwhile, the scene in which Louise and Thelma blow up an oil tanker was a *huge* deal to shoot. We only had one chance at it, of course, because there was only one tanker. Ridley had eight cameras set up to catch it from every possible angle—and Susan and I were asked to clear out of the way. "Hey, you should shoot our reaction at the same time it blows. You'll be able to get our *real* reaction, instead of us pretending later!" we said. After a safety check, Ridley was willing to do it, so they set up another camera just for us. Everyone was finally ready, Susan and I were standing in the car, holding our guns up as if we'd just shot the tanker, and then . . . KABOOM! It was amazing! And that extra camera was able to capture our *real reaction*—which was absolutely nonexistent. Inexplicably, Susan and I did not react in the slightest. We just stood there, utterly expressionless.

Ridley came over and said, "WHAT WAS THAT?!"

I honestly don't know why that happened; I think somehow both of us *forgot* to react? It was like we were watching it on TV or something. So they had to do a whole other fake setup, where orange lights would suddenly light up our faces instead of fire, and a huge fan provided the wind from the explosion. And *this* time we managed to be appropriately amazed and whooped and celebrated.

(Evidently Marco St. John, who played the truck driver, was worried about the future of his career, after having played such an odious character. But Ridley Scott noted later to *Vanity Fair* that Marco went on to play Hamlet in Canada, so all's well that ends well.)

The final scene was the last one we shot for the whole movie. That's usually not the case. For example, the very last scene that ends *The Accidental Tourist* was actually shot *first*. This is not uncommon in movies, where scenes are regularly shot out of sequence. We were on a tight schedule, too; Ridley was due to leave to go make a different movie, and the sun was going down. There was no way we could go over—planes were booked, etc. We had to nail that scene then and there.

Now, Ridley shot the whole film in a really smart and fabulous way. He captured both of our close-ups at the same time, which I'd never seen anyone do before, and haven't since. He always operated the A camera (the main camera) himself, but he always had both cameras going so he could use the same take—and that was the case here. We had the two cameras set up, it was late afternoon, and the sun was just about to go down behind the mountain. When the cameras were rolling Susan and I looked at each other and I realized—and I'm sure she did too—that this was the end of an unmatchable experience. We'd become so close and this movie had meant so much, and this was the moment it all ended, for the characters *and* for us. So I didn't have to search for the emotion of that moment; I felt it all. Instead, we turned to each other, said as little as possible . . . and Susan had the brilliant idea that we should kiss goodbye. This wasn't her first superb read: After Thelma sleeps with Brad Pitt's character, Louise was originally supposed to be mad at her the next morning in the diner, but Susan sagely pointed out that a real friend would be happy for her, hence her smiles and the added line, "Aw, you finally got laid properly!"

And then the sun disappeared, and *Thelma & Louise* was a wrap. What came next surprised everyone.

. . .

The movie had been made with a low enough budget—$17 million—that we were just hoping people would go see it. We'd felt all along that it might end up being viewed almost as an art-house movie. Everyone working on it knew that it was a *brilliant* script, and that Ridley had magnificently expanded the scale of the movie, but none of us could have predicted what a nerve it would strike when it came out.

As it happened, two weeks after it opened, Susan and I ended up on the cover of *TIME* magazine—and that issue included *two* editorials about the movie, both negative. So many people loved it, but there were a number of passionate editorials denouncing it—*"Oh my God, the world is ruined—now the women have guns"* type of stuff. Some people from both left and right of the political spectrum adopted a kind of "tut-tut" attitude. Some on the left felt that the violence perpetrated by the protagonists shouldn't be thought of as liberation for women; the other side just hated that some of the male characters were shown in a bad light.

Regarding the supposed high level of violence, *Entertainment Weekly* humorously suggested that people deeming the movie violent get a grip, by publishing a chart comparing *Thelma & Louise* to *Lethal Weapon*:

THELMA & LOUISE	LETHAL WEAPON
Gunshots: 11	Gunshots: 425*
Gunshots Fired at People: 1	Gunshots Fired at People: 300*
Total Violent Deaths: 3	Total Violent Deaths: 22
Men: 1	Men: 21
Women: 2	Women: 1
Explosions: 1	Explosions: 3
Car Crashes: 4	Car Crashes: 4
Torture Scenes: 0	Torture Scenes: 2
Kickboxing Fights: 0	Kickboxing Fights: 1

* Figures are approximate due to inherent difficulty in counting individual machine-gun bullets.

. . .

Sometime during the making of *Thelma & Louise*, Jeff Goldblum and I split up. Ultimately it had been my decision to end it, but I also regretted it terribly. We still saw each other quite a lot at first, which eased the transition a bit. But I feel now that I was too hasty;

I should have given us more time. I've only ever wished him happiness. It was a truly magical chapter in my life.

A few months later, I saw Warren Beatty at a party, and he told me how sorry he was to learn that Jeff and I weren't together anymore.

"What a shame . . . you know, I rode in an elevator with you two once," he said, "and you were such a cute couple that I thought, 'You know what? I'm not even going to fuck her.'"

. . .

Before *Thelma & Louise* came out, if people recognized me in the supermarket or whatever, they'd usually say they liked one of the movies from my "bug phase:" *Beetlejuice* or *The Fly*. But after this movie came out, people who recognized me had a lot they wanted to share with me: This is how many times I saw it; this is who I saw it with; this is how it changed my life . . . or even: "My friend and I acted out your trip!"

Really. *Which part?*

. . .

Ever since then, I've made my acting choices with the women in the audience in mind. What are they going to think about my character? And I'm not looking to find "role model" parts, mind you—I kind of hate that term. I think if you set out to create a "role model," the character is likely to have very few interesting flaws.

I mean, think about Thelma and Louise: We kill a guy, evade the law, drive drunk, hold up a liquor store, have sex with a random hitchhiker, lock a cop in his trunk at gunpoint, blow up a fuel tanker, and kill ourselves. Sooo . . . *"We acted out your trip . . ."*

Right.

When you think of it that way, how *were* those characters able to inspire women to such an extraordinary extent, to strike a nerve the way they did? How to explain that after seeing a movie that ends with the leads sailing off the edge of the Grand Canyon, women emerged cheering, feeling inspired and empowered? I was profoundly struck by this. It brought home for me in a very powerful way how rarely we give women the chance to feel that way coming out of a movie. Men can come out of almost every movie having identified with the lead character or one of the important male characters and feeling empowered.

I think it's because even though we—Thelma and Louise—kill ourselves, we retain control of our lives to the bitter end; we never give up being in charge our own fate, once we experience freedom. We may have made horrible choices along the way but at least they're *our* choices.

Driving off the cliff was a metaphor for getting away. It was the only way Thelma and Louise could remain in charge of their lives—any other choice would mean putting someone else back in control of them. This made me want more parts where my character decides her own destiny. I mean, is there anything more "in charge of their fate" than driving a damn car off a cliff?

By the way, Callie Khouri always had the best answers when talking to the press about the movie. If an interviewer asked *me* about why the male characters were portrayed negatively, I would say "No, they weren't! There are seven of them in important roles, and they cover the gamut: a very sensitive and decent cop; a sweet but commitment-phobic boyfriend; a guy who steals their money—but gives Thelma a six-thousand-dollar orgasm . . . and then, yes, all the way down to a rapist." That's what *I* would say—until I heard Callie answer the question about male characters being treated unfairly. She simply said, "So what?"

So yeah, Thelma and Louise were "role models." Badass role models.

. . .

Before its release, *Thelma & Louise* premiered as the closing-night film at the Cannes Film Festival in 1991. Susan couldn't attend, but Ridley and I went. This was the first time a European audience was going to see it. It was shown at the enormous Palais des Festivals theater, and Ridley and I were excited to see how the audience would react. After all, at earlier screenings in the States, the film got lots of laughs, especially in the first ten minutes.

The movie started . . . and there was no reaction at all to any of the moments that typically got big laughs. Ridley and I kept looking at each other, concerned. The whole first section of the movie went by in total silence. Now we were very worried, and Ridley whispered that maybe we needed to make a quick exit; this was not going well. Then came the moment when Louise shoots the would-be rapist . . . and the audience EXPLODED. They roared and cheered; they gave a standing ovation *during* the movie.

Then Ridley gave a little smile and said, "Well, I guess they like it after all."

Ridley was nominated for an Academy Award, as was Adrian Biddle, the cinematographer, and Thom Noble, the editor. Callie was nominated—and won!—for Best Original Screenplay (also winning the Golden Globe and Writers Guild awards—she swept them all). Susan and I were both nominated for Best Actress; Jodie Foster won for *The Silence of the Lambs*.

Before the awards were handed out, Susan and I were sitting next to each other, and she leaned over and said, "If I win, I'm bringing you up with me."

I thought, *Why didn't I think of that?* If I'd gone up, I would've praised her to the skies, of course, but for Susan to think of that (I don't believe that has ever happened at the Oscars) was just another sign of why I love her so.

Thelma & Louise became a cultural landmark; it was hailed as a bright new beginning for films starring women. Whether the press loved the movie or not, they were unequivocal in predicting that it would "change everything." Now there would be *so* many more movies starring women—female buddy pictures, female road movies—films for and with women would now explode. I thought, *I can't believe it—I got to be part of something that's going to change things for women!*

Turned out its impact on Hollywood culture was very easy to measure. Nothing changed.

But I did.

Years later, Susan and I were brought together to take photos for the twentieth anniversary of the movie, and as we stepped onto the set, I noticed that the photographer had set the camera at a low angle. And *both* of us immediately said, at the same time, "Could you raise that camera a bit?"

And then we looked at each other, and we were back in that car, sailing on to a better future—or at least, a future we chose.

Chapter Nine

I Love When You Do That Chicken Dance

When it came to learning and growing from the roles I've played, you can imagine what an extraordinary double-header it was making *Thelma & Louise* and *A League of Their Own* back-to-back. It was life-changing enough to be in *one* movie that struck a nerve, but to have my very next movie also become a cultural phenomenon caused a tremendous shift in my life.

Back then (thirty years ago, ye gods!), I never thought about how long movies I was in would live on, but just about the same number of girls and young women come up to tell me that they play sports because of *A League of Their Own* as when it first came out. (Those are my favorite interactions, by the way.) In fact, none other than Abby Wambach (you know, the two-time Olympic gold medalist, World Cup winner, and member of the National Soccer

Hall of Fame—*that* Abby Wambach) told me she took up soccer because of *League*.

You're welcome, soccer fans.

And every time someone tells me that the movie inspired them into athletics of some kind, I can honestly say, "Hey, me, too!"

I'd never considered myself athletic in any way. In high school I was already taller than 98 percent of the population (a small handful of boys was taller), so why would I want to go play a sport and invite everyone to look at me? This obviously begs the question of why I would be so determined to become an actor, where potentially *millions* of people would look at me . . . but I think that may have been because, with acting, I wouldn't be *me*; I'd be someone else completely.

But when the chance to be in *A League of Their Own* came around, I didn't hesitate for a second. I'd started playing catch with my first husband, Richard, on the beach in Montauk during the summers we were together, and he helped me develop a pretty good throw. I was sure that with training I'd be able to learn good-enough "movie baseball" to pull it off. (Here's a perfect example of "movie baseball": as good as I eventually got at playing, for any home run my character hit—and as I recall she *only* hit home runs—I would shoot the close-up of the mighty swing, and then the props guys would use a giant slingshot to hurl the ball over the fence.)

My developing ability to stick to my guns was never more tested than during my first meeting with the director for the movie. I was to go see Penny Marshall at her house on La Presa Drive, and my agents gave me just one instruction before the meeting: Whatever you do, do *not* get suckered into throwing a baseball.

"This meeting is simply about your ability to play the role, not play sports, so don't go near a baseball," they told me. "And she *will* ask you to throw a ball, so be prepared."

No problem, I thought—I'd been so recently schooled in backbone by Susan Sarandon, not to mention Thelma herself—that following this instruction seemed as easy as a four-pitch walk. All the same, I purposely wore a miniskirt and spiky high heels, just in case, so there was no way I could go out onto Penny's lawn and acquiesce.

The meeting went along fine, and as I was preparing to leave, Penny said, "Okay, less just see you trow da bawl . . ." (That Bronx accent, you know!)

I was prepared for this.

"Ah, haha! You know—no," I said. "And here's the funny thing: My agents told me you'd ask me to do that, but I'm under strict instructions—"

"Come on," Penny said, "just for one second, come on, just one trow . . ."

Nope. No *way* was I going to touch a baseball. I stood firm.

Fully five minutes went by before I was out on the fucking lawn, throwing a fucking baseball.

Agent: "How did the meeting go, Geena?"

Me: "I threw the ball."

Silence.

Penny had won that little test of wills, and I successfully revealed myself to her as a wimpy pushover. (I tell you who is not a wimpy pushover: Debra Winger—at one time cast as Dottie—who quit the movie because Madonna had been cast.) I later wondered if trowin' da bawl was less about my skills than Penny trying to see if she could *get* me to throw it, even though I'd been ordered not to, because then she'd know I wouldn't be a problem when we made the movie. Or she simply wanted to see me throw a ball and was going to make it happen no matter what anyone said.

Bottom line, she rolled right over my fledgling badass.

I was determined, then, that the shooting of the movie would be different. This little failure to remain strong would be an aberration, because, of course, this was the me *after Thelma & Louise*, *after* an intensive crash course in standing up for myself, courtesy of the example set by Susan Sarandon. I knew how to do it now.

Here is a multiple-choice problem, the answer to which neatly describes how different I was from the old me while making *League*:

My driver on the film has the air-conditioning in the car blasting at the coldest setting on the first day. Do I:

a. **Just reach over and turn it down myself (after all, the car is *for me*)?**

b. **Ask him politely to turn it down?**

c. **Hug my arms and say "Brrr!" in an adorable way so he'll know to turn it down?**

Answer: Bring blankets in the car every day and pretend I need to sleep. Both ways, to and from the set.

For four months. Can you imagine?

Making this movie turned out to be a very important milestone in my journey: After doing *Thelma & Louise* and feeling so empowered, I slipped right back into a hefty amount of passive, don't-stir-the-pot behavior; it was stunning to see how quickly I'd given up my voice, let my guard down, gone back to old patterns. The big change at least was that now I was fully aware of doing it. I could see it all, which was a painful but enlightening step.

. . .

Once I was cast, I met with the scriptwriters Babaloo Mandel and
Lowell Ganz, who offered to tailor the role to me now that I was
Dottie. The script was fantastic; the only thing I asked for was
if Dottie could be a little funnier. Pretty much everyone in the
movie was funny, but Dottie seemed to be the straight man most
of the time. They happily agreed to punch it up for humor for me.
A few days later the script came back with some additions—but
in each case, it seemed like my new line teed up a new joke for
Tom Hanks's or Jon Lovitz's characters.

"It can't be that hard, guys," I found myself saying.

"No, it *is* hard," they said. "It's actually pretty hard to come up
with jokes for women . . ."

So I said, "Why not imagine I'm Billy Crystal—just pretend
you're writing funny lines for *him*, but then it will be me who says
them."

But jokes for me didn't materialize.

So Dottie wasn't going to be a barrel of laughs . . . just as well.
Because now I'd decided I was going to become Gary Cooper.
Someone with quiet strength, someone who when a job needed do-
ing, would get it done.

Years later, when Rosie O'Donnell was doing her talk show and
had me on, she told me that she'd been surprised at first by how
little I seemed to be doing by way of acting when we were shooting.
(She didn't know I was secretly stoic Gary Cooper, I guess!) *Geena's
not doing anything—she's not acting!* Rosie remembered thinking.
But as things went along, she came to appreciate the calm nature
of my performance and started calling me "Geena the Macheena."

. . .

Now my biggest challenge was learning how to convince movie-goers that I was the *best baseball player that ever was*. There's a line in the script where an announcer says, "Mighty Dottie Hinson steps to the plate . . ." So, yeah, not just any old ballplayer—I had to believably portray a woman you'd describe as *mighty*.

Tiny problem, as I said: not knowing how to play baseball, or any other sport.

So for about six weeks before the shoot (and during the actual filming, too), I was lucky enough to be paired with some big-time baseball coaches, like Bo Hughes, and trained with them every day, soaking up their expertise. My character was a catcher, and the first week or so my shins were polka-dotted from all the round bruises I had; I remember one of the coaches saying, "You know, it works a lot easier to catch the ball with your glove than your shins."

But soon, to my surprise and delight, Rod Dedeaux (one of the most successful college baseball coaches ever) said, "You know what, you have some real untapped athletic ability."

This was the best compliment I could have ever gotten, and certainly nothing I ever expected to hear in my life. Turns out, I *am* coordinated—it just took until I was thirty-six to find that out! Well, now I was feeling confident I could pull off playing the superstar athlete Dottie Hinson . . . and I think I must have pulled it off *very* well, because a few years after *League* came out, I was invited to play in an MLB exhibition game—like, in a real game, with real Major League ballplayers! (Obviously, they didn't know anything about slingshot home runs.) I thought they were insane to think I could possibly hit a professional pitch, but that's the magic of movies, right? Still, I didn't ever say, "*Are you insane?*" I just said I was too busy. No way was I going to ruin the reputation I now had of having truly outsized skills.

While I was able to act being the "best" ballplayer, there was one superlative I could not claim: being the nicest person on set. Tom Hanks *is* the nicest guy in the world, in real life, which was wonderful . . . and pissed me the eff off. I felt I'd built a solid reputation for being the nicest person on the sets of my movies—but you simply can't out-nice Tom. He's *also* funny as hell, up for anything, and ready to go, at all times.

The kind townsfolk of Evansville, Indiana, came out in droves to play the fans in the sweltering stands, despite the heat and humidity. Sometimes, Tom and Rosie O'Donnell took it upon themselves to entertain them; Rosie would do standup or get everybody singing; Tom would do things like lead them in spelling out Evansville: "GIMME AN E!" and one time put on a makeshift puppet show with baseball caps on bats, hiding behind the dugout.

Here's what a typical day was like: First, every morning in the makeup trailer—literally *every* morning—we'd put on the cast album of my favorite musical, *Jesus Christ Superstar*, and all sing along. Your role assignment in the musical was based on when you came in to be made up. Tom had less to do in the makeup chair, so he'd wander in later than most to sing the role of Caiaphas. The makeup guy had gorgeous long hair so he obviously had to be Jesus; I cast myself as the high priest Annas.

I tried to convince everybody that we should perform it for the crew, only we should wear grass skirts and strum ukuleles and call it *Jesus Christ Superstar Goes Hawaiian*. Tom brought his sweet son Colin to set a lot of days—he was about fourteen years old back then—and Colin figured out for us how to make a helmet out of a watermelon for the Roman Guard.

We never did end up performing it, and we never cast the actual superstar singer in our midst either, because Madonna got made up in the other makeup trailer. (As far as I know, they never put on a show in *their* trailer.)

After hair and makeup, during the many weeks we shot baseball stuff, all of us Peaches were on set all day, every day, often in the actual dugout, in case the weather caused a change in the shooting schedule. We'd hang there in our uniforms; in the morning we'd be given a "clean" or "dirty" uniform, depending on whether the scene took place before playing or after. This is where we really bonded, which was Penny's goal—all of us in this together, all equal.

. . .

Penny clearly knew what she was doing. She was a brilliant director, handling a huge, unwieldy movie. But she was also so self-deprecating that it seemed like she couldn't think of herself that way. Penny was evidently famous for shooting a lot of coverage in her movies, and that proved to be the case here, in spades. I've wondered if that was partly a result of those insecurities . . . the feeling that she had to cover her bases thoroughly?

Evidently, she set the record for the most footage ever shot on a movie—word was you could have made four movies out of it! We ended up going months over schedule. At one point I had T-shirts printed for all the girls that said, "Free the Peaches," which Penny rolled her eyes at. But she was masterful in the editing room; she polished all that footage into something that has meant a great deal to millions of women and girls—something truly lasting. One night Penny had the idea to film us just playing a real baseball game—not a specific scene, just playing—and see if anything special happened. There were cameras all over the place, being continually reloaded. Now, a lot of the women were really excellent ballplayers . . . but spontaneous baseball magic was hard to come by. We ended up having to make it a short night because we used up ALL THE FILM WE HAD!

Another time, Tom and I were preparing to shoot a night scene in which he ends up kissing me on the mound (and by that, I mean the pitcher's mound, not a part of my anatomy). I commented to an assistant director that given it was only two people standing in one spot, and a mere page and a half—*and* the only thing on the schedule—we'd at the latest be done by 5 a.m., to which the producer, Robert Greenhut, responded, "If we're done before the sun comes up, I'll buy you a car."

This was all I needed.

"Okay, everybody," I called out, "let's get 'er done! I'm getting a car out of this!" I thought there was no way we wouldn't finish before the sun came up. I started to wonder if he'd buy me a really *nice* car—an Audi? A BMW? Maybe even a Mercedes?

And then we filmed the scene, and honestly, the only way it *wasn't* shot was from a satellite in space. The first shot was extremely wide, taking in the whole ballpark, then a little bit closer, then closer still, then closer . . . then finally up to our feet, then our hips, then our faces . . . and from every conceivable angle. In the end, the crew had to erect black curtains around us as the night became dawn became ten o'clock the next day.

Needless to say, I never got an Audi or a BMW . . . or even a

Dodge Colt. (And that scene didn't make it into the movie. It turned out the original players advising on the movie hated the implication that a married player would kiss another man while her husband was at war, and test audiences didn't like it either.)

I didn't end up watching all that footage at dailies, either, as it turned out. Ever since *Tootsie* I'd always gone to dailies, knowing the advantages it gave me. But not on *League*. When I told Penny I'd like to come to dailies, she said, "No, no, you can't, please— because that's when we get to make fun of how all of you play."

Ouch. Well, if that was the case, thank God she cut it in a way to make us all look great.

• • •

About halfway through the shoot, my parents came to Indiana to visit, which caused a little bit of confusion on the set. The people playing fans in the stands had been admonished not to wear their own "modern" eyeglasses when the cameras rolled, lest they ruin the 1940s authenticity. Mom and Dad were standing down by the dugout with me, when an extras wrangler came and urgently told them to get back in the stands—they were not allowed down there, and my mom should remove her "modern glasses" immediately. The confusion came from the fact that the extras in the stands were wearing period costumes—and my parents still dressed like it was the 1940s.

On another day, I asked my dad to play catch with me— something we'd never done when I was a kid, but so touching and wonderful to do with him now. We overheard someone in the stands say, "Oh look, Geena Davis is so nice, she's playing catch with that old man." Again, he must have been just some old guy from the extras, since he was apparently in costume.

One day, my folks and I were in my trailer and Penny came in to talk to me. Mom jumped up and said, "There's my GIRL! Oh, I love when you did that chicken dance." Mom was a huge fan of *Laverne and Shirley*.

Penny was very sweet with my mom, then turned to me to tell me something about a delay. "So, the fucking light changed, we have to switch to a different fucking scene, so it's going to take I don't know how the fuck long for that . . ." Mom and Dad were just beaming at her the whole time, not understanding a single word she said because of the way Penny mumbled and that accent. My folks would have fallen to dust if they'd understood what she was saying.

. . .

Very often during the shoot, members of the press would visit to do interviews on location. There were so many interviews, in fact, with such predictable questions—"What's it like to work with Madonna/Tom Hanks/a woman director?"—that I started making up different answers to amuse myself. "Did you already know how to play baseball?" was a very common question, to which I'd variously answer: "My mom taught me how to play"; "No, but I was the center on my high school basketball team"; "Never touched a ball"; "I was on my college softball team."

One question they *all* asked, male or female, was "Would you say this is a 'feminist' movie?" delivered with an amused, conspiratorial tone—the subtext being "What a naughty question I'm asking!"

And I would simply say, "Yes."

Interviewers were always taken aback that I would say that without qualifiers; in fact, they were taken aback that I would say that at *all*.

"Wait—are you saying . . . you're a *feminist?*" they'd ask.

"Yes, yes, I am."

Their reactions to that were so big it was as if I'd said, "I have sex with animals." Like, mouth-open shocked.

They'd say, "Wait—what—can I *write* that? That you *said* that?"

Even the copy on the back of the original VHS case used a review by Joel Siegel that describes the movie as being about a male character—oh, and Jon Lovitz:

> *Tom Hanks, Geena Davis, and Madonna star in this major-league comedy from the team that brought you* Big. *Hanks stars as Jimmy Dugan, a washed-up ballplayer whose big league days are over. Hired to coach in the All-American Girls Baseball League of 1943, while the male pros are at war, Dugan finds himself drawn back into the game by the heart and heroes of his all-girl team. Jon Lovitz adds a scene-stealing cameo as the sarcastic scout who recruits Dottie Hinson (Geena Davis), the baseball dolly with a Babe Ruth swing. Teammates Madonna, Lori Petty and Rosie O'Donnell round out the roster, taking the team to the World Series."*

This might seem hard to believe these days, but that was the way things were back in the '90s: the backlash against the women's movement was in full swing, and most people avoided using any term related to "feminism." In fact, Susan Faludi's breakout critique *Backlash: The Undeclared War Against American Women* came out the same year we shot *League* (which also saw the testimony of Anita Hill). I'd read plenty enough articles denouncing that term to convince me to say it unequivocally and often. These were the days of "I'm not a feminist, *but* . . ." and I was not having it.

The other extremely common question I got was "So, with so many women on this movie . . . I assume there's a lot of *cat-fighting*?" asked with a wink-wink, "you know how you gals are" tone. The fact is—as you might expect—there was tremendous camaraderie among us; we cared about one another a great deal and looked out for one another. I loved my li'l sis, Lori Petty, and all our teammates. I have to think we were feeling something like what the original Peaches did, back in the day—bonded by this extraordinary experience we all shared. And we're all still very close to this day.

. . .

Years later, I had an idea for a sequel to *A League of Their Own*, because that's evidently my jam, dreaming up sequels for me to be in. I figured it could be kind of *Ocean's 11*–style, with the Rockford Peaches—you know, the old gang—getting back together again for one last shot at immortality. The original movie had been such a big hit, and cultural touchstone; I thought surely it deserved a sequel.

It turned out Lowell Ganz and Babaloo Mandel were already hard at work writing a sequel . . . in which none of the women appeared. It was about Tom Hanks's character, Jimmy Dugan, getting recruited to coach the Negro League. So, a sequel to a movie about women, where the only character to reappear would be the male coach. To me it was unimaginable that the idea would even come up.

The movie didn't end up getting made; evidently they were never satisfied with the script.

Years after that, I had an idea for a *different* sequel—*A Little League of Their Own*. (Admit it, that title is genius, isn't it?) In this story, I would have a couple of sons; a girl wants to join my sons' Little League team and she's not allowed—and Dottie decides she has to step out in public again to make sure the girl gets to play. I'm still holding out hope that we could make that someday, although I'm probably too old by now. (Someday soon it could be my *grandsons* playing Little League—yikes.) Well, I can't seem to let go of things, as you can tell, so we'll see . . .

Thanks to *A League of Their Own* I had finally found my sporting muscles. Playing a sport dramatically improved my self-image: It made me feel that—finally—it was okay to take up this much space in the world, and to feel good about my body. And I now knew that I was athletic. In the future, I would be psyched to train in several other sports for movie roles—I would learn horseback riding, sword fighting, ice-skating, pistol shooting, then ice-skating and pistol shooting at the same time—and whatever the verb for tae kwon do is. ("Tae kwon doing"?)

Once again, the demands of the movie and the character spread out in a magical way into my real life. I was using acting to fill out the persona of someone confident in their abilities—someone I was determined to be more like in real life.

. . .

Baby me, evidently telling a joke.

Dressed-up Dan and me, who always insisted on having a hat, purse, and gloves for every occasion.

Dan and me with our grandparents, Pappy and Gam, behind their house in Vermont.

My best friend
Lucyann and me,
inseparable.

Holding the gun that I got from Santa to my head.

Mom, Dad, and me with the homemade trailer Dad built.
Evidently we dressed up to go camping.

Queen of the Ball at a sixth-grade dance.

My glamorous Aunt Gloria,
wearing a kimono.

Class

is . . .

1. not laughing out loudly
2. not lying
3. not going around the house like a slob.
4. not wearing loud clothes
5. not being overweight.
6. maturity
7. being responsible
8. a clean house + self.
9. not showing off.
10. keeping promises.
11. not being loud.
12. not fonyness
13. poise
14. good taste
15. tackt
16. respect
17. being able to listen.

This stationery (and list) is from when I was around fifteen years old—clearly very fixated on not being loud when laughing, in dress, and in general.

The Trip fashion log

take off! In a nifty little kackie suit—short jacket, baggie pants. Accent these with a red halter, red heart pin and shiny red patent sandals.

You've arrived! Now for a quick change, out of those mussed clothes into a spiffy set to meet new friends in— a ribby cardigan duo. It's a tiny daredevil dress topped with a clingy sweater. And those ankle-strap chunkies will go well, don't you think?

Ahh! Off to the beach with a new pal. You can't converse but your outfit says it all— a puckered tube top and matching baggies. Super!

My fantasy wardrobe for going to Sweden, with captions styled after fashion magazine articles: "You can't converse, but your outfit says it all."

My first "model" shot, taken while still at BU— in anticipation of the modeling career I was banking on.

Stepping out of my hometown church with my new husband, Richard Emmolo, and best man, Tommy Southern.

One of the Victoria's Secret catalog shots that helped me land the part in *Tootsie*.

First day of work with Dustin Hoffman on *Tootsie*.

Jeff and me—
two peas in a pod.

Trying to hide Melanie Griffith's kiss imprint at the 1989 Oscars.

My mom imitating my Oscars speech when she won "Best Supporting Mother" the next day from the other faculty at her school.

My mom's "Oscar," mine for the Jean Hersholt Humanitarian Award, and the one for *The Accidental Tourist*, worse for wear.

Parade marshal for Wareham's semiquincentennial anniversary.

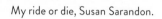
My ride or die, Susan Sarandon.

One of my favorite photos, because of the way Ridley is looking at me, with Michael Madsen and Susan on the left.

Chris McDonald and me, clowning around at the New York premiere of *Thelma & Louise*.

Tom Hanks and me chatting between takes.

I've spent enough of my life being afraid of things. I was shy and scared—and now I'm over it.

In *Vanity Fair*, thirty years ago—and I still look exactly like this.

At a surprise birthday party I threw for my boyfriend Gavin de Becker.

Renny Harlin and me, a couple of blonds, arriving in Helsinki.

Pony giving Donkey Hody the side-eye.

Competing at the archery Olympic trials, August 1999, in Bloomfield, New Jersey.

Not only have Nina Tassler and I been best friends for forty-seven years, but we are also a sight gag.

I'm not really so tall—this is me in a normal-size chair.

The height of my pumpkin-carving obsession.

This is how presidents greet each other— Martin Sheen of *The West Wing* and me at the Screen Actors Guild Awards.

My mom, Lucille Davis . . . but even my kids think this is a photo of me.

My handsome dad served in World War II.

The Bourne Bridge, which my dad used to walk across the top of periodically to check the paint.

Dad jumping a ravine at Berea College.

My parents posing on their
newly chosen grave plot.

The folks hamming it up at church on
their golden wedding anniversary.

Dad at ninety-three with his 1939
Cadillac, in his old hippie look.

For years I'd had a close relationship with Gavin de Becker (he wrote the incredible best-selling book *The Gift of Fear*), and by this time we'd fallen in love. I had long been aware that he was the smartest, funniest person I knew, so it wasn't a big surprise that we found our way to more than friendship. The biggest surprise, which I've realized only in hindsight, is that I didn't change when our relationship changed.

Twice before, I'd had a male friend where the relationship eventually switched to intimacy, at which point—again, this is insight I gained long after the affairs were over—I immediately turned into someone else. (One of these was in college; the other after I'd been working in the film industry for a while.) Suddenly, instead of being the person they'd known, I turned into what I guess was my mental picture of a "girlfriend."

In each of those relationships, I started wanting my now "boyfriend" to make the decisions; I became intensely focused on trying to figure out how to please him. I became, I guess I would have to call it, girly: almost to the point of batting eyelashes . . . all of which was exceedingly strange and unwelcome to them. They *both* said, early on, "What happened to you??" unable to understand how their strong, confident friend had suddenly turned to mush. Both relationships ended very soon after that, and this had the effect of unfortunately killing the friendships, too. It makes me sick to my stomach to think they fell for me as I was, and I inexplicably became who I wasn't. They simply wanted the real me, and I'd taken that away from them. And from myself. I regret it deeply.

But with Gavin, I stayed exactly the same me that had been friends with him from the start. It would have been ludicrous to become suddenly girly when we knew each other so well. It was amazing to luxuriate in a relationship where I could say or feel anything I wanted to from the beginning—or rather, that I didn't shut off my authentic self. It just happened naturally; we liked each other so much that everything sprang from that shared affection. We would talk for hours on end, only stopping if one of us had to, like, eat or sleep.

...

My parents grew close to Gavin, too, and on one of their visits to Los Angeles, he invited them to come spend a long weekend at his house in the woods near Lake Arrowhead, high up in the mountains northeast of Los Angeles—super rustic and serene.

We were out on a long hike, and Dad found a huge piece of wood and insisted on carrying it back to the house single-handedly.

"This'll make great firewood," he said, refusing any help with the lugging of the wood. Gavin was horrified that I was going to let the old man hike all the way back to the house carrying an enormous piece of tree. But I didn't bat an eye; he was always scaring people with the stuff he did.

"Make him put it down!" Gavin whispered to me. But I knew better.

Another time we were all staying at my house in Los Feliz, and coming back from lunch in the rain, we found that a whole lot of water was spilling out of the gutter right by the front door. Turned out the gutter was full of fallen leaves. We all stood on the stairs, watching the cascading water, wondering what to do. My father knew what to do: without so much as a pause he jumped up on the soaked and slippery banister railing, hoisting himself halfway onto the roof, and proceeded to empty the gutter by hand.

My father was born in 1913. This was 1992. You do the math.

Gavin was terrified.

"He's a thousand fucking years old," Gavin said. "You have to get him down. GET HIM DOWN!"

But I never worried about him; my dad could do anything. I also knew it would be useless trying to convince him to come down.

. . .

Gavin invited me to go on an African safari with him not too long after we became lovers. Even though it was one of those fancy-tents type of tours, we managed to put ourselves in some not-prearranged danger while there. At the camp, we heard about a place hours away where you could go to see elephants, so of course off we went, in a jeep with two staff members—and saw plenty of elephants. We stayed there the whole day. At one point I went off to pee somewhere and came upon a big-ass snake out in the open, kind of . . . standing up. I was a good way off, so I stayed there; then, deciding there was no reason not to move closer—to test my courage—I ever-so-slowly stepped closer, then closer, and the snake did nothing but continue to stare at me. I had assumed there was nothing the snake could do to hurt me—how could it bite me from all the way over there? I really wanted to know if I could be brave enough to get close to a huge snake . . . and I did. I watched it for a while, and then went back to the group, describing the quite long (about six foot) creature I'd encountered, and how I'd bravely gotten even closer to it—but not close enough to get bit.

The stunned drivers told me that it was a spitting cobra, a snake that can spit at your eyes with nearly perfect aim from as far as eight feet away, with venom that can blind you. If I needed a lesson—and clearly, I did—this taught me that it's never a good idea to make assumptions about *wild animals in Africa*. Dumbass.

The sun was starting to set as we began the long drive back to our camp. Driving through a shallow river, the open jeep suddenly tilted into some deep hole and stopped.

The driver jumped out to look at it, and everyone spent a while trying to push the jeep out. It was almost dark when they discovered that the axle had broken. We weren't going anywhere. Gavin and I began an inventory to see if there were matches in the jeep to maybe build a fire, and discussed how we'd stay warm through the night. We felt like, *oh well, an adventure*. But the drivers started looking absolutely panic-stricken. It was officially dark now, and their faces resembled what I assume people in a shipwreck look like when they're suddenly in an inflatable raft in the middle of the ocean. With breathless urgency, they tried to rouse base camp on the walkie-talkie, to no avail. We were too far away. Spending the night in an open-top jeep was evidently bad, very bad. Our fears only increased—every sound from the jungle made us startle and pull closer together—until eventually we heard the thrum of an engine, and another jeep from base camp appeared to rescue us. So yes—adventure!

Later in the trip, we made the most ludicrous decision possible. There was the opportunity to go to a different camp, hundreds of miles across the Kalahari Desert; against all advice, we decided to drive ourselves there. Whenever we told anyone we were planning to drive rather than fly by bush plane, they'd ask incredulously, "Driving? Driving to Kasane?" We were equal parts determination and naivete. The gates into our destination (Chobe National Game Park) closed and locked at 5:00 p.m. sharp, at which point we'd be stuck in the dark (again), so we set out very early. Because the road was a straight shot all the way, we thought *what could go wrong?*

Within an hour of setting out, we found ourselves in a blinding sandstorm. Visibility was near zero, but we could just make out the taillights of the truck in front of us, allowing Gavin to navigate somewhat safely. He was stressed to the max but kept us within sight of the truck's lights in impossible conditions. After about half an hour of this tense and difficult drive, something occurred to me.

"Gavin," I said, "I don't think this is a sandstorm. You should stop for a second."

"Are you insane? I'll lose the taillights, and then we're lost! We're not going to do this by committee."

"I think it could be the dust kicking up from the truck that we're following."

I finally convinced Gavin to pull over, which he did just so I could see I was wrong. As the car came to a stop—so did the sandstorm. The whole drama *was* caused by dust kicked up by the truck on this dirt road. Gavin said, "I've found a way that this dumb mistake was your fault: You should have picked a smarter boyfriend." Okay . . . now back to the fun drive! Which was not fun at all, really, with the ticking clock, and the memory of how panic-stricken the drivers had been the night we were outside in the dark with a broken axle.

Hours in, we switched jobs and I was now driving the jeep. Driving fast to meet our 5 p.m. deadline, we occasionally saw mirages of objects, ponds, hills—all stuff that would disappear as we got closer. One time I saw, straight ahead of us, right in the middle of the road, a huge bull elephant. Only this mirage didn't disappear. I hit the brakes and the car slid toward the alarmed giant. Gavin said, "Yeah, I thought it was real, too." But it immediately proved it was very real. It started stomping its feet at us and trumpeting, ears flapping.

Maybe the worst few seconds of my life were when I realized I had to back up . . . and it was a stick shift. I very much needed to *not* screw this up. Gavin said quietly, "Don't stall." Teeth rattling, I backed up quite a way from the elephant, but now we had a new problem—the elephant was just staying there, with no indication it ever intended to move . . . and still that ticking clock.

Gavin said, "Try honking at it," and I screeched, "WHAT IF IT CHARGES? Or something!"

Finally, the elephant started moving off the road back into the bush, glowering at us the whole time, as if to say, "I've got my eye on you . . ." It vanished instantly into the thick foliage, and all I could think was it was standing right there, ready to ambush us if we tried to slip past. I edged the jeep forward until it was about level with where we'd last seen the elephant, and then floored it.

We'd left the original camp with hours to spare but had used them all up—the guard was just swinging the gate closed when we screeched up in desperation. We asked what would have happened if we hadn't gotten there in time.

"Oh, that would be bad, very bad," he said, shaking his head at the thought. "We would probably have only found parts of you."

But that trip, and the many other adventures Gavin and I had, really brought out a side of me that had been lying dormant: the adventurous, almost daredevil side I'd gotten from my father. Gavin loved seeing that part of me.

Gavin was scary smart, funny, and full of surprises. One night we were walking past the Hollywood Wax Museum on our way to dinner when he said, "You know, I just read they have a new wax figure of Tom Hanks in there. Let's go see it."

But the museum was closed. Gavin caught the attention of someone inside and asked through the door if we could pop in quickly and just take a peek at the Tom Hanks wax figure. The guy recognized me and let us in, telling us to be quick. We eventually found Tom, in an outfit from his movie *Big*. I gazed in wonder at what a great likeness it was, truly impressive.

"Wow, it looks so real . . ." I said, leaning in. At which point the figure came to life and Tom Hanks jumped toward me and said, "SURPRISE!"

The museum staff had advised Gavin to stand behind me when it happened, because he might need to catch me if I fell backward in horror. I don't know how many *other* times a wax figure had come to life, but Gavin took the advice. A big group of my friends burst out of hiding, and we had a great party right there in the museum. Gavin told me later he had scheduled the party to be after the Oscars when I was nominated for *Thelma & Louise*, so that the party could be either celebratory or compensatory, depending on whether I won or not. It was one of the most fabulous surprises I could imagine, and Tom doing it, well . . . shows what kind of guy he is. (And this was before I worked with him on *A League of Their Own*, too.)

Eventually, Gavin's and my relationship turned from romance back into friendship, but the love will always be there. He's one of the most important people in my life.

. . .

Sometime in the late '80s, I met with the director Stephen Frears about a movie he was going to direct called *The Grifters*. Frears was considering me for a part, but worried that I'd been in comedies mostly and might not be convincing in something more serious. I told him the answer was to shoot me from the right side—my serious side—not my left, where my funny is. I kind of made that up, because I was a huge fan of his work and thought it would be so incredible to work with him . . . but eventually I asked him to take me out of the running. I was too uncomfortable with the scene in *The Grifters* where the character has to have sex with a gross, seamy landlord. Stephen said, "But you sold me on the whole face thing!"

However, the minute we wrapped *League*, I was rushing off to Chicago to start filming a different Stephen Frears movie, called *Hero*, with only two days off in between. This was the first and only time in my career that I knew what I was going to be in next before finishing what I was currently working on. You always read about actors who have their next three or four movies lined up; it must be so affirming, but that had never been the case for me.

In *Hero*, I play Gayle Gayley, a TV reporter who survives a plane crash; a stranger appears and rescues Gayle from the wreckage, then disappears, leaving behind a Cinderella-like shoe. Andy Garcia later shows up with the other shoe, and love ensues, but (spoiler alert) it turns out that she was really saved by Dustin Hoffman.

It was great to be reunited with Dustin ten years later; we fell right back into our old *Tootsie* ways. We still had a shorthand with each other, and Dustin continued to mentor me, just as he had before. One day we were shooting my close-up in a scene where I have a bit of a speech. So Dustin, off camera and not in the script, started interjecting comments between my lines, making it feel like a conversation. He was essentially coaching me off-camera, making it more alive and spontaneous by my not knowing what he was going to say. It was a wonderfully inventive thing to do for a fellow actor, and it was really helping me . . . but Stephen Frears started pulling on his hair. (This was what he did when he was frustrated.)

"Stop, Dustin! Stop!" Stephen said. "I can't concentrate."

When Dustin wouldn't stop doing it, Stephen appealed to me.

"Geena!" Stephen said. "Tell him to stop doing that! I shall go *mad*!"

"But Stephen," I said, "I don't want to stop him. He's helping me, and he's not overlapping. You can just cut his lines out . . ."

And with that, Stephen went back to trying to pull his hair out of his scalp.

There was scene in *Hero* in which I'm supposed to peel an onion during a speech I'm giving, so that when I tear up, we're not sure if it's the onion or real tears. The night before we filmed it, I bought a whole bag of different types of onions and tested them all out for how much they would make me cry . . . and asked the props department to buy the ones that produced the most tears. Next day, we were shooting the scene, and *no tears* would flow. Nothing would work—actually crying didn't work, and neither did the onions. I'd worn out my crying thingie. We even tried putting the juice of an onion near my eyes, then *in* my eyes . . . still no tears.

Poor Stephen Frears! He said, "Why did you have to *practice*?"

. . .

At the end of the movie—as it was written in the original script—Gayle Gayley never found out it was Dustin's character that saved her; no one besides Andy Garcia's and Dustin Hoffman's characters ever knew. It seemed clear to me that my character would need to find out the truth about who saved her: as essentially a proxy for the audience, I felt that it was essential for *someone* in the movie to find out who the real hero was for it to be truly satisfying.

In fact, I accepted the role with the provision that the ending scene would be changed so that my character would find out it was Dustin's character who was the hero. There had been a meeting before I accepted the role, with Stephen Frears, Dustin Hoffman, the writer, a producer, and myself, and Dustin had strongly backed me up on this point; everyone left that meeting in agreement that the scene would be rewritten. At that point I didn't know enough to think to ask my agents to add it to my contract; I thought it was enough that everyone, including Dustin, had heard it confirmed.

But by the time the shooting was at about the halfway point, no rewrite had shown up; I kept looking at the schedule and seeing the final scene getting closer and closer, but still nothing, so I brought it up regularly. I was always told the writer was working on it, but days and weeks passed, and still no sign of the new pages. More time passed, until the scene appeared on the following week's schedule; I spoke with the writer directly, and he told me it was coming—that it was taking so long because he was having a hard time finding the right way to write the change.

Finally, it was the night before, and I called the producer in a panic to say that I still hadn't gotten new pages.

"Oh, no, no, no, don't worry, it's just *tricky*, you know? Tricky to *write*. But you'll have it by the morning."

"But it's not that tricky," I said. "It can be very simple. I can just say, 'It was you,' or even just 'Ahh . . .' I could even just *nod* to him like, 'I know it was you . . .'"

Morning came, no rewrite.

The producer said, "The writer *really tried*, he tried so *hard*, but he just couldn't find a way to write it after all. It just didn't work."

"But this was agreed to as a condition for my saying yes to this movie," I said. "In fact, I may have turned it down if the ending wasn't going to be changed."

There was something bigger at play here than just the scene. An agreement had been tossed aside; I had expected to be treated like someone whose opinions were valued. I knew what I was doing by this point in my career. I believe what happened was that Stephen and the producers fully expected the writer to change the ending, but he decided he didn't want to change it after all, and felt there wouldn't be any repercussions if he didn't.

I had no way of knowing exactly what happened, but I did know that I couldn't let it stand. Dustin, having agreed with me, emboldened me. I called my agents and told them what was going on, and they agreed that I should stand my ground.

So back to the set I went, visibly shaking, and said, "There doesn't even need to be any different *dialogue*. It can just be looks exchanged, but it has to be clear that I figured out who saved me."

The best they said they could do was to shoot the scene both ways . . . which, of course, meant they could use the original version in the final cut.

I said, "I'm sorry, I just can't shoot it like that. That isn't what I was promised."

This was the strongest stance I had ever taken in my *life*. I was told that if I didn't shoot it, we'd have to shut down the film for that day.

Deep breath.

"I'm sorry, I can't."

And with that, wrap was called for the day.

I was shaking so hard my teeth were rattling, but I'd stood my ground, and no one could take that away from me. (As I'm writing this, I'm picturing how this would have gone down if it were Susan Sarandon in my place; to imagine *her* shaking is simply ludicrous—she would have been cool as a cucumber.) About fifteen minutes later, I got a call from my agent.

"Geena! You did a great job. Well done, standing up for yourself."

"Thanks," I said, still quivering.

I was terrified, wondering what was going to happen. A few days later, the scene was back on the schedule. Dustin's character still refused to admit to being the hero, and my character still thanked him anyway for saving her life . . . *but there was a change:* Dustin had a new line as I was about to walk out the door:

"You're welcome."

[insert fireworks gif here]

It had been a terrifying way to make myself heard, but in the end, it worked—and the studio clearly wasn't bothered by it, because I worked for them again on three *Stuart Little* movies. But I was left wondering: If it had been a male actor, would he have had the same experience?

I guess I'll never know. *A League of Their Own* had hit cinemas just over a year after *Thelma & Louise*, and just three months after that, *Hero* came out, to very good reviews. I thought this would last forever, or at least for as long as I had strength in my swing.

Intermission

Things people have said to me:

"I like your movie." (This always means *Beetlejuice*.)

"I love your body, Larry!" (I played Larry in *Fletch* and there are
  some big "Fletchianados" out there.)

"Hey, it's Gena Rowlands!"

"Didn't you used to be famous?

"Didn't you used to be Geena Davis?"

....

Stranger: "Have you ever heard you look like Geena Davis?"

Me: "Yes, I hear it all the time."

Stranger: "So, are you?"

Me (modestly): "Well, yes, I am."

Stranger: "No, you're not."

Me (slightly less modestly): "Yes, I am."

Stranger: "Well, you're *not*. Nice try."

Me: [silence]

....

In an airport newsstand:

Cashier: "Oh, my God . . . Julia Roberts!"

Me: [amused]

Cashier: "I can't believe you're here, Julia Roberts!"

Me (picking up copy of *People* magazine with Julia Roberts on the cover and holding it up next to my face): "So . . . we're *sure* I'm Julia Roberts?"

Cashier: "Oh, Julia, will you please autograph that for me?"

Me (signing "Julia Roberts" on the picture): "Here you go."

....

Stranger: "I think you're famous. What movies have you been in?"

Me: "Oh, gosh, I'd rather not . . ."

Stranger: "No, come on, I really think you might be famous!"

Me (modestly): "Well, *A League of Their Own* . . ."

Stranger: [blank stare]

Me (still modestly): "*Thelma & Louise* . . ."

Stranger: [nothing]

Me (desperate now): "*Beetlejuice*???"

Stranger: "Nope. I guess I was wrong."

....

Sitting at lunch outside at a restaurant in Beverly Hills, my lunch date admitted that he'd been really worried about where to go in case I got bothered.

"Oh, no, as you can see, no one ever bothers me," I said.

A passing tour bus stops in traffic. Over a loudspeaker: "And everyone, on your right you'll see we have Geena Davis! There's Geena Davis! Hello, Geena Davis! Could you please come get on the bus and say 'hi' to your fans?"

....

Stranger: "Oh, oh, oh, I know you, I know you! I just can't think of your name . . ."

Me: [nothing]

Stranger: "Please, I know you're famous, you've gotta tell me your name!"

Gavin de Becker: "Me or her?"

Stranger: "Yes, that's IT, I knew it—Mia Hearn! Mia Hearn! Oh my God, look everybody, it's Mia Hearn!"

(And now back to our original programming)

Chapter Ten
I Bought a Goat to Keep the Donkey Company

It was just meant to be a general meeting, the kind of thing that happens all the time in Hollywood. It turned into something else entirely.

I had wanted to be in an action movie for a long time. I love nothing more than going to a theater to see one on its opening Friday night; one of my life's goals is still to be a kick-ass villain in a Marvel movie—*or* in a Wonder Woman movie, since I am an AMAZONIAN ARCHER IRL. When *Hero* came out I was approaching thirty-seven and had never felt more physically adept. The baseball of *A League of Their Own* had convinced me that my body was no longer my enemy: I was strong, capable, coordinated— the kick-ass part of me was growing, even bursting out. Even before *League*, *Thelma & Louise* had given me a taste of how great it felt to be *doing* stuff onscreen. I enjoyed the stunt driving and the gun shooting and all that. It was thrilling to me that I was getting roles where I could be seen taking control, including physically . . . and not being relegated to the girlfriend of the person doing all the cool stuff.

I wanted more of it.

So my agents, knowing this, suggested I meet with a director named Renny Harlin.

Renny was hugely famous in his native Finland; his first film, *Born American*, was at the time the most expensive Finnish movie ever shot. He'd then made one of the *Nightmare on Elm Street* movies, and one of the *Die Hards*, too, and had just finished shooting the Sly Stallone vehicle *Cliffhanger*, in which three valises of cash go missing in the Rockies. The movie itself would eventually go on to make many more than three valises of cash, generating a quarter of a billion dollars worldwide. So Renny was hot at the box office, and when I met him, I noticed he was also, well, hot . . . in person. He was very tall (big plus for me), with long blond hair, and the clincher was that he was Scandinavian (as you know, I had a history with handsome blond Scandinavians). The meeting went on for much longer than it probably needed to. It's tough to meet men anyway, but when you meet a Nordic god, well . . . I asked my agent if he was single; Renny, in turn, tried to get my number (this is sometimes how it happens in Hollywood), which they wouldn't give him. They gave me his number instead—and the game was afoot.

But right after we started dating, I decamped to New York to make *Angie*, and this character really made me work to justify her actions. As I've said, I crave to play characters who drive their own destiny, for good or ill, but Angie makes some choices that are so contrary to expectations that it would be a big challenge to redeem her in the audience's eyes. She's a Brooklynite who gets pregnant by her plumber boyfriend Vinnie (played by the late great James Gandolfini, five years before he became Tony Soprano), but who decides to go against the mores of the community and have the kid alone.

Bill and Lucille Davis came down from Massachusetts to visit while we were in NYC shooting, and I put them up at the Ritz-Carlton, hoping they'd be able to withstand the rather fancy surroundings without worrying too much about the cost. I was very relieved that they seemed to be enjoying themselves; I didn't find out for a few days that instead of ordering room service for breakfast as I'd insisted, they were walking many blocks every morning to a McDonald's for coffee and Egg McMuffins and could not be talked out of it.

When we spoke after they got home, Mom told me what happened when they were checking out: They'd called for help with their bags, and she laughed in embarrassment about the bellman overhearing her call out to Dad, "Well, I've taken everything that's not nailed down," as she packed up the little shampoo bottles and soaps. When I got the bill, I noticed she really *had* taken everything not nailed down. There was a charge of about three hundred and fifty bucks for the *entire contents* of the minibar, which she'd also loaded up into her suitcase. She would have *died* of mortification if she'd known all that stuff wasn't complimentary, so of course I never said anything. And it did come in handy to have all the little bottles of vodka and whiskey there when I visited, since they rarely kept booze in the house.

In *Angie*, I finally got to use the Brooklyn accent I'd picked up from my first husband, Richard, and there were some great fun moments, too: At one point Angie dresses up as Santa—a Santa who wears thigh-high black leather boots, that is—and dances for her work pals while throwing gifts around, but being nine months pregnant all the pelvic gyrations make the baby want to come *out*. (My best friend in the movie, who helps me into and out of the cab to the hospital, is played by Aida Turturro, who would later star as Tony Soprano's sister, Janice, in *The Sopranos*; the movie also starred Michael Rispoli, who would play Jackie Asprile Jr. in the show, giving *Angie* a pre-*Sopranos* trifecta.)

At the hospital, the obstetrician on call (played by the diminutive actor Ray Xifo) is so short he carries around a box to stand on so he can reach the delivery table. When it's time to push, he tries to convince me to sing "One" from *A Chorus Line* to help me relax and get into it. ("It's a medical fact that you can't panic while you're singing Marvin Hamlisch.") Not unreasonably, as the OB, two nurses, and Aida Turturro all cheerily sing the song at me—already in agony from the birth—I wail, "What's *happening* to me?"

That funny scene takes on a dread seriousness when the baby is born with a deformed arm. After a few days, Angie does something unimaginable—she runs off without the baby to find the mother who abandoned *her*. So what I needed to do was make the audience empathize with what could have led her to do that, and to forgive her when she returns to make amends with her little son.

I found this challenge fascinating.

I wanted to explore playing a woman who makes irredeemable decisions and to redeem her. I was learning that in choosing your own path, you can go wildly off course, and still find a way to come back stronger.

. . .

On our first date, Renny took me to a tiny Japanese place, very exclusive (six people only, that kind of thing) and not for the faint of heart. This was the type of sushi restaurant where the chef just keeps sending over his works of art to you—there's no menu—and though I *like* sushi, I'm more of a salmon and tuna type of gal; I'm not particularly brave when it comes to the exotic stuff. Renny realized that I was giving the food the fish-eye, so to speak, because of the challenging nature of the so-raw-it-still-has-a-face-on-it fare. I was embarrassed, as ever, but honestly, you have to believe me when I tell you that it was genuinely wall-to-wall *what the hell is that?* So Renny asked the chef if there was anything he could do to help out . . . and he *very* kindly sent over a beautiful tray with a very hot rock and some thin raw fish, inviting me to cook it to my own liking. I thought this was absolutely the coolest thing ever—and leave it to Renny to find a place like that.

Here's what really drew me to Renny: it turned out he was not only a physically big guy; he had a big *life*, to which I was enormously attracted . . . I mean, come on, owning an amusement park in Finland? Geena bait! (I've always wanted to have my own amusement park, like Dolly Parton has Dollywood. Mine would be called Geena-Would, as in, "Try all these crazy-ass rides—Geena would!")

I'd always tried so hard to avoid being big that someone with an outsized view of life inspired me in that direction as well. It's weird, but everything the wrong size appeals to me, whether it's a deck of playing cards the size of your pinky fingernail, or the twelve-inch-tall fiberglass chicken I used to have in my bedroom (and wish I still did). At one house I had fifty tiny working cuckoo clocks tick-tocking in the guest bathroom, creating a delightful sense of insanity when you went in there. My current fireplace is surrounded by a gigantic fifteen-foot-tall carved face of Neptune; his wild hair (filled with seashells) kind of looks like Renny's did back then. So yeah . . . (In college I drew a poster for my friend Joe's play that was supposed to say, "The Big Finish," but because I can't spell for shit, I accidentally made it say, "The Big Finnish." Prophetic!)

There was something else I noticed fairly early on in our relationship. It started quite subtly: On a date Renny said he liked my jacket and asked where I'd gotten it. I realized it had been Jeff's, which I'd had tailored down for me. Renny said, "Oh, that's cool . . . but maybe don't wear his clothes on a date with me." I thought that sounded reasonable and I was kind of embarrassed I hadn't thought of it. But more incidents along this line were to come. He soon suggested it would be fun to only go to restaurants I hadn't been to before, to make our dates special. Seemed worth a try, but there were two problems, one being that I had already been to a million restaurants in the ten years I'd been in LA, and I also had a *terrible* time remembering where I'd been.

It turned out that nearly every other restaurant we'd go to I was greeted with "Welcome back!" no matter how hard I tried. I know it probably seems obvious where this is going, but it started so small. He told me that he'd been horribly burned by being cheated on in the past, and that was why he had a bit of a problem trusting people. (More on this later.) Suffice it to say I wish that I'd read one of those "10 Things to Watch Out for in a New Relationship" articles back then.

In Finland, Renny Harlin was an absolute megastar; it was like traveling with Michael Jackson in his prime over there. And I was soon christened "Suomenen Miniä" by all the Finnish press, which translates to "Finland's Daughter-in-Law."

Things moved quickly. We were married within six months. The wedding was big, naturally: a three-day extravaganza on a farm up in Wine Country. Friday night we threw a country-western-themed barbecue in the barn, with line dancing. (I'd been obsessed ever since Susan and I learned on the set of *Thelma & Louise*.) The day of the actual wedding we filled with crazy fun activities on the big grounds of the farm. Needless to say, it was the only one of my many weddings with an elephant ride, and a hot-air balloon tied to a rope so you could go up and down in it. The property had an island in the middle of a lake which we turned into a "Dessert Island," with little rowboats you could take back and forth until everyone was sugared to the max.

The actual ceremony took place in the early evening, in a romantic, broken-down stone building with no roof; we decorated the shabby-chic walls with silk banners. Unfortunately, the press found out about the wedding (probably because Sylvester Stallone was there!) and helicopters hovered overhead during the ceremony and part of the dinner, almost drowning out "The Geena and Renny Waltz," which had been written for us by a Finnish composer (and which Finnish couples still play at their weddings). It was all so much-much . . . but taking things to the max was Renny's way, and I was all in.

We became quite the public couple for a while, partly having to do with *Cliffhanger*, which would become a huge hit. We attended multiple premieres of it, including at the Cannes Film Festival, where I wore a gorgeous vintage couture Halston evening gown that I'd begged the owner to lend me. The night of the premiere, at the last minute we had to get out of the car and walk to the theater because of the terrible traffic; a few police officers formed a V and walked ahead of us to part the crowd. The skinny tie on one of the shoes I was wearing came undone. Renny knelt down in front of me and tied it; the French crowd exclaimed, "Oooh!"

For that same trip a wonderful designer I'd never met named Melinda Eng just out of the blue sent me a giant box of evening gowns—each with its own wrap, too—and each fit perfectly. That'll make you feel like a movie star! They were silky, flowy, beautiful things, and I wore them all, because every night there was some kind of black-tie event or premiere.

For the LA premiere of *Cliffhanger* I borrowed a dress from the set of *Angie*, and added a little velvet bow around my neck like a choker. All the newspapers in Finland covered it—we were on the front pages constantly—and there were even articles on how to get my look, replete with the velvet choker. Our lives were fast and fun . . . but at the same time Renny's suspicious side was coming more and more to the fore.

For example, when it was time to get some new sheets, he asked that we go to a store I'd never been to before. This kind of thing was getting pretty standard. He had become fixated on never wanting to go somewhere I might have been to with another man. I picked out a bedding store I'd never even heard of, let alone been to, and we went in. Sure enough, the clerk said, "Nice to see you again," to me. Renny's face darkened . . . we left quickly. In the car Renny wanted to know why I'd taken him somewhere I'd obviously shopped at before—and *I* wanted to know why the hell the guy said that—so I called the store.

"Hi, this is Geena, I was just in your store. Why did you say 'nice to see you again' when I've never met you?"

"Oh, it was just—I live on the same street you used to live on, and I'd see you coming in and out of your car."

Oh, brother. I was hooked into this escalating situation for two reasons: I convinced myself that once he realized I was profoundly *not* going to cheat on him, all this would go away; he'd see I was nothing like whoever had cheated on him, and then he'd always be the fun, loving Renny. Second, I couldn't bear to be accused of something without defending myself—rather than putting it back on him. Neither of these were healthy tactics: I clearly bought into the idea that *I* needed to twist myself around, rather than this being *his* problem.

I was becoming so careful of his feelings that I managed to take myself out of the running for a part I really wanted to accept. What happened was there was a movie script Renny was trying to get made, and he wanted to know if I'd play a role in it. I didn't love the script or the part he was thinking of . . . but I didn't want to hurt his feelings about it, so I decided to say I just wasn't looking to play a supporting role at that time, and it worked. But soon after that I was offered what seemed to me at the time to be a supporting role in the Mel Gibson movie *Maverick*, to which I very much intended to say yes.

I excitedly told Renny about it, but he looked at me expressionlessly and said, "But obviously you won't be doing it, though . . . since it's a supporting part."

. . . and I turned it down. I was losing ground, losing myself. I'd always operated on my instinct when choosing roles and trusted myself completely. But for the first time I was turning something down that I *wanted to do* because I wouldn't be honest with Renny. I could have said, "I'm sorry, I just didn't like your script"; I could have said, "No matter what I said before, I've decided to do *this* movie." Unfortunately, there would be another movie for which I gave up my precious instincts.

About a year after we married, we went nuts and bought Las Tejas, an estate in Montecito, east of Santa Barbara; you can look it up online and see pictures. At Las Tejas we threw some great parties—usually for not more than twenty people, but quite extravagant. One Fourth of July we had a picnic on the lawn, then took everyone in an open-air bus down to the water to watch the fireworks from a boat, then back to the house to lie on lawn chairs with blankets and popcorn to enjoy an outdoor showing of—what else?—*Cinema Paradiso*. That house . . . was crazy. There were sixteen acres of gardens, for a start. Parties might begin in the Japanese garden with Japanese music and sushi, then move to the Mexican garden, where there would be a mariachi band and shots of tequila, then off to the barn where the animals lounged around, and we'd do some country-western dancing—before heading off to the Italian garden for dessert.

This was a different kind of life than I'd *ever* had—an over-the-top, oversized way of moving through the world. This was me doing peak Hollywood, a lifestyle I'd never had before, nor since. We visited Finland often. Renny had warned me up front that Finns can seem introverted and stoic . . . but I found them to be just the opposite; guys would sometimes suddenly burst into song when they saw me . . . but that may have been simply prompted by an excess of cocktails. Finns, by the way, can drink you under each and every table. I remember once going to a party during crayfish season (small lobstery things) and the deal was that we were supposed to do one shot of vodka per crayfish. Suffice it to say that the Finns ate *far* more crayfish than I . . . long after I'd needed to go get to bed.

. . .

Who wouldn't want to get to be a pirate? (Kenneth Turan once wrote in the *Los Angeles Times*, "Who would have guessed that Geena Davis harbored a secret desire to be Errol Flynn?") Well, I didn't know I wanted to be one—I could never have imagined I'd *get* the opportunity to be piratical . . . but swinging from ropes and jumping off the fo'c'sle and climbing up the mizzenmast and peering off the quarterdeck at some distant storm a-brewin' . . . ? How fun is all *that*? Not to mention, SWORD FIGHTING!

Well, it turned out that Renny's next movie was a pirate movie, and I did get a chance to climb up the ol' mizzenmast.

There's a backstory to how that movie got made. I was originally attached to a Paul Verhoeven pirate movie called *Mistress of the Seas*. (Seems pirates were having their moment back in the mid-'90s.) According to one source quoted in *Entertainment Weekly*, Verhoeven "had in mind . . . a sexy film that, oh, by the way, had a couple of ships in it." Verhoeven asked me if I'd be willing to gallop along a beach on a horse naked, and I said sure, though that was before I had properly thought it through. Lady Godiva, sedately meandering through the streets of Coventry in the English Midlands, is one thing, but galloping naked along a beach, as your breasts do . . . *what*? I couldn't imagine how that would be even remotely attractive.

At the same time that Verhoeven was trying to put his project together, Renny was *also* preparing to make a pirate movie, called *Cutthroat Island*, starring Michael Douglas. Michael told Renny he wanted a woman with a name to play the female pirate captain, and Renny implored me to come on board, as it were. I was still floating around Verhoeven's project, but at dinner with Renny and his producer, Mario Kassar, Mario begged me to join *Cutthroat* and offered me a lot of money. This was to be the last big shot for Mario's company, Carolco, which was facing bankruptcy.

The problem for me was that the female character was the *captain* of the ship, yet almost all the derring-do was carried out by the men in the story. In fact, at one point, she was tied up in the hold for thirty pages! I wasn't especially interested when I happened to be attached to play a *different* pirate queen who did all things piratical. But the Verhoeven project was getting shaky, Mario had offered me a very substantial pay increase, and Renny was begging me—so I signed on. It's the only time I'd signed on to a project reluctantly.

I've always been able to be very picky about which roles I choose because I can afford to wait for something good to come along. (So if you ever hear that I'm playing William Shatner's comatose wife in some movie—I think that's about the right Hollywood age difference—you'll know I'm broke.) In the case of *Cutthroat*, the money was going to be incredible, and Renny needed me, so— what the hell.

Then it got more complicated. Soon after, Michael told Mario Kassar that, given he only had a tiny window between the end of the filming of *Disclosure* and the start of *Cutthroat*, he would have no time at all to learn sword fighting and other skills, and . . . you can probably guess where this is going: Michael was out.

It would make sense that this would be a cause for wailing and gnashing of teeth—but not so. When we heard Michael had dropped out, Renny and I cried for joy, jumping up and down in excitement and running from the Japanese garden to the Mexican garden to the Italian garden. Not that we didn't love Michael and didn't want to work with him; we very much *did*. It was because without Michael the movie would fall apart and spare us. You see, Renny knew that Carolco was going belly-up before *Cutthroat Island* even went into production. Now, without Michael, the reason to make the movie had gone away, which was actually a very good thing for both of us.

My agent let Mario Kassar know that naturally I would be dropping out too. But Mario wouldn't hear of it.

"Absolutely not," Mario said. "She has to do this movie, no matter what. What did I offer her, five million? Make it eight!" At the time, that was the highest salary any woman had gotten, I believe, but I would have walked away from that money in a heartbeat if I could have gotten out of doing it.

Renny was speaking directly with Mario, begging him to let us go, begging him not to put us in this position . . . But Mario would not relent.

Oh, and the extra money I was getting? Mario Kassar cut Renny's salary by, you guessed it, $3 million, and Renny spent a million dollars of his own money to hire Mark Norman—who would go on to win an Oscar for *Shakespeare in Love*—to try to make the script work without Michael.

We were going to have to make *Cutthroat Island*.

· · ·

Despite having wanted to run screaming from the movie, Renny and I loved *making* it. We shot it in Thailand and on the Mediterranean island of Malta, where (once you erase the TV antennas and power lines) the cobblestone streets and yellow stone houses make the island look like it's still the 1500s. Adorable Matthew Modine was cast as my romantic partner, and I had so much fun stuff to do. I had scenes in which I was fighting four guys at once with a sword and knife and swinging on ropes, and further sword fighting on the rigging, and looking through a spyglass with a little monkey on my shoulder, drinking rum . . . everything, in fact, you might imagine a pirate doing. At one point in a scene, I drop my sword, and do this thing where you step on the handle and it flies up back into your hand, and on I went, swashbuckling. I loved it.

I also had to ride a horse. I'd never ridden much as a child, and now had only a week to learn how. One of the first shots in the movie is me riding along a beach (*not* naked, in this pirate movie) in a flat-out gallop. My stunt double, Ángel, was teaching me how to ride between setups, but we were running out of time to turn me into a true horsewoman. With little time left, Ángel came up with a brilliant suggestion: "What if you just *act* like you know how to ride?" *Genius! Are you kidding me, of course I can do that!* After all, I was the queen of faking it till making it, and I was surprised I hadn't thought of it first. Suddenly the rehearsals went brilliantly. I looked like a fierce, commanding rider, even though it was always the horse who was fully in charge.

My "acting" like a rider seemed to work just fine for the horse: He already knew that when I kicked him, he was to thunder straight down that beach toward the cameras. But there was a new problem: I was wearing a walkie-talkie so I could hear the crew's instructions, and the horse was a smarty. The word "Rolling!" would come over the walkie, and the beast learned that the *next* thing would be "Action" and *then* the kick, so the horse decided not to wait for "Action" or the kick and just boom—took off as soon as he heard "Rolling!" The solution was to whisper the necessary word.

When shooting another scene, I was galloping through some trees, escaping from something or other, and suddenly my horse decided to take a sharp left turn (it had seen some of its friends off camera and wanted to say hi). Unfortunately, I wasn't expecting the left turn and chose to keep going forward, off the horse, in an almost perfect parabola. I wasn't hurt, thank God, but one of the breast enhancements that was in my bra, a kind of chicken-cutlet-looking silicon pad, must have parabola-ed up and out of my shirt—which I realized later in the trailer when I found one missing. My dear friend Howell Caldwell, the second AD, launched a search party to find it, while trying not to reveal what it was they were looking for. He found it, bless him.

The first of the *many* horrifying stunts I did myself over the two movies Renny and I made together was shot in Phuket, as well. The characters Matthew Modine and I played are trying to escape bad guys and end up hanging from ropes above a three-hundred-foot drop. First, we shot our close-ups of the scene on land, pretending to be hanging from the ropes; we acted hella scared, of course, because of the danger our characters were in. Then we're put in harnesses . . . and sent over the *actual edge* of the three-hundred-foot cliff for the wide shot. The cameras were set above, so they could capture the ocean churning far, far below. The harness was attached to a wire about the width of a pencil—but which, we were assured, was able to hold three thousand pounds or something. I trusted the stunt crew, so over we went, holding on to fat ropes, but actually fully held up by the wires.

We were told to sit into the harnesses, putting our weight directly on the wires, not on the fake ropes we were holding. But I began to cling desperately to the rope, which made me feel like my arms were the only thing keeping me from falling to my death. The dialogue *this* time sounded as far from what we'd shot on land as you can possibly imagine. I could barely breathe enough to get out my strangled lines. We ended up having to completely redo our close-ups on land, trying to re-create the insane level of fear we'd just experienced. Stunts! Fun!

Horses, sword fighting, pirating . . . *What woman gets to do this stuff?* I thought. Sadly, though, our joy at making the movie didn't extend to the box office numbers. Carolco had indeed gone bankrupt while we were shooting the movie, and MGM, the distributor, had been sold. There was virtually no marketing push.

The day before its release, the *Los Angeles Times* published a huge article about the expense of it all, noting that we'd even had the shoelaces made by hand. It was true that we'd used a talented Italian costume designer . . . but the shoelaces part had to be made up. We all wore boots! There *were* no shoelaces. Yet the next day, the *Los Angeles Times* reviewer Kenneth Turan wrote, "Full-size ships, impressive waves, thousands of costumes accurate down to the shoelaces, anything and everything an unreasonable amount of money could buy has been press-ganged into service here."

Mr. Turan picked up the shoelaces thing from the negative article the day before, not from actual observation, because, as said: Pirates don't have shoelaces!

There was something of a situational problem, too. *Cutthroat Island* came out five months after one of the most notorious flops of all time, *Waterworld*, had bombed spectacularly at the box office. Much more attention was now being paid to how much movies cost.

Well, whatever it was, *Cutthroat Island*—at least amusingly translated as *Throat Surgery Island* in Finnish—sank like a pirate ship. But for me what made up for all the bad reviews was that Quentin Tarantino really liked the movie. When I met him years later, he told me he'd watched one of the action scenes involving a carriage over and over to figure out where the stunt was, because it looked as if I had actually done this clearly impossible stunt *myself*. One reviewer agreed with him:

> *If that's not really her faux cold-cocking foes, barreling through windows, rolling off balconies into a moving carriage and riding away from explosions during a fiery siege on Port Royal in Jamaica, "Island" has some of the best stunt doubles of all time.*
>
> —*Nick Rogers, November 30, 2015, thefilmyap.com*

And now I want to make one thing clear: If I happen to drink rum before noon, it does not mean I have a drinking problem. It's because I'm a PIRATE!

. . .

I'm a silver linings kind of person, and there's one thing I haven't told you yet about *Cutthroat Island* that made the whole experience so much better.

One afternoon we were filming a scene in Malta when I noticed a mournful extra standing off to one side. My heart filled with love for her; she was short, and lonely, and altogether too hairy, not to mention entirely unimpressed that she was on a major movie set.

She was also a donkey.

I knew already that Renny was the king of the romantic gesture, but his next move topped it all: He'd seen me fall in love with that sweet animal, and a few days later I came home to our rental in the beautiful coastal town of Marsaxlokk to find a gigantic wooden box with an enormous bow on top in the living room. Renny had had the carpenters on the movie build it—and inside was Hody: full name, Donkey Hody. (Say it out loud.)

The only way to get a donkey from Malta to Los Angeles was to put her on one of those fancy planes that they use for transporting racehorses, so that was how we got the little hundred-dollar donkey home. Fortunately for us and for "Don Quixote," Las Tejas came complete with stables and a fenced-in pasture; up till then we'd had nothing to put in them, but soon we'd have a veritable menagerie. You see, once home, I didn't want Donkey Hody to be lonely, speaking only Maltese and all, so we got her a pony for company— which I named Pony. The pony was supposed to be the donkey's friend, but it turned out that Pony hated Hody, so what to do now? Well, I tried again: I bought Hody a fifty-dollar goat from our gardener, the kind with the eyes on the side of its head (the goat, not the gardener), which I promptly named Goaty. But Goaty didn't like Hody either and now I was worried that *Goaty* might be lonely (I'd given up on Hody), so we bought him a little twenty-five-dollar goat named Scampy. But Scampy was too busy escaping to spend much quality time with anybody.

Let the record show that Pony loved the goats. But besides that, I now owned a Donkey named Hody, a pony named Pony who hated the donkey, a goat named Goaty who had an attitude problem, and a little goat called Scampy who was forever wandering the streets of Montecito.

Donkey Hody, though, was worth anything: I still have her,

twenty-seven years later! When you walk around, she follows you, and if you stop, she stops, as though she were engaged in an endless game of Statues. I got her the smallest size of these special clothes made to help keep off the flies. It's like a too-big clown outfit, and off she goes, hippy-skipping around the ring. Her feet are so small you want to die of the cutes, and when we put her in her stall, she was too short to see out, so we added a little step for her to stand on.

But she wasn't just cute, it turned out. She was also a *badass* bad ass. One night, a mountain lion slunk onto our property and tried to drag Goaty under the fence and away, but Hody was having none of it. In Africa, cattle herds often include donkeys, as they are no-

Donkey Hody's feet are so small.

torious for sounding the alarm (they're clever little animals). Hody went crazy that night, and scared off the mountain lion, proving, I suppose, that even though Goaty didn't like Hody, the feeling was not mutual. Poor Goaty's leg was ripped up by the lion, though, and he stayed at the vet for six months. We ended up spending a fortune on him, but we saved the fifty-dollar goat and that was all that mattered.

Renny later bought me a reindeer in Canada during the filming of our next project together, *The Long Kiss Goodnight*, which I would have named . . . Rainy? Deery? but we were barred by customs from bringing it into the United States.

Probably just as well.

Renny was still living large, no matter what. One Midsummer Eve in Finland (which is huge there, celebrating the longest day of the year in that northerly clime), Renny and his friends rented two helicopters to fly us around the country all night and land at whatever big bonfires and gatherings we found. Eventually we touched down at a concert by the Leningrad Cowboys, a very popular Finnish band—and Renny talked them into letting me join them on stage to help sing their cover of the Mary Hopkin hit "Those Were the Days"—to a crowd of 50,000 people. My singing voice is, in fact, very much like Mary Hopkin's sounds on that song, all girly and warbly. I sound like I'm a sweet little old lady.

• • •

I was the opposite of a sweet little old lady in my next movie, again directed by Renny.

The Long Kiss Goodnight was as far from a pirate movie as you could imagine, and to this day I think it's one of the best I've ever made. If forced to choose among characters I've loved to play, I put mine in this movie at number two right behind Thelma. In *Long Kiss* I essentially play two different characters in the body of one person: Samantha Caine, a Honesdale, Pennsylvania, mother whose previous life has been wiped out by a bad case of amnesia; and Charly Baltimore, an assassin. The key to it was to keep the two sides plausibly related, which was a terrific acting challenge, and there was so much crazy physical stuff to do again. (When the movie came out Roger Ebert commented, "Geena, give yourself a break.")

I went nuts with the prep: I worked out for two hours nearly every day, took tae kwon do lessons, and got weaponry training out in the middle of nowhere at a police training facility. I learned to clear rooms and buildings, and soon my instructor told me I had a "natural skill for this; I think if you wanted to, you could *compete* in pistol shooting." I'd never competed in anything, but his words served as a Post-it note on my brain, one I'd return to in the not-too-distant future.

...

The screenwriter on *Long Kiss*, Shane Black, reported that he'd been advised to write the script about a man, not a woman.

"It might have made more money, they told me, but it *had* to be a woman. The lead had to be female."

Fortunately for me, Shane stuck to his guns.

"What I wanted to do is not be afraid to give a woman character as serious a role as I would a man character," Shane said. "The temptation is to keep a woman soft and fluffy."

Opposite me in *Long Kiss* was the wondrous Samuel L. Jackson. To this day he cites Mitch Henessey as his favorite character he's ever played. He and I got along famously; he's incredibly funny, and we were just crazy about each other. We loved the script, we loved everything about it—even the fact of having to film in Toronto in the middle of winter only served to bring us closer. The temperature on the night shoots could dip as low as 20° below zero, and the days weren't much warmer.

In scenes where I was holding a gun, the props guys would wrap it in a heating pad between takes—I guess so it wouldn't stick to my hand, like a tongue on cold metal? (They heated *me* between takes, too, mercifully.) In the outdoor night scenes, I was wearing only leggings and a sleeveless T-shirt under a big coat, and before every new scene I'd say, "I figure now is about when Charly would zip up her coat . . ." but Renny would always insist I looked tougher with it open—and so it was, even when I had a big wet patch of fake blood all over the front of my paper-thin tank top.

That character, Charly Baltimore, was tough, all right. I had the honor of being the first woman to say "Suck my dick" in a movie, so . . . proud of that. I say first because there was a second time just a year later: Demi Moore said it, too, in *G.I. Jane*—directed by Ridley Scott!

I did most of my own stunts on this movie, too, including a harrowing torture scene with a water wheel (I'll let you watch the movie to see what that was all about). Early in the movie I hit a deer with a car and go flying out through the windshield—losing my shoes as I go—and get knocked out, which causes some of my assassin memory to start coming back. I'm all bleeding and dazed but I want to put the deer out of its misery, so I walk through the snow in my bare feet—because it looks cool!—then wade through a half-frozen stream, until I kill the animatronic deer by breaking its neck.

This was the first instance of the phrase that became a kind of signature on the set of *Long Kiss*: *"You married him."* My beloved friend Howell, who was second assistant director on this movie, too, coined the phrase in answer to my amazement at some of the things Renny wanted me to do. *I* very much wanted to do whatever stunts I could, but sometimes Renny took it way too far. (He really *believed* in me? Was he trying to *kill* me?)

I'd ask Howell, "Let me get this straight: He wants me to climb out of a racing Santa sleigh, walk across the top of the car next to it moving at top speed, and then jump onto the side of a moving tanker truck?"

Howell would just shrug. "Hey, you married him."

A few scenes after the deer kill, a one-eyed guy with a shotgun shows up at my suburban home; there are all kinds of punches thrown and bullets fired, until my "Charly" side takes over and does something he couldn't have expected: kill him with a lemon meringue pie—I presume a first in cinema history. (It was technically the glass pie pan that did it.).

Earlier in the scene, I'm hiding behind the refrigerator door when One-Eye blasts it, and I'm supposed to go flying back. The stunt coordinator put me in a rig with a harness, and when the gun went off, they zipped me backward until I crashed into the cabinets—stunt fun!

The special effects guys were tasked with blasting me with a huge fan at the same time and throwing lettuce and other vegetables at me as if they came flying out of the fridge; on the last take, they had the idea of using the enormous fan to propel lettuce my way. "Let's put it in the fan and it'll go flying faster!" they figured. So, without testing it out or telling me, they dropped lettuce into the massive fan, which unfortunately caused it to instantly turn into flying lettuce needles that pierced my skin—and which the makeup artist had to pull out of my face, one by one, with tweezers.

Oh, but that was just in the *morning*; the same day, we shot a scene in which Sam Jackson and I fall into a lake through a hole in solid ice. We'd been forced to jump out a window to make an escape and the script had me using a machine gun to shoot a hole in the ice as we fell so we wouldn't die when we hit it. Right up until that day I *of course* assumed the scene would be shot in a studio with a fake ice hole . . . Nope, it was planned for an actual frozen lake, through the surface of which they'd chainsawed a hole. Yes, we had wetsuits on under our clothes, and there was a hot tub set up for when we got out to make it less horrific . . .

. . . but it was *horrific*. On Renny's call of "Action!" Sam and I were to go under the water, as though we'd just fallen into the hole, then pop up and climb out. All I could think about was Houdini under the ice in the 1953 film, desperately trying to find the hole.

It was unfathomably cold. As soon as I went under, I pretty much blacked out, with an instant skull-crushing ice-cream headache; it was as if I'd been hit with a cinder block, and I couldn't see or think or hear.

But up we came, roaring, and crawled out of shot as planned, and kept crawling over into the hot tub. Sam lit up a cigarette.

"Oh, oh, oh, we did it!" I said, my entire body in agony from the deep freeze.

"Oh, shit, I'm glad that's fucking over," Sam said.

"Yes! Thank God we never have to do it again . . ."

We were almost crying with relief, or at least I was.

Just then Renny appeared:

"We've got to do it again," he said. "You didn't go down far enough."

A moment's pause as that sank in. Then, "Sure," Sam said, "whatever you need." This was Sam; always cool, always willing, totally unflappable.

The second time didn't work, either—seems the explosive, popping-up thing didn't look explosive *enough*, so on the third— THIRD—attempt, we pushed on the bottom of the ice to get as deep as possible before fireworking up out of the water.

· · ·

The Long Kiss Goodnight hit movie theaters nine months after I'd turned forty. I was panic-stricken about my parents seeing the movie, with the very R-rated "suck my dick" of it all. So much so that I asked Renny to make a special video version of it just for my folks, with all the swearing cut out—I told them it was so they didn't have to bother going to the theater to see it. *Long Kiss* got some great reviews and did well enough, but it's gone on to be a cult classic, and I'm very happy about the number of times people (mostly guys) stop me to say they loved it.

Before the movie came out, test audiences did *not* want Sam's character to die in the end, which was how it was shot. ("You can't kill Sam Jackson!") So Renny shot a new ending in which his character, Mitch Henessey, survives. Which meant Sam and I could do a sequel! My dream! But the movie wasn't successful enough to warrant one. I haven't given up, though. He didn't die, so we *can* still do a sequel—just twenty-five years later. (I shall never give up on my franchise dream!)

Just about a year after *Long Kiss* premiered, I filed for divorce from Renny. He had betrayed me in one of the worst ways you can imagine. I don't intend to go into the details here; back then the news, such as it was, didn't register all that much in the wider world, and I see no reason to make it register now.

But I will say how profoundly painful it was. I had held fast through years of being mistrusted because I thought that once he *did* trust me, he would always be the incredibly loving person he otherwise was. So, at the end, my overwhelming reaction was less to do with the nature of the betrayal than the tremendous feeling of loss—I'd realized I'd soldiered on through all of that and yet didn't get the prize in the end. It was shattering.

I toyed with the idea of naming this chapter "You Married Him," but given how it ended, I decided to give the donkey first billing.

Chapter Eleven
Not for Nothing, But I Haven't Retired

In the song "Busy Man" by Billy Ray Cyrus, there's a lyric that says, "Have you ever seen a headstone with these words, 'If only I had spent more time at work'?"

Well, if you haven't, then mine will be the first. Because I do, with all my heart, wish I'd been able to work more in my forties and fifties. I mean, you can imagine how incredibly spoiled I was, considering that (in my opinion) I'd landed some of the best roles out there—juicy lead parts with big arcs and so much to do. But I was deeply aggrieved to find that the work for which I'd been previously known, and which I'd loved with great passion, became harder to come by past forty.

When I was first starting out, I'd already heard that roles typically become scarce for women after forty, but I was sure it wouldn't be the case anymore by the time *I* hit forty. When I watched the Oscars, every year it seemed like Meryl Streep was in some incredible movie, and Sally Field, Jessica Lange, Glenn Close—they seemed to be working all the time. Surely they were going to keep working past forty, paving the way for all of us. Or, failing that, it would not happen to me, the evidence being the great parts I was getting. But their accomplishments didn't fix it, and I didn't break the mold. After I turned forty, like everyone else, I faced a downturn in the number of roles I was being offered, and the quality of them.

It was devastating. I wanted to do more of the job I lived for, not less.

I did find myself turning down several ill-conceived movies, though, many of which never even came out. See, I know right away whether I want to do a part. The signal is when I'm reading a script and start to feel like, "Oh, I want to say that; I want to be in that situation"—that's how I know to go after it.

I'd always waited patiently for the next great thing to come along. I'm good at amusing myself in the meantime and the next great thing always *did* come along.

But this gap between movies was becoming worrisome: three years. (I'd been averaging one movie a year.) I thought about taking an ad out in the trades: a full-page photo of me with only the caption:

NOT FOR NOTHING, BUT I HAVEN'T RETIRED, YOU KNOW

. . . as just a little way to remind folks that I wanted to work. (I wouldn't be the first showbiz Davis to publicly lobby for more work: At fifty-four years of age, *Bette* Davis posted an ad in the "Situations Wanted" section of *The Hollywood Reporter* in which she listed, "thirty years' experience as an actress in motion pictures. Wants steady employment in Hollywood.") That said, there were *very* few movies that came out where I thought, "Dang, I wish I'd gotten *that* role . . ." Most all of us over forty were facing the same predicament.

I started to joke that I'd get lots of work again when I entered my "Don Ameche years"—that I just had to wait until I was as old as he was when he was in the smash hit *Cocoon* to be in demand again.

But I did find something else to obsess over.

. . .

After learning lots of sports and skills for movie roles, I was spurred on to set a goal for my newfound athleticism. I decided I wanted to learn a sport the *real* way, not just the movie version: to become an actual athlete.

Once we finished shooting *The Long Kiss Goodnight* in May 1996, I was left with a few months off until it premiered in October. And fortunately, I had the upcoming Atlanta Olympics to look forward to. I've always adored the Olympics—something about the single-minded effort of those athletes toward excellence, toward their one big shot—for someone extremely goal-oriented, the Olympics are fascinating.

And the Atlanta Olympics featured great drama—Kerri Strug vaulting for the team gold with a busted ankle, and 137-pound Naim Süleymanoğlu from Bulgaria ("Pocket Hercules") lifting 336 pounds to get his third gold medal. But one sport in particular caught my attention for the first time.

That year that there was a ton of coverage of the men's archery competition on TV because the American men were dominating, and I vividly remember watching, spellbound. The star of the whole deal was Justin Huish, and in NBC fashion they'd produced a "get-to-know-him" video of Justin training at home in California. He'd wanted to practice at his house, but the yard just wasn't big enough—the target is 70 meters away in Olympic-style archery. No matter: the video showed how he'd open the front and rear doors of the family garage, then go across the quiet residential street to his neighbor's front yard and fire the arrows across the street, through the garage, and into the target in the backyard (pausing if a car or person went by, naturally).

This seemed spectacularly cool to me and gave me an idea: Evidently, I was good at shooting pistols, and a bow and arrow is also a kind of weapon . . . but that you can practice at *home*? Archery looked so beautiful; could this be my sport? So if any of you heard I'd taken up archery a while back and thought, *random!* this is why.

Justin Huish was a hip-looking twenty-one-year old dude wearing wraparound shades and a backwards baseball cap—and he took the gold in the individual *and* team events. He brought the sport firmly into the twenty-first century, and I was so impressed with how dramatic-looking it was. On the back of my new fixation with archery, Renny bought me a complete set of equipment for our anniversary in 1996. Then I asked my treasured assistant, Jill Johnson, to find me a good coach.

A week later she said, "Would you mind if your teacher is Justin Huish?"

"Who's that??" I'd forgotten the name, and she reminded me who he was. "You called the *Olympic gold medal guy*?!" I couldn't believe it; how had she even found him?

"Oh, his mom's number was in the phone book, and I called her."

So the actual Olympic gold medalist very kindly came over to Las Tejas; I told him I wanted to become a serious archer, and he shot some arrows to demonstrate—*amazing* to see him shoot in person!—but Justin just didn't feel comfortable about being too encouraging.

"I'm not really a coach, I just thought I'd come talk to you about taking it up . . . It's just *so hard*," Justin said. "I mean, people can get fairly good in this sport, but to achieve becoming that indefinable *extra bit* good—to where you can flawlessly reproduce a perfect shot . . . well, that's basically impossible."

Okay, but can you give me the name of a good coach? When the double-gold medal winner said that to excel in his sport was basically impossible, it didn't change my mind; I knew myself, and knew that if I decided to be a badass at something, I was going to be a badass at something. Actually, please: just *tell* me I can't do something. I'll handle the rest.

Justin gave me the name of a top Olympic-level coach, Don Rabska, who also worked for Easton Sports archery division, so he knew equipment inside and out. (I would discover that correctly calibrated, finely tuned equipment is one of the keys to success in archery.)

Many, many years earlier, ten-year-old me had sent a letter to my parents from camp that read, "I like everything except arcery [*sic*] because I don't know how to do it." Now here I was, forty-one, meeting my new archery coach for the first time, and Don brought all the equipment we'd need.

Now he *claims* that I started the first lesson by asking, "So, how old is too old to go to the Olympics in archery?"

But that's silly. I hadn't even touched a bow yet, let alone shot an arrow!

I'm sure I waited until the second lesson—till, you know, I was more experienced.

. . .

I was instantly and completely hooked.

I loved archery. Learning it to the level that I eventually did helped me gain a huge boost of internal confidence, for a simple reason: You can measure how well you're doing. Your success is not predicated on the opinions of reviewers, and it doesn't matter if people don't like what you wore to the tournament. You either score the points or you don't. There's nothing subjective about it—unlike my day job, which is *utterly* subjective.

I'd been worried that not having learned archery as a kid would be a disadvantage, but at that first lesson Don pointed out that it could really work in my favor: because I hadn't ever shot before, I had no worn-in flawed technique that I might fall back into if nervous . . . so, advantage!

Don began teaching me the basics of technique but put equal emphasis on the mental game. He taught me that the vital key was the ability to let go of the outcome. You must be able to repeat the best version of your shot as many times as you can, exactly the same way, whether you're in your backyard or at a major tournament; with no one watching or with a big crowd. Any shot where you try *harder*—what Don referred to as trying to do a "fancy shot"—will throw off your technique. So, if you're down to the last arrow to win the gold medal, and you have to score a 10 to win, rather than trying for an *extra good* shot, mentally you need to be in a place where you can think of it as "just another shot."

Not being invested in the outcome—how profoundly difficult! Can you imagine being in the situation where you will reach your ultimate dream—but the only way to do it is not to care if you do? This happens in other sports as well: a golfer, for example, tries to swing the same way every time, but might fall into trying an extra fancy shot if they're behind. There's a perfect eye of the storm into which you have to go—the exact opposite of trying harder—and it's a fascinating and impossible thing to strive for.

But perhaps the greatest thing archery—and Don—gave me was the silencing of the damaging voice inside my head. One day, fairly early on in our lessons, Don asked, "What were you just thinking after you shot that arrow?"

"I was thinking I suck," I said.

A few minutes later, he asked again what I was thinking.

"Uh, I was thinking that *you* think I suck."

"We've got to get rid of that negative self-talk," Don said. "You can have all the skill in the world, but not believing in yourself will bring you down."

As I tuned in to it more, I realized that in fact I was hearing this negative self-talk about everything—it wasn't just when I was shooting, the voice was interested in trashing me *all day long*. I think a lot of people are subject to that, to hearing an ongoing internal monologue about how we're going to get laughed at, or that we're not good enough; as if life isn't hard enough already, we need to beat *ourselves* up. Once Don helped me realize what the self-sabotaging voice in my head can do to archery, I started to work on eradicating it from the rest of my life as well.

Whenever the voice started in, as it always did, I'd change it around by thinking, "I'm doing the best I can." I worked like crazy on that and got good at putting those thoughts away. It was like what I taught myself to think about acting: What you did on that day was the best you could do at that time.

And it changed my life dramatically.

A quote I gave to *Good Housekeeping* around that time sums up what this new mindset gave me: "Becoming confident in my physical abilities, acknowledging that I had a right to take up space and be happy with my performance, was the final piece of the puzzle. I started to believe that people weren't judging me every second of my life. I began to really like myself."

I can't overstate how important archery was in quelling my hypercritical inner voice. It also helped that I got good, and fairly quickly . . . and that *no one was watching.*

Archery is the worst spectator sport in the world, in my humble opinion. (Archery competition is different in the Olympics and very exciting to watch.) Picture standing on the goal line of a football field, trying to shoot the 4.8-inch center ring of a target three quarters of the way down the field. Observers can't see where your arrows hit (*you* can't either!—you have to look through a spotting scope to see where they land), and nobody knows who's ahead because the archers all shoot at the same time.

Also, most tournaments last *all day.* Since nobody except a parent here and there ever watches archery tournaments, the public had no clue that I was doing this. Archers are very cool, laid-back people, so they didn't make a fuss, either. No one called TMZ to say, "Hey, Geena Davis—bizarrely—is now competing in archery!" So, for a long time, it was all very comfortable—no pressure and no audience.

Archery is also a sport in which you must keep up your muscle strength for a particular bow. For example, let's say your bow takes thirty-two pounds of effort to shoot. If you don't shoot for two weeks, you will unlikely be able to still pull it with the same control you had two weeks prior, and have to build up to that weight all over again. This type of fine control is slow to gain and fast to lose! I had been training hard for more than two years and was really improving; Don was starting to believe I might indeed make it to the Olympic trials semifinals, but first I had to qualify at the USA Archery Target Nationals.

About six weeks before the Nationals were set to begin, the designer Hugo Boss invited me to attend a big fashion show in Italy. His company was offering an all-expenses-paid trip, so who was I to say no to a luxury vacation in Tuscany?

Don, though, was concerned: He didn't want me to go a week without shooting, with the Nationals just over the horizon. So Don—somehow!—arranged for me to enter a tournament in Tuscany while I was there.

As I've said, archers are totally laid-back people, but there I was being chauffeured to a rural archery competition by a driver in a black suit. Those Tuscan archers saw me arrive and must have thought, *What the—?* Some of them clearly kind of recognized me. Their faces seemed to say, "Is she shooting a movie here? What the heck is this?"

At the end of the day, I was tied for first place on the women's side with the local number one shooter. For the tiebreaker, they tallied up which of us had the most Xs (hitting the tiny X ring in the center of the center); there was a pause, then the tournament director announced the results. I had won! There I was, somewhere up a beautiful hill above Florence, walking away with this big-ass trophy they gave me.

"Thanks, everybody!" I said. "Arrivederci! Bye!" and with that I walked back to the Mercedes while the driver put my gear in the trunk.

I looked at the sea of bemused faces as we pulled away, each probably thinking, *"Che cazzo?"*

Geena Davis, archer—that's what just happened.

· · ·

In the middle of all this—after a three-year movie drought—I got offered something great. I was to play Eleanor Little, mother of Stuart, in *Stuart Little*. This meant I could now claim to be the only actor to go from playing an amnesiac assassin straight to the parent of a rodent. I'm pretty sure the filmmakers thought of me because I'd already had so much "interspecies" experience—you know, being the girlfriend of both a fly and of a blue alien and having had a run-in with a giant sandworm in *Beetlejuice* to boot.

(Tim Burton: "And . . . *you see a giant sandworm!*"

Geena: [shocked reaction]

Tim: "No, the sandworm is really *tall!*"

Geena: [shocked reaction, looking up]

Stuart Little promised to be darling because it was very well written—when you base something on the work of E. B. White it's hard to go wrong—and I got to work with the fabulous Hugh Laurie, who is also a darling, as smart and witty and colorful as you'd hope he would be. The challenge of playing opposite an invisible mouse was . . . weird; Hugh and I had to interact with our son the mouse as though he were real and present and corporeal, which was a problem, because he wasn't and wasn't and wasn't. Our director, Rob Minkoff, told us that the more matter-of-fact Hugh and I could be, the more real it would make Stuart seem.

But I can't tell you how bizarre it is when you have to interact with an absence. You probably imagine that there would at least be a little mouse doll or something to look at, but truly there isn't anything. You're acting with, and reacting to, nothing (there has to be nothing there, so they don't have to erase it to put Stuart in). And we always had to keep in mind how Stuart would be added in. When I shot a scene in which I was holding Stuart in my hand and kissing him, Rob Minkoff had to point out that my hand was clenched shut, so if a little mouse had indeed been in there, I would have just squeezed him to death. And that when I was kissing him, I was kissing the top of my hand, so it would mean he was missing a head, too.

Later, when we made *Stuart Little 2* (finally, a real sequel! and honestly, I hoped the franchise would go on forever) there was the added complication of a new baby in the Little family, Martha, to go along with George, played by Jonathan Lipnicki. (It was my suggestion to add a girl baby to boost the number of female characters in the story.)

Young children are almost always played by twins—first because they can only work very limited hours, and perhaps even more important, so that if one gets tired or cranky, the other one can be drafted in to cover. Anna and Ashley were cast as Martha— they were adorable, about twenty months old, and well aware of when they were separated from their actual mother—which meant that each new scene tended to be preceded by a not-unreasonable crying jag, no matter how much I tried to comfort and distract Anna or Ashley. Once they were calm, though, they were a little pooped, and it was then hard to get them to be interested in whatever was going on in the scene. At one point, the baby needed to be looking at me intently in her close-up, but none of my clowning around could catch her interest; Rob Minkoff decided to try shining a laser pointer on my forehead, and boy, that worked. She was suddenly staring at me with rapt attention.

But this was just a little part of what working with babies can entail: The opening scene was a particularly complicated crane shot: the camera being lowered down from an attic window to me and the baby sitting at a bedroom window, and then on down to the street. It was taking a long time to shoot, but the baby on my lap was in a great mood, so I didn't dare change anything—including her diaper, when it became sodden; soon her pee was running down both of our legs. But I soldiered on—anything for the shot! (I once overheard a director I worked with say the experience of *making* the movie is the most important part; I assume he meant if everyone is having a good time on set it will show up on screen. But I have the opposite view: It's great if people enjoy the experience, but the most important thing is getting what is required *on film*, because that's all the viewers will experience. It doesn't matter if shooting it is hell, as long as the movie comes out good. *Whatever it takes*—that's my motto.)

In the first *Stuart Little*, there's a scene with a remote-controlled boat race on the lake in Central Park, and I happened to be watching as an assistant director set up the child extras. I noticed he was giving all the remotes to boys, and then choosing girls to stand behind the boys, to cheer them on. I went over to the AD and quietly said, "Hey, what would you think about giving half of the remotes to girls?" He looked at me as though thunderstruck—"Yes, yes, of *course!*" he said, and winced. He couldn't believe that he hadn't thought of it himself . . . but the point was, he couldn't: All he was doing was what the culture dictated—"Only boys like mechanical things"—and he fixed it immediately when he realized how unconsciously he had followed gender stereotyping. (He still talks about it, all these years later.)

That little thing—which probably no one watching the movie even noticed—would grow into one of my deepest passions over the intervening years: the representation of girls and women in films for young people.

I would come to think of that tiny spark from *Stuart Little* many times in the years to come, but soon I had something else unexpected on my mind: I found out I had a brain disorder that suddenly explained so much of my life.

. . .

On the set of *Stuart Little*, my ability to hyperfocus became very apparent: apart from archery, I was now also obsessed—with pumpkin carving.

With Halloween approaching, I asked my driver to go out and get me the biggest pumpkin he could find. To my utter delight he brought back a 200-pound gourd, a yard across and two feet high. Each day, whenever I sat in the chair having my hair done, and during down time, I'd carve away at that thing (I'd bought myself a Martha Stewart carving kit, which is what launched this new fixation) and spent weeks working on it. Pro tip: a pumpkin won't start to go bad until you open it, and with Martha's tools I was just carving on the outside of the shell.

When I finished, I had put an illustration of the boat-racing scene from the *Stuart Little* book on the side of the massive pumpkin. Now I could finally open it at the back and hollow it out; the shell was so thick I asked one of the electricians to set up some high-powered lights inside it, and it looked amazing. Happy with my creation, I called the office of the head of the studio, Lucy Fisher, asking if she could come down to the set.

I didn't even think for a second that when one of the actors in one of your movies asks you to COME TO SET RIGHT AWAY, that's a very alarming call to get. Lucy rushed to set, terrified there was a big problem.

"Ta-da!" I said, showing her the carved pumpkin all lit up and glowing. "Whadda ya think?"

By the way, with the strong lights inside it, it had rotted by the next morning.

Where did this laser-like focus come from? How could I spend *weeks* carving one pumpkin? And I was also still fixated on archery—I practiced on an empty stage on the Sony lot between every scene (Sony posted guards at either door so I didn't inadvertently skewer someone) and I reached thirteenth in the nation that year. I'd always loved a challenge, and I needed things to be difficult; I have to be careful what I choose to get interested in because, eventually, I will want to go to the Olympics in it, whatever it is.

And it was all because of three letters.

• • •

At the same time that I took up archery, I started with a new therapist, and after only a few sessions, she said, "Have you ever been told you have ADD?" (People most often used ADD back then, rather than ADHD like today.)

Well, that just couldn't be, I told her. I'm the oppositive of hyperactive (I think of myself as a slow, lumbering bear), but as she started to pepper me with questions, it seemed more and more likely that she might have a point. She suggested I go get properly tested.

"This won't be able to show if I have ADD," I told the woman administering the tests. "I love tests, and I do really well on them. I'm very good at concentrating really hard."

"Well, we'll see," she said, and we began.

The testing was very extensive, with many parts; one task was watching a monitor and pressing a button every time I saw a little dot light up. How could I possibly screw that up?

"Well, Geena," the doctor said, after reviewing the results, "you have a very pronounced case of ADD." She told me that during the long press-the-button test, there were a lot of times I pressed it at the wrong time—and that there was a *twenty-minute* period where I didn't press it at all. How could that possibly be true when I was concentrating so hard?

Learning I have ADD rocked my world. Everything in my life suddenly started to make sense. The many, many times I was tortured by not being able to finish assignments? Couldn't practice the piano until right before leaving to go to the lesson? Starting a million different projects and never being able to finish any of them, which caused me such agony? ADD.

Turns out that I have one of the best possible careers for someone with ADD (as if you can just choose to be a movie actor!). Everything about it holds your feet to the fire, and I need to have my feet held to the fire to be able to fully engage. You are going to shoot *this* scene on *this* day, in a limited amount of time, and it's your only chance to get it right . . . with a hundred or so crew members relying on you to do so. This means I can remember the lines and the blocking flawlessly. If there's a scene in which I'm eating or drinking, and I have to replicate the same movements for subsequent takes? No problem. I am so hyperfocused that all those things lock in my brain like cement.

This diagnosis created a tremendous sense of relief in me. I now knew the explanation for the torture I'd been putting myself through by not being able to accomplish many important things in life . . . and also why I was able to focus so intensely on other things. (After seeing one of my pumpkin creations, a friend claimed I had Attention *Surplus* Disorder.) The revelation came with a deep sadness, too, for not having learned all this much earlier. No one back then could have suspected that a shy girl with no hyperactivity could possibly have ADD. (Just as no one suspected that my brother, Dan, had dyslexia.)

Whenever I failed at something at school, I'd tell myself over and over, "Just remember, ten years from now, you won't remember this." But those things *did* stay with me; they were just part of the crushing shame I felt for not being able to function properly, which I had to hide at all costs . . . but now, at last, I knew why I'd always been this way.

My therapist compared people with my kind of ADD—the non-hyperactive kind—to lions. Lions sleep 90 percent of the time, but when they hear something walking around they're like: "WHAT

WAS THAT??" and instantly have 100 percent focus. I'm just like that. If it lights up, spins, blows bubbles, and plays music I'm *there*. And now I knew why. I was an actor; I was an archer; I was a lion.

. . .

Could a lion who is an archer make it to the Olympics?

Unlike a lion, I was training about four hours a day, six days a week, shooting more than 4,500 arrows a month, with Don refining my skills. I'd finished twenty-ninth out of three hundred at the national championships in July 1999—being in the top thirty-two of that competition automatically gets you into the Olympic trials semifinals, so there I was in Bloomfield, New Jersey, in late August 1999.

The thing was, I'd been shooting completely under the radar up to this point, with zero attention from the press; now that I was going to the Olympic trials, the news broke. Even the *New York Times* covered them ("Geena Davis Zeros in with Bow and Arrows" read the headline).

On the day of the actual semifinals there were fifty news crews in attendance, almost all of them standing behind me, their cameras whirring every time I touched an arrow . . . and then whipping to the target to see where they landed. I'd been at it quite a short time and had never practiced in a high-pressure situation like this. My nerves completely took over, and my hands were shaking for the first time ever when I pulled back the bow. I didn't make it to the finals.

Not that I would have. It would have been a long shot (tee-hee) to go from twenty-ninth to suddenly being in the top four, but I decided to believe I could do it, so I'd do my best at the trials. (I did move up to twenty-fourth, so yay!)

During a press conference after the trials, a woman reporter asked what had led me to think I could take up a sport I'd never tried and excel at it. I whipped out the best quote I'd ever come upon, and which has become my personal motto: "If man can do it, I can do it." (Unfortunately, I don't remember who said it.)

There was a slight pause, then the (again, female!) reporter asked, "And is that your aim, to prove you can do things men can do?"

There were groans from the other reporters gathered there— mostly men, for the record—and I said to the throng, "No one else misunderstood what I mean, right?"

No one else had misunderstood. Nevertheless, from that moment on I amended my life's philosophy so as to be categorically clear:

If a human being can do it, I can do it.

—*Geena Davis*

• • •

Little did I know a huge, unexpected thrill was coming my way.

The 2000 Summer Olympics were to be held in Sydney, and the organizers planned to stage *a full trial-run* of the Olympics to test all the facilities, a year before the actual event. For archery, there was an official Olympic "Test Tournament," and all of the very same archers who would compete in the 2000 Olympics were there. The USA team amazingly offered me a wild card spot! I got to wear the team USA uniform, the whole deal—and have the full experience of competing in the Olympics, after all. There, when I made a shot, I was up on the jumbotron! Incidentally, one of my USA "teammates" *won*; instead of a gold medal, they presented her with a trophy of a golden arrow.

It seemed I had turned myself into an actual athlete with my "real life" sport. And I'd made peace with my ADD diagnosis—or, rather, my diagnosis had brought me an element of peace that had been missing for so long.

• • •

As a kid, I spent a lot of time fantasizing about what I'd be like as an adult, and it always centered around New Year's Eve 1999, what I imagined would be the most important night of my life. I pictured that by that night I'd no longer be the odd kid; like my aunt Gloria, I'd be cool and sophisticated. I'd be at an elegant party, wearing a chic cocktail dress, martini glass in hand, and having witty conversations with other sophisticated people. The main point was by that New Year's Eve I'd be someone else. And now here it was, 1999.

As an adult I was well aware that New Year's Eve was more often than not a big disappointment, so I was determined to make this one match my childhood fantasy as much as possible. I organized a masquerade ball with a small group of my closest friends. Ahead of the big night we all took ballroom dancing lessons, and I hosted a mask-making party. I tried to think of everything—I even created a tulle skirt that I could make light up at midnight. We served breakfast at 3 a.m., which I thought was the best part.

The turn of the century was *not* a disappointment. It lived up to all those years of my fantasizing.

. . .

The next summer my parents' fiftieth anniversary was upon us, and Dad wanted to make a real celebration of it—by singing a duet with Mom! So much of their life revolved around the church, so we arranged to have a party in the church hall right after Sunday service and invite the whole congregation, just as they'd done fifty years earlier when they got married. I was visiting very frequently in those days, and Dad would ask me to play the piano for them to practice their duet over and over again. They were going to sing a "golden anniversary" song from 1909, and my dad was going to make sure they nailed it.

My sister-in-law, Marilyn, a brilliant seamstress, was in charge of headgear. She supplied my dad with an old top hat and decorated a very old-fashioned bonnet for Mom. And sure enough, on the day, they killed it—belting out "Put on Your Old Grey Bonnet," with Mom hilariously hamming it up like a vaudevillian.

> ". . . And through the fields of clover,
> We'll drive up to Dover
> on our Golden Wedding Day."

This was despite her having had symptoms of Alzheimer's for several years by then. Every word and note of the song had gone into her hard drive *decades* ago and had stuck there, never to be dislodged. It was only things happening in the present that floated away immediately.

This was history sadly repeating itself. My mother's mother had developed dementia late in life, and it occasioned a most poignant situation: My grandmother, Florence Cook, had led a life consumed by bitterness, ever since she became a young widow. Every Saturday when Dan and I were kids we'd go visit her, and the spigot of martyred complaints would turn on again as she harangued my mom in a most un(grand)motherly way.

But as my grandmother's dementia developed, she very unexpectedly became happy and untroubled—at the same time that she began to not recognize us, which only broke my mother's heart further. "Ma" eventually had to be placed in a nursing home, and we'd go visit often, sometimes taking her out for ice cream—but she'd always want to hurry back; she was convinced she was a nurse at the home and needed to return in time for her "shift." As we'd reenter the place, the staff would say, "Florence, your shift hasn't started yet, why don't you go relax for a bit," and she'd give us all hugs goodbye.

"All my life I've wanted her to be nice to me," my mother said, crying quietly on the drive home, "and now she is . . . but she doesn't know who I *am*."

Now, sadly, that dread disease was reappearing in my mom.

It first became apparent while Renny and I were still together. My folks were visiting us once at the same time Renny's sister and family were there, and Mom was very interested in my sweet niece, Linnea. As we were driving in the car one day, Mom caught sight of Linnea and said, "So, are you in high school?" Linnea explained that the Finnish school system was different, and how the grades were ranged . . . which satisfied Mom—until five minutes later, when she'd ask her again: "So tell me, are you in high school?"

Linnea would repeat the whole story again, with every detail, and then again—until it was clear that Mom would not stop asking, and neither would Linnea stop patiently giving her the full answer. I finally said to Linnea, "It's okay, sweetheart, really . . ." and the next time Mom asked, Linnea softly replied, "Yes. Yes, I am in high school."

For all of her illness, until the very last part, Mom lived at home, and still knew who we were. A lot of her friends didn't even realize that she had stopped recognizing them, so good was she at acting (I guess I did get it from her after all). Whatever energy those friends put out, Mom matched.

"So good to see *you*, too!" she'd say, convincing them that she was perfectly aware of who they were. Then when they left, she'd turn to me and say,

"Who *was* that? She certainly seemed to believe we know each other!"

My dad proved incontrovertibly during this time that he was a saint. He never once—for years, mind you—said anything like "You just asked me that." He was always very happy to tell her a story over and over again, leaving nothing out—and thinking of some new, interesting details to add for her enjoyment.

My mother, like her own mother, had developed what I'd come to call "happy Alzheimer's," and found delight in everything.

"What are we doing now?" she'd ask.

"Well, Mom," I'd say, "we're going to go on this plane."

"Oh! That sounds good," she'd say, perfectly contentedly, before asking me again what we were up to.

We were getting on a plane because I was taking Dad to his sixty-fifth college reunion in Berea, Kentucky. Mom was in such good spirits and with it enough that it was very easy to have her come too. I think only a very few people there realized she had dementia, she was so personable and fun. And Mom could swan her way through anything. When her doctor asked her, "Who is the president?" she gave him a sly smile and said, "Don't you know?"

Dad was thrilled to be going because he'd been to only two reunions across the years. There were eleven members of the class of '51 there, all remarkably hale and hearty. Well, it makes sense that it would be the healthiest eighty-eight-year-olds who could attend; one even arrived in a miniskirt and beret. As soon as they met up, they started ribbing one another about how old they were—"I didn't think *you'd* make it, you old geezer"—and they made a lot of jokes about who among them would make it to their seventieth reunion.

There was a banquet on Saturday evening, and each class had its own table with the year of their graduation on a placard. Close by our group was the seventieth class table, empty but for two elderly women, which caused the sixty-fives to sober up . . . briefly, because they were soon teasing one another again. "Well, sorry, fellas, looks like only us gals will be sitting at that table next time!" (It turned out it was only my dad and his friend Delmas Saunders—and me—sitting at the seventieth reunion table five years later.)

The desserts had been preset on the tables above each place setting, and before the meal was served Mom tucked into her pecan pie; then, a little while later, she said, "Well, why does everyone have pie, but I don't?" I told her I was sure it had been a mistake and gave her mine. She was so heartbreakingly sweet in her illness, and I followed my dad's lead in never acknowledging her slips.

Not too long after that trip, Mom would hurt her knee quite badly in a fall and would be admitted to the hospital, where her mental status deteriorated severely; she went from there to a nursing home to recover. She still knew who we were, but when she got aspirational pneumonia, her decline was precipitous.

Dad put her in hospice care to bypass any feeding tube or beeping machines. I'd just gone home to LA but flew back immediately with this sudden turn of events. When I walked into her room, she seemed utterly unresponsive, but when she heard my voice, she looked straight at me and smiled.

"I love you," Mom said, clearly, holding my gaze.

"I love you, too, Mom," I said . . . and then she drifted away again.

My mother never spoke after that. For five days she hung on, and then one morning my father and I decided to take a brief break to go get breakfast at a local diner, and when we got back, Mom had passed.

It was the morning of November 15, 2001. Lucille Davis, my mother, was eighty-two years old.

Chapter Twelve
The Mother Gets Killed Gruesomely in the First Five Minutes

When my daughter was two years old, we were watching children's TV together when . . . oh, yes, by the way, in my forties, I became a mother (three times over). This turns out to be my favorite role of all, but it's also the one I plan to talk about the least.

Here's a little story to illustrate why: At a Golden Globes press conference for *Stuart Little 2*, a male reporter said, "You just had a baby girl, congratulations. Was it in vitro or natural?"

I hardly need to point out to you how unacceptably intrusive this was, but the gathered press leaned forward as one, sure that a reply would be forthcoming. Fortunately, I had an answer prepared—yes, I knew I needed to be ready for this kind of question, as the Hollywood Foreign Press members tended to veer toward the inappropriate.

So, without a pause, I said: "Oh, no, no, you're confused: Stuart Little was *adopted*."

The original questioner was the only person who didn't laugh, and then compounded the error by going on to say, "No, but *was* it in vitro?" as if I truly owed him an honest answer. (I didn't use the other comeback I'd considered, which was inspired by the then-president George W. Bush's newly released colonoscopy results: "Look, it's okay for the press to climb up the president's ass because that needs to be public knowledge, but stay out of my vagina!")

Given the expectation that because I'm an actor I should naturally share every detail about my family life, I've been wary of sharing *anything*, and honestly, I value my family's privacy over everything. And also, if I were going to talk about my kids, I would need a whole second book to do justice to them.

So, for the purposes of this book, I have a daughter and twin boys . . . their dad—my ex, Dr. Reza Jarrahy—is an extremely gifted and compassionate surgeon who specializes in treating craniofacial deformity in kids. Reza spends a lot of time every year traveling to Guatemala and other countries on medical missions, which tells you what kind of person he is. He's also a fantastic father.

Where was I?

Ah, yes—when my now twenty-year-old daughter (!) was a toddler, I decided I wanted the data on one very specific thing: How many female characters were there in movies and television made specifically for kids?

See, when Alizeh was about two, I sat down with her to watch her very first kids' TV show. And probably because of the Spidey sense I'd developed about women's representation over the years, I was floored to see that there seemed to be *far more* male characters than female characters—in a show designed for the youngest kids!

Really!?

Then I saw it—as well as gender stereotyping—in almost everything we watched together, with some exceptions (the Teletubbies are gender-balanced, don't know if you could tell). It occurred to me, as a mother in the twenty-first century, surely kids should be seeing boys and girls sharing the sandbox equally by now!

Well, in the beginning I didn't intend for it to take over my life. First I just checked with my mom friends to see if they had noticed there was only one female character in an animated movie that had just come out (except for the mother who dies gruesomely in the first five minutes). Not one of them had noticed.

By the way, why is that? Why does the mother die so often? I posit that if we're going to reach true equality, we must kill off the *fathers*, too.

So I decided to bring it up with people in my industry. If I had a meeting with a studio executive or producer or whomever, I'd casually ask: Have you ever noticed how few female characters there are in movies made for kids?

And *to a person* they'd say, "No, no, that's not true anymore, that's been fixed." And often they'd name a movie with only one, *maybe* two female characters in it as proof that gender inequality was a thing of the past.

But here's the thing: No one took the question lightly. They truly felt a responsibility to do right by girls in their movies and TV shows, *and thought they were.* How could that be? How could the people *creating* these movies and TV shows not notice the huge gender imbalance?

Now I realized that I needed the numbers. If the actual creators of kids' media couldn't see the dearth of female presence, maybe the data would help them to become aware.

This took my life in an entirely new direction, which I never would have anticipated. Obsession time: I was going to go to the Olympics in this.

· · ·

I became a middle-aged data geek by sponsoring the largest research project ever undertaken on the representation of female characters in kids' entertainment—which took two years to complete because it was so extensive.

This initial research showed that in kids' movies and TV shows, for every one female speaking character, there were three male characters; that female characters tended to contribute very little to the plot, and often served as "eye candy." (Oh, and one of the most common occupations for female characters in G-rated movies was royalty, which, hey, is a great gig—if you can get it.)

Our research also revealed that when female characters do exist in children's media, they are often either narrowly stereotyped and/ or hypersexualized. The effect of that hypersexualization was seen in a study conducted by Christine Reuter Starr at Knox College in Illinois. First published in the journal *Sex Roles*, Starr and her faculty advisor, Professor Gail Ferguson, found for the first time that little girls were self-sexualizing by the age of six. (When shown two dolls, one of which was wearing "modest but still trendy" clothes, and the other dressed in revealing, "sexy" clothes, 68 percent of the girls said they "wanted to look like" the sexy doll, and 72 percent believed that doll would be "more popular.")

As far as the occupations of female characters go, in family films 81 percent of the jobs were held by male characters. The most troubling finding was that the percentage of fictional women in the workforce was even *lower* than the one that exists in the real world. Despite women holding 21 percent of global political positions worldwide, out of 127 characters holding political office, only 12 were female. In the legal sphere on screen, male judges and lawyers outnumbered females 13 to 1, and in computer science and engineering, the ratio of men to women was 15 to 1. In other words, however abysmal the numbers in the real world were, they were far worse in *fiction*—where you *make it up.*

So what message are we sending girls and boys at a vulnerable age if female characters are one-dimensional, sidelined, hyper-sexualized, or simply not there at all? We're saying that women and girls are less valuable to our society than men and boys. That women and girls don't take up half the space in the world. We're teaching them to have unconscious gender bias from the beginning.

That's why I chose to focus on what kids see first. It's just common sense: Don't create a problem that needs to be solved later. Just show kids from the beginning that boys and girls do equally interesting and important things, and that girls and women are, by the way, half of the population. Think of how dramatically different our world would be if children grew up free from these biases! By feeding our youngest kids seriously imbalanced worlds from the beginning, we are unwittingly training yet another generation to see women and girls as less valuable than men and boys.

. . .

My plan for all this data was not to try to educate the public. I wanted it for a very specific reason: to take it directly to the makers of kids' entertainment, and share it with them in a very private, collegial way. I already knew that these smart, creative folks simply didn't realize there was a problem. I also knew that the people who go into the business of creating kids' media do it because they *love kids*. So everything was primed for the possibility that opening their eyes could bring about very significant change.

My first move after I had the research in hand was to ask Disney if I could present it to them. They were very obliging and gathered about forty people in a conference room for me, culled from live action and animation and everything else Disney does. I made the presentation, having no idea how they would react—were they going to doubt the research? Feel defensive in some way?

As it turned out, their reaction was better than anything I could have hoped: They were *staggered*, every one of them. One of the men present, an animator, spoke first.

"Just this morning, I was drawing a scene in a restaurant. And I made every single character, from the diners to the wait staff, male. I have no idea why I did that," he said. "I'm the problem!"

Bless him, it broke the ice and drew a laugh, and others chimed in. The head of casting for the studio was crestfallen. She said, "Every movie we do here, my staff and I go through it to see who could become Asian-American, who could become Black or Hispanic. And we never once have said, 'Could this character be played by a woman?' I have no idea why we never thought of that."

Creators' reactions to hearing the research was exactly the same at every studio, network, and production company. They were *stunned*. They thought they were doing right by girls, and they were floored to learn that they were not.

In all these years there was only *one* person who pushed back on the need to make the gender ratio more balanced in their movies; the head of an animation company told me, "Well, we've already figured out how to please girls—50 percent of the audiences for our movies are female, so we know we're doing right by them!"

Uh, or maybe parents take *all* the kids when they go to the movies?

...

The great thing is, my plan is working. The data really was the magic key to making change. In the fall of 2019, something historic happened: For the first time, female leads and co-leads in family films reached gender parity. In early 2020, our research found that the same has happened in television made for kids. And in 2021, gender parity for minor and secondary female characters in popular television programming was achieved for the first time in history. All of this came about in great part due to the efforts of our president and CEO, Madeline Di Nonno, whose talent and passion know no bounds.

I'm happy to report that the Geena Davis Institute on Gender in Media has become the go-to resource for research and insights into onscreen bias in global family entertainment and media—be it biases of gender identity, race/ethnicity, LGBTQIA+, body size, age, or people with disabilities—and I was honored to receive a second Academy Award in 2019, the Jean Hersholt Humanitarian Award, for the work I've been doing.

. . .

Why should only guys named Robert have their own film festivals? Turns out I have a film festival, called BFF: the Bentonville Film Festival.

Bentonville, a charming city in northwest Arkansas that calls itself "the great American town," has proved itself to be the perfect location, with its burgeoning creative ecosystem, its new luxury hotel, its award-winning cuisine, and a world-class art museum, Crystal Bridges. (It is also the home of Walmart, our founding sponsor.) There was just one hurdle we had to overcome: Bentonville had no movie theaters! The first year, we made the festival possible by outfitting churches, meeting rooms, conference rooms, and even the downtown square to screen festival entries. In later years, we began to bring in mobile theaters and created a large outdoor event.

The festival is solely dedicated to championing women and diverse voices in front of and behind the camera. One event at the festival that's a real crowd pleaser is "Geena and Friends." Some of my female actor friends and I act out classic movie scenes originally cast with all male actors. Flipping the dynamic on its head, it's a fun and funny way to expand our vision of who can play what roles. We've done everything from *City Slickers* and *Wedding Crashers* to *The Fast and the Furious* and *Top Gun*.

BFF is working hard to live up to its initials. With the charm of our location, and the hospitality that's extended to everyone, we want it to become known as a festival for filmmakers without velvet ropes. We now get more than 70,000 attendees each year.

Wendy Guerrero, president of both the foundation and BFF, has built an amazing creative community among our alumni filmmakers, and what we've learned from them is that it's still difficult to get their *second* project made, even after a success. So we created the BFFoundation, a nonprofit that continues the work of the festival year-round.

We were one of the first film festivals to create an online platform for viewing films with the rise of the pandemic, and we saw a global appetite for our content at BFF almost immediately, making it even more accessible.

We've seen tremendous change happening in the industry since we launched in 2015. Corporate sponsors and studios are proving to have dedicated policies for diversity and inclusion within their companies. We've seen major blockbuster films directed by female and diverse filmmakers break box office records, and we see audiences demanding more inclusive representation on and off screen every day.

And Bentonville finally got a movie theater—pretty proud of that!

...

Here's my theory of change: there's one category of gross inequality in our culture where the underrepresentation of women can be fixed *overnight*:

On screen.

In the time it takes to create a new television show or movie, we can change what the future looks like, so that media itself can be the cure for the problem it created. In other words, we can create the future through what people see.

Yes, there are woefully few women CEOs in the world, but there can be lots of them in films. How long will it take to fix the problem of corporate boards being so unequal? Well, they can be half women tomorrow, on screen. How are we possibly going to get a lot more girls to go into science, technology, engineering, and math careers? There can be droves of women in STEM jobs right now, in *fiction*—and girls and women will see them and say, "That could be me, too."

So, get this: When we were looking at careers of characters on TV, there was one occupation that really stood out as being very well populated by women: forensic scientist. I don't have to do any work to get more female forensic scientists on TV. The phenomenon has a name, too: the CSI Effect. And the percentage of women studying forensic science in college has skyrocketed, from *seeing it*.

Media images are incredibly powerful.

"Seeing it and then being it" doesn't just apply to occupations.

A few years ago, my archery coach Don called and said he'd been looking at some charts regarding competitive archery; girls always had the lowest numbers for participation. But suddenly, in 2012, girls' participation shot up by 105 percent—to the top.

So what happened in 2012? Both *The Hunger Games* and *Brave* hit theaters, *both* movies featuring a badass female archer as the protagonist. Girls left the theater and bought a bow.

My institute wanted to check that out and confirmed this was no coincidence. We asked girls who took up the sport what made them decide to do so, and seven out of ten of them said that Katniss from *The Hunger Games* or Princess Merida from *Brave* made them decide to do so. (Some of the others named me!)

Here's what I say: If they can see it, they can be it.

And it's true.

. . .

After our visit to Pixar in 2013, the director Dan Scanlon came up to talk to me. He told me that what I'd said during a previous visit had really stuck with him. I'd encouraged the directors and writers to look to background characters and group scenes as an easy opportunity to improve gender representation and diversity. He'd just finished making *Monsters University*, a prequel to *Monsters, Inc.*, and said, "Anyway, I just hope you like it."

The day *Monsters University* came out I ran to see it. An early scene depicts a college campus . . . *And there it was*, finally: a panning shot in which half the characters were female, half male. And in a movie about fraternities, there were an equal number of sororities featured. We ran some numbers and were able to show that there was a 350 percent increase in female characters from *Monsters, Inc.*

My heart filled—and so did the theaters: *Monsters University* grossed $743 million worldwide. The movie was a hit. The data proved it.

. . .

I had long told my agents that I never wanted to do an hourlong TV show. I'd heard all the stories: It's like doing a movie that never ends, with horrible hours and years of commitment; it's generally thought of as the toughest lifestyle in Hollywood for actors, so my plan was to stay far away.

One day, when I was forty-nine, my agent called and said, "You've been offered an hourlong TV show, and we know you don't want to do one of those, but when it's an offer, we are obliged to tell you."

"Well, I appreciate that . . ." I said.

"You'd be playing the president of the United States," they said. Pause.

"Do I have to read it first or can we just say yes immediately?"

This was 2005—I was approaching my fiftieth year, and now I was preparing to be the president of the United States in *Commander in Chief* for ABC. (Hillary Clinton would be a candidate for the Democratic presidential primaries three years later.)

Finally, the drought was over; this was the role of a lifetime. The script, written by Rod Lurie, was genius; the rest of the cast (headed by the incomparable Donald Sutherland, whom I adore) was stellar, and here was female representation at the highest possible level— what could be more iconic than playing the leader of the free world?! Ever since *Thelma & Louise*, the issue of women's representation had been at the forefront of my mind, and I thought this role could potentially become very significant, and not only for me.

Whenever I was between jobs, I knew something great would come along—something *always* did. This time, though, I'd had to wait most of a decade, but now I had a truly groundbreaking role, and I was thrilled. Even though I had three small children, I knew I could make it work.

We shot the pilot—brilliantly directed by the show's creator, Rod Lurie—in Virginia, and the kids came with me. One scene during our time on location really stands out in my memory. The First Gentleman and I were simply to get out of a limo and head into (a stand-in for) the White House. We shot the scene multiple times, while a crowd that had formed behind some tape watched.

When we were finished, the tape came down before the actors had left, so the onlookers began to pour onto the set; it wasn't a big deal, but I had to go get ready for another scene. I looked over at the president's Secret Service detail as if to say, "Um, are you not going to help with this?" When they looked perplexed, I realized, holy shit: being the president has already gone to my head—here I was expecting the extras *playing* the Secret Service to behave like the real thing—when we weren't even shooting. Oh my God.

This was humiliating, but also funny . . . I somehow panto-mimed to the guys that they should *pretend* to be the real thing, and they immediately jumped in, putting their fingers to their ears like those fellows do, and saying, "Sorry, the president needs to be somewhere . . ."

I found it profoundly fulfilling to be on that show. My kids got to grind Goldfish crackers into the Oval Office carpet, and I got to play at being the most powerful person on the planet. (My dad, when asked what it was like to be the father of the president, would say it was nice, but that he was "more proud of being Stuart Little's grandfather," which says everything about his sense of humor.)

. . .

We were the number one new show of the season. *Commander* had been nominated for a Golden Globe, and I won the Globe for Best Actress in a Drama Series in January. (At the ceremony, I started my acceptance speech by saying, "As I was coming in, I felt a little tug at my skirt, and there was a little girl, maybe eight or ten, in her first party dress, and she said, 'Because of you, I want to be president someday.'" I took a pause as the Golden Globe crowd awwed at this; then said, "Well, that didn't actually *happen* . . . but it very well *could* have. If I was in the farmlands of Nebraska, or somewhere, there could have been a little girl tugging at my dress, and were that to be the case, then all of this would have been worth it.")

People loved *Commander in Chief*; the ratings were good, and we were getting plaudits and prizes. However, something huge happened partway into the season: The creator, Rod Lurie, was *taken off the show*. I was absolutely stunned: Rod had been brilliant, irreplaceable. How could we do it without him? Even though I was an executive producer on the show, I wasn't told why this happened . . . or even that it was *going* to happen. (I would find out later that it was basically to do with a turf war between Touchstone, the studio, and ABC.) But a new showrunner was immediately brought in: Steven Bochco, stalwart of *Hill Street Blues*, *L.A. Law*, and *NYPD Blue*, among a host of other hit shows.

When Steven came on, I had the idea to take him out to lunch, figuring he'd want to get to know me—*why did I think that yet again?*

I said, "So tell me, what interested you in taking over *Commander in Chief*?"

"Well, it's not like that," he said. "I just made a deal with Touchstone, and they asked me to, so I thought I'd do them a favor."

Uh-oh.

Almost immediately, it was felt that my character (the president of the United States, mind you) was making too many decisions on her own . . . and that she needed more men in the room telling her what to do. With that in mind, a new character was added to the show, a campaign strategist.

The blessing was that it was Mark-Paul Gosselaar who would play the role; he's a fantastic actor, and a prince of a guy, so it was a delight having him join us. However, despite my compulsion to be unfailingly kind, I for some reason decided we should prank him on his first day.

The plan was that we would tell Mark-Paul that I'm *always* in character. So evil. I don't know what possessed me. On that first day, before bringing him to the makeup trailer, the second AD took him to one side and said, "By the way, just so you know . . . and obviously some actors work this way: Geena is always in character as the president. It's no big deal. Just remember to address her as 'Madam President,' and, you know, stand up if she enters the room, that kind of thing. No bigs."

(As I'm sitting here writing, I can't believe we put Mark-Paul through this.)

I waited until he was seated in the makeup trailer, and then stepped in. Of course, everyone in the trailer except Mark-Paul was in on it, so they immediately dropped what they were doing, hopped up, and said, "Good morning, Madam President." Mark-Paul was down at the far end, and sure enough, when I reached him, he, too, stood up and said, appropriately sheepishly, "Good morning, Madam President."

I proceeded to shake his hand like all of this was perfectly normal and said, "Welcome to my administration; I'll see you in the Oval Office."

But that evidently wasn't enough.

Later, on set, all the grips and boom operators and best boys—the whole dang crew—called out "Morning, Madam President!" as I entered.

I said, "I'd like to make an announcement. This is a new member of my staff, Richard McDonald. He's my campaign advisor, a political strategist, and he goes by 'Dickie.' Please welcome him."

Poor Mark-Paul. Apparently, he'd called his wife first chance and said, "Oh my God, you won't BELIEVE this shit. Geena freakin' Davis stays in character the *whole time*."

. . .

Eventually, Steven Bochco got fired from the show too, and neither the network nor the studio wanted to hire a new showrunner. That meant our excellent head writer, Dee Johnson, took over. It had seemed scary to lose two showrunners, but Dee was awesome, and we would do whatever it took to keep our beloved show going.

Suddenly, shockingly—ABC took us *off* their schedule. They didn't want us opposite *American Idol*, as it was chewing up all competition back then, so we went on a three-month hiatus. During that time, we shot the remaining six episodes, with a view to coming back once Simon Cowell had stopped tormenting people.

All right. Time to step up.

"We're a great team," I said. "We can do this—we're going to save our show!!" We were determined we would survive this rough patch, and be on for many more seasons; of course we would. We were on a mission.

With *American Idol* complete, it was our time to return . . . but for some inexplicable reason we'd been moved to Wednesday night, instead of our original Tuesday, *and* at a different time; there had been zero advertising to tell viewers where to find us. Back then, before binge watching and streaming, TV viewing habits were just exactly that: *habits*. Folks knew that Tuesday was "that great new show about the female president," but if you moved it to a different night and didn't tell anyone, you were pretty much guaranteeing that ratings would suffer.

And so it was.

I wish I could tell you that it didn't matter, that viewers found us and stayed loyal, but in 2006, your time slot was everything.

Right about this time, an organization called the White House Project—a nonprofit that worked to promote women's voting, political participation, and leadership—decided to present awards to both Rod Lurie and me for *Commander in Chief.* Marie Wilson, who founded the WHP, loved the show; it was emblematic of everything they stood for. At the awards ceremony, Rod and I were standing backstage, about to be introduced, when I got a call.

Commander in Chief had been canceled. I took the deepest breath imaginable, went out on stage, gave my speech, and walked off.

Rod said, "Wow—you really held it together. You could have said, 'By the way, we just got canceled.'"

But what was the point?

I was too devastated to even think about telling anyone publicly that night. I loved that show, I loved that character, the audience had loved it . . . and most important, we'd brought the representation of women in the culture to a new high. And it had all been taken away in an instant. (Talk about the power of media images: A survey conducted by the Kaplan Thaler Group showed that after our one season, 58 percent of respondents [519 women and 503 men, divided equally between Democrats and Republicans] were more likely to vote for a woman candidate for president than before it aired.)

There was no possibility of thinking, "That's all right. Something better will come along." This show *was* the something better; this show was *everything* to me. The pain of losing it, after pinning all my hopes and dreams on it, was unbearable. The loss felt like something tangible. There's a Portuguese word that describes this: "saudade," which roughly translated means "the presence of the absence."

The cancellation of that show—in other words, the brevity of my administration—saw me carry that absence for many years.

A few years later, when Hillary Clinton didn't become the Democratic candidate for president, I told my dad that I was despairing that we still seemed so far away from having a woman president. So I shared my latest ambition with him: "Dad," I said, "I think I'm going to have to become the *real* president."

Dad just looked up thoughtfully and said, "Oh? Okay. You sure you *want* that job?"

. . .

In the intervening years, I've found a way to look at what happened with *Commander in Chief* that I find comforting. I've read a bit about the theory of parallel universes: the idea that there are alternate planes co-existing with our own, and each of them depicts how events here in our sublunary lives could have unfolded differently. I've decided I believe in parallel universes. And I further believe that in these parallel universes, I am not Geena *Prime*—the one all the other Geenas are a copy of. Because surely the *main* Geena, the real Geena, would not have had her show canceled. Geena Prime's *Commander in Chief* ran for eight seasons; it changed everything, and women got elected to the presidency. Just knowing that Geena Prime is out there and exists makes me feel better about my life.

Why is this comforting? Because another version of me did get to keep playing that character, and I admire her and look up to her, and she made the kind of changes the world desperately needs.

And I hope that Geena Prime knows about, and thinks fondly of, me.

Chapter Thirteen
Not Dying of Politeness

During a trip home to visit my folks, before Mom's Alzheimer's had kicked in, Dad said he had great news: He'd picked out their grave plot and was very pleased about it.

"You have to think ahead with things like this, you know," he said. "You can't leave it till the last minute."

In other words, Dad was sure he was really getting a jump on this burial-plans thing . . . at eighty-nine years old. (Turns out he was right, though; he bought the plot well before his time came.) He wanted to show it to me, so the three of us drove to this little hidden-away cemetery. I told him it really was a beautiful spot. Then he had me take a picture of the two of them, smiling, standing on top of the plot.

My dad's can-do spirit—much of which I inherited—meant that he really could do anything . . . and he was also a *daredevil*, it turns out. My favorite photo of him was taken while he was in college in Kentucky: He's in midair leaping across a big gully, the kind where you fall to your death if you don't make it. But there he is, sailing over, sure he would reach the other side.

All his life my dad worked for the Corps of Engineers at the Cape Cod Canal, and one of their jobs was to check the condition of the 274-foot-high Bourne Bridge (that's twenty-five stories!). Once a year they had to inspect it to see if it needed a new coat of paint. So my dad would climb up and just *walk across* the high arched top of the bridge. No safety rope or anything, just strolling across. I remember Dan and I being horrified when we learned of that as adults: "How could you *do* that?! What if you fell off?" And he said, "Why, it's almost as wide as a sidewalk! You wouldn't fall off a sidewalk, would you?"

He ended up living eight years after my mom passed, and we spent a lot of time together. On one visit I arrived to find a massive pile of gravel in our long driveway. My father pointed out that it cost extra to have it spread out on the driveway, so he was planning on doing it himself.

This, now, was a thing too far—surely this would kill him. So I got a shovel and started into it, too, figuring the more I did, the less chance he'd have a heart attack or something. I could hear him shoveling away on the other side of the gravel pile, and so I went faster, faster, working myself into a fine state—now wondering if I was going to be the one having the heart attack.

I'd read somewhere that if a person can carry on a conversation, they're not exerting themselves too much, so I went around to the other side of the pile to get him to talk, as a test.

"Dad . . . hey, how you . . . whoo! How ya doing?" *I* could barely talk, I was puffing and panting so much.

"Oh, good, Geenie, gettin' along . . ." he said as he happily shoveled away, accomplishing three quarters of the job himself.

He was ninety-three at the time.

. . .

So yeah, my father could walk across the tops of bridges; could shimmy up drainpipes in his eighties; outwork me spreading gravel across a driveway. He was insanely fit, infinitely calm, and could handle anything. And in the last five years of his life, he let his hair and beard grow until he looked like an old hippie . . . or the Ancient Mariner. So much so that when he was in the hospital toward the end of his life, the doctors and nurses thought he was some crazy old fella that needed to be slowly yelled at in order to understand. "MISTER DAVIS, CAN I COMB YOUR HAIR?" He'd just chuckle and ignore how nutty this was, but it really bothered me that they would just assume he was senile.

So I pinned a note up on the wall behind him: "I have perfect hearing, and more marbles than you."

He was ill for only the last six weeks of his life—and during that time, he had very little discomfort. He just kept on enjoying his life. Soon after he was admitted, an ingenious young doctor made the leap to realizing my dad had celiac disease—something he'd had all his life, but which hadn't been diagnosed in the past, oh, *ninety-five* years. He'd never stopped eating wheat because he never knew he should. He probably could have lived to a *hundred* and five if he'd known to cut out wheat.

. . .

There was a point during his hospitalization when a cranky old German doctor brusquely told us he was sure that Dad was going to die that very night. Dad was unresponsive, so it seemed like the time had come. We—Dan, his wife, Marilyn, and I—took turns going in to say goodbye. I held his hand and poured my heart out to him.

We slept in the waiting room chairs to be there when the time came . . . and when we crept into his room in the morning, there he was, sitting up, smiling at us. "Oh, hullo there—you up so early?" he said. Dad being Dad, he hadn't gotten the memo about kicking the bucket.

• • •

To pass the time in the hospital I'd read aloud to him for hours—*Moby-Dick* and *Treasure Island*. He'd tire and close his eyes; then say, "How 'bout reading a little more, there, Geenie?"

He was getting stronger. He had believed that he would never want a feeding tube when he got old and sick, but once he did get old and sick, he realized he was still sharp as a tack, with a great quality of life, so he thought, why not get the tube? When it came time to take it out, they did a test to see if he could swallow properly—sometimes you lose your muscle power for swallowing food when you don't do it for a while—and the test went great. He would be moving on to a rehab place the next morning.

That night, after all his friends and neighbors had gone home (everyone loved my dad), I was sitting with him, knitting. You know me by now—I'd picked the hardest possible pattern, even though I hadn't ever knitted before. Dad had drifted off to sleep, and when he woke up, he looked at me.

"You're still here, Geenie?

"Yeah, Dad."

"Whatcha doin'?"

"Oh, just knitting," I said.

"You don't have to stay," he said. "Why don't you head on home?"

I kissed him.

"Good night, Dad," I said. "I love you."

"Love you," he said. "We had a really good day today, didn't we?" he said.

"We had a great day, Dad," I said. "It really was."

By the time I got to the house five minutes later, the phone was already ringing. It was April 2, 2009. My dad was ninety-five years old.

. . .

My father loved Jesus deeply. He never talked about it with us, but you could tell when he said grace at dinner; it was integral to his life. The year before he died, Dad decided to celebrate his ninety-fifth birthday by singing his first ever solo in church, despite having been in the choir for sixty years. In his sweet tenor voice, he sang,

> *"Jesus, the very thought of thee,*
> *with sweetness fills my breast;*
> *but sweeter far, thy face to see,*
> *and in thy presence, rest."*

After he died, I found I was consumed with worry about him. Having been so closely and intensely involved with him and his care in the hospital (and Dan right there with me), I couldn't seem to let go. I started having recurring dreams about him—I'm at my house with a few friends over, Dad is there, and everything is normal; then I look at him again and think, *"Wait a minute . . ."* and go over and say, "Dad, I thought you died?"

"Oh?" he'd say. "No, I'm fine, I'm okay . . ."

I had this dream so many times that once, while I was *in* it, I remembered that something similar to this had been only a dream, so I wanted to prove that this time it wasn't a dream. I thought, "If I can hug him, that means this is real"—and I gave him a huge hug. He was solid! He was hugging me back! It *was* real . . . But of course I woke up again.

But still I didn't, *couldn't*, know how he was doing, if he was all right. I told a friend, "He was sure he was going to see Jesus, but I'm so worried about him. I just don't know where he *is* now . . ."

My friend said, "Maybe he *did* see Jesus."

Ah yes, of course—maybe he *did*. Why had I been so worried about him? I also believe that in the dreams he was *actually visiting* me. After all, in them he always said, "I'm okay, I'm fine." I found great comfort in that, and still do.

. . .

In recent years, I've invented a whole alter ego for myself in the chat section of a jigsaw puzzle site I frequent. Mostly people comment about whether they liked a particular puzzle: "Fun and colorful! Took me a while to put together, though!" They also share things about their lives, their health problems, family affairs. I've joined in the chatting as "Amy," who is deeply, profoundly sweet and kind: "I'm so sorry to hear about your hip troubles, Sew-Kwik19; I hope tomorrow will be a brighter day! Know that all your friends here are thinking of you with great affection. Big hug."

I've been wondering why I choose to talk like that—even why I think of "Amy" almost as if she's a real person. I'm wondering if I invented her supremely polite persona because I needed her to take over that formerly dominant side of me, the uber polite part that still sometimes wants to show her face. If so, I've given her an outlet.

I'm still working hard on what I said is my goal in life—closing the gap between when something happens and when I react authentically to it. It might always be a challenge, but I've gotten profoundly better at it. A good example happened when we were making *Commander in Chief*: I came to the set in the morning one day, and as usual we all hugged one another in greeting. The director of that episode greeted me also, and as we were hugging, he said, "Ah, my favorite part of the day, when I get to feel up Geena Davis." (He wasn't; we were just hugging.)

Without the tiniest pause, I cordially but firmly said, "Oops, *that's* inappropriate!" He had a *huge* reaction to that—"What?? Are you serious? You don't mean that, right? I would never . . . I'm a feminist!" He brought it up again and again throughout the day and couldn't let it go. But all I'd done was to say what I'd felt right when it was happening.

It's such a small incident, but I can't tell you how rewarding that moment was—to know what to say with no pause to think about how to say it, or even if I *should*. It still stands out in my mind because it was a time when I really felt how empowering it can be to live authentically. I'd always had a problem with *l'esprit de*

l'escalier—"the spirit of the staircase"—the French term for thinking of what to say after you've already left the party. But oh boy, it's
fun when you do it right in the moment. It's very rare now for me to
have regret on the stairs.

I recently read a great quote from Reese Witherspoon in an
interview with Gayle King for *InStyle* magazine: "LeBron James
doesn't go, 'I'm kinda, sorta good at basketball.' He's like, "I'm
the best there ever was,'" Reese said. "So, yes, I do think I'm very
good at what I do. I've been doing it for thirty years. I know what
I'm doing. Give me the ball."

I know exactly how she feels, and I echo that. I'm confident in my
abilities and feel very good about how I handle things.

In other words, I got this.

. . .

Nowadays, I very much feel in charge of my own destiny, ready
to take on the world. But if what I've written here has led you to
believe that I have become a certifiable, *full-time* badass, don't be
fooled. It's still very possible I may yet die of politeness. Why, at
the beginning of the pandemic, when we were all still washing vegetables in Clorox, a woman was hand-delivering a package to my
house. I'd texted her to say just leave it on the front steps. But right
as she was about to do so, I happened to come around the corner
from the backyard. I stopped in my tracks; she did too, seemingly
considering if she should now just hand it directly to me.

Neither of us was wearing a mask, by the way.

After a beat she very haltingly started approaching me, leaving
me oceans of time to say something like, "That's okay, you can

just leave it there, thanks," or, "Oops, this dang pandemic, huh? I'll just grab that later." I could have even pretended to be a funny robot and say, "Danger. Must. Create. Distance." Instead, I stood frozen and gaped at her until she finally stood two feet away and handed me the no-doubt-plague-coated box. So yeah—fifty-eight years later, and still in danger of dying from politeness. Despite everything, I can really only claim to be *working* on being a full-on badass. Either Thelma or Louise, it doesn't matter which, but definitely one of them.

. . .

I wasn't able to change the world before my daughter grew up, though she's amazing and powerful and gloriously self-possessed anyway. But my fond hope is that, one day, she will be able to say to *her* daughter, should she be so blessed, "You know, once upon a time, women and girls were thought to be less important than men and boys." And my granddaughter will turn to her with an incredulous look, then laugh and say, "Mom, are you making this up?"

Acknowledgments

I would like to thank Jason Weinberg for giving me the idea to write this book, and then making me do it.

Thank you to Alizeh, Kian, and Kaiis.

Many thanks to Mollie Glick at CAA, and to Rakesh Satyal, Judith Curr, and everyone at HarperOne.

Thank you to Madeline Di Nonno and everyone else at the Institute.

Thank you to my irreplaceable team: Kevin Huvane, Ben Dey, Ali Trustman, Greg Clark, and Peter Jacobs.

Thank you to the people I can't live without: Nina, Jerry, Howell, O'B, Mary, Doug, Billi, and Alan.

I love you, Gav.

Thank you, Daisette McKelvie.

Credits and Permissions

Insert page 6 (*top left*): Victoria's Secret

Insert page 6 (*top right*): United Archives GmbH / Alamy

Insert page 6 (*bottom*): Ron Galella / Getty Images

Insert page 7 (*bottom left*): Leo Paduzzi

Insert page 8: Jerry de Wilde

Insert page 9 (*top*): Fotos International / Getty Images

Insert page 9 (*bottom*): Robin Platzer / Getty Images

Insert page 10 (*top*): Columbia Pictures / Photofest

Insert page 10 (*bottom*): Michel Comte / Vanity Fair (September 1992)

Insert page 11 (*bottom*): Heikki Kotilainen

Insert page 12 (*bottom*): Matt Campbell / Getty Images

Insert page 13 (*top*): Joh Shearer / Getty Images

Insert page 14 (*top*): Robert Hallowell

Insert page 14 (*bottom*): Vince Bucci / Getty Images

Insert page 15 (*center*): Ken Wiedemann / Getty Images

About the Author

Geena Davis is one of Hollywood's most respected actors, having appeared in several roles that became cultural landmarks, such as Thelma in Thelma & Louise, *Dottie Hinson in* A League of Their Own, *and Mackenzie Allen in* Commander in Chief. *She is also a two-time Academy Award winner, a world-class archer, and a tireless advocate of women and girls, as founder and chair of the Geena Davis Institute on Gender in Media.*